Remedies

BLACK LETTER OUTLINES

Remedies

THIRD EDITION

Russell L. Weaver
Professor of Law & Distinguished University Scholar
University of Louisville
Louis D. Brandeis School of Law

W. Jonathan Cardi
Judge Donald L. Smith Professor of Law
Wake Forest University School of Law

BLACK LETTER SERIES®

WEST ACADEMIC

860 Blue Gentian Road, Suite 350
Eagan, MN 55121
1-877-888-1330

Published in the United States of America

ISBN: 978-1-68561-376-1

To Laurence, Ben and Kate, with love, RLW

To Juliana, Mia, and Kate, WJC

Summary of Contents

Table of Contents

Capsule Summary

■ CHAPTER ONE: EQUITY AND EQUITABLE REMEDIES

A. HISTORICAL PERSPECTIVE ON THE DEVELOPMENT OF "LAW" AND "EQUITY"

At common law, there existed a dual court system that included "law" courts and "equity" courts.

1. **The King and the Law Courts**

   In Early England, although the people could seek recourse to the King's Courts (which we also refer to as the "Law Courts"), they also could petition the King to grant them justice.

2. **The Medieval Chancellor**

   The Chancellor was a minister of the king who also served as a high church official. As a minister, the Chancellor functioned more like a prime minister who performed various functions for the King. One function that the Chancellor performed was to issue "writs" authorizing litigants to bring suit in the King's Courts.

3. **The Provisions of Oxford**

   In 1258, the Provisions of Oxford prohibited the creation of new forms of writs absent the consent of the King and the King's Council (composed of Lords). A later statute relaxed this rule by authorizing new writs that were factually similar to existing writs. Statute of Westminster II (1285).

4. **The King's Residual Authority**

   Despite the Provisions of Oxford, the King retained his equitable power to grant "justice."

5. **Development of the Chancellor's Equitable Power**

   As the quantity of petitions to the King grew in number, the King asked the Chancellor to hear and decide these matters.

6. **The Growth of Chancery**

   Over time, the petitions became too much for even the Chancellor to hear and he began delegating his authority to subordinate officials. As these subordinate officials began to hear cases, they began to function more like judges in that they developed facts, applied the law to facts, and (began to develop legal precedent). Over time, a separate and coordinate system of justice began to develop.

B. DISTINCTIONS BETWEEN LAW AND EQUITY

There were fundamental differences between law courts and equity courts including their governing principles and the way they issued their judgments or decisions.

1. The Relationship of Equity Courts to Law Courts

Equity courts were not bound by the Provisions of Oxford and could readily hear new forms of action. But, true to their roots, equity courts refused to act except when the common law courts could not provide the plaintiff with an adequate remedy.

2. Equitable Relief Distinguished from Legal Relief

Equity courts also differed from law courts in regard to the types of judgments they rendered. A common law court would make an award of monetary damages. Equity acted *in personam.*

3. Governing Principles of Equity

True to their religious roots, equity courts were referred to as "courts of conscience," and were supposed to use their powers to bring about "justice" or "equity."

4. Equitable Maxims

Equity was governed by the various "equitable maxims."

C. THE DEVELOPMENT OF EQUITY IN THE UNITED STATES

Just as the English common law was transplanted to the United States, equity and equitable principles were transplanted as well.

1. The Field Code and Early Attempts to Abolish Equity Courts

In 1848, the State of New York adopted the Field Code, a civil procedure code, which abolished the distinction between law courts and equity courts.

2. Variations of Merger

In the United States, merger has taken a number of different forms. Most states, following the Field Code model, abolished the distinction between law and equity. Other states maintained separate equity courts in the common law mode (although some states provided for more liberal transfer of cases between courts). However, a very few states retained the common law model.

D. EQUITABLE REMEDIES TODAY

Despite merger, distinctions between law and equity have not completely disappeared. Indeed, although courts no longer distinguish between "legal actions" and "equitable actions," they do distinguish between "legal" remedies and "equitable" remedies. Equitable remedies continue to be subject to many historical distinctions and limitations that have applied to such remedies.

1. Equitable Remedies are Based on "Conscience" and "Equity"

As we have seen, equity courts developed as "courts of conscience."

a. Equity and Conscience Today

Today, even though equity courts no longer exist, equitable remedies are only available when "equity" and "conscience" demand them.

b. **Equity Versus Law on Conscience Principles**

The description of equity as a "court of conscience" was always somewhat misleading. Courts of law had their own "rules of conscience" (e.g., invalidating contracts that violate "public policy") although they did not necessarily label their rules as such.

c. **The Difficulty in Defining Terms Like "Equity" and "Conscience"**

In deciding whether a particular result is "conscionable" or "equitable," Equity courts relied on the equitable maxims discussed earlier, as well as on the chancellor's own sense of morality and justice. But many question whether the maxims are consistent with each other, and whether they really provide the basis for judicial decisions (as opposed to justifications for decisions already made).

2. **Equitable Remedies Are Granted in Personam**

Another historical distinction that has survived is the rule that "equity acts *in personam*."

a. ***In Personam* Remedies Defined**

When a court renders an *in personam* judgment, it orders the defendant to do, or refrain from doing, some act. A defendant who refuses to comply can be held in contempt and subjected to prison or fine.

b. **Legal Remedies Contrasted**

By contrast, a law court usually renders a monetary judgment.

3. **Inadequacy of Legal Remedy/Irreparable Harm**

Another equitable maxim that survives today is the principle that equitable relief is not available except when plaintiff's legal remedy is inadequate.

a. **Example of an Adequate Legal Remedy**

The classic example of an "adequate legal remedy" involves items that are readily purchasable on the open market (e.g., a current model Chevrolet).

b. **Other Examples of Inadequacy**

When damages are difficult or impossible to calculate; when defendant is insolvent or it is otherwise impossible to collect a monetary judgment; when plaintiff will be required to bring multiple proceedings to vindicate his rights; and when the plaintiff's injury is of such a nature (e.g., deprivation of civil rights) the remedy of damages is substitutionary and ineffective.

c. **The Adequacy Requirement Today**

The common law requirement of irreparable injury survives today, albeit in somewhat more flexible form.

d. **The Wisdom of Retaining the Adequacy Requirement**

Today, commentators debate whether it makes sense to maintain the historical requirement of inadequacy as a predicate to equitable relief. One reason for maintaining the requirement is illustrated by the problems that can develop if antagonistic parties are forced to work together.

4. Equitable Relief Is Discretionary

Another fundamental principle of equity is the notion that equitable relief is discretionary. Even if the plaintiff is suffering irreparable injury, a court has discretion to deny equitable relief.

a. Discretion May be Exercised to Deny Relief When an Injunction Would Involve the Court in Continuing Supervision Problems

Although they will sometimes do so, courts are generally reluctant to issue injunctions which enmesh the court in continuing supervision of the parties.

b. Discretion May Be Exercised Against Relief Based on Public Policy Considerations

Equitable relief may also be denied when public policy considerations demand it.

E. EQUITABLE DEFENSES

A number of common law equitable defenses are used today to prevent an award of equitable relief. The major defenses are "unclean hands", unconscionability, laches, and estoppel. All these doctrines are grounded in equitable principles.

1. Clean Hands Doctrine

The "unclean hands" (or "clean hands") doctrine states that "he who comes to equity must come with clean hands."

a. The Classic Example: The *Highwayman's Case*

In the *Highwayman's Case,* the court refused to help two robbers divide up the loot.

b. The Unclean Hands Can Apply to Many Types of Misconduct

"Unclean hands," includes all misconduct and wrongdoing that is sufficiently related to the plaintiff's claim.

c. Potential Inequities Caused by the Clean Hands Doctrine

Of course, when the clean hands doctrine is strictly applied, the doctrine can lead to potential inequities. For example, in the *Highwayman's Case,* if the court leaves the parties where it found them, then one of the robbers will be left with all of the loot.

d. Unrelated Transactions Exception

Courts will generally refuse to apply the clean hands doctrine when the plaintiff's misconduct is unrelated to the transaction at hand.

2. Unconscionability

Since equity developed as a "court of conscience," courts have always felt free to deny equitable relief on the grounds of conscience

a. Classic Example

The classic example of unconscionability is provided by the case of *Campbell Soup Co. v. Wentz,* 172 F.2d 80 (3d Cir.1948): "We [think] that a party who has offered and succeeded in getting an agreement as tough as this one is, should not come to a chancellor and ask court help in the enforcement of its terms."

b. U.C.C. § 2–302

U.C.C. § 2–302 also contains an unconscionability provision.

3. Laches

A third defense that can be used to defeat an equitable claim is the defense of "laches," which is associated with the maxim: "Equity aids the vigilant not those who slumber on their rights."

a. Laches Defined

Broadly defined, laches is any unreasonable delay by the plaintiff in instituting or prosecuting an action under circumstances where the delay causes prejudice to the defendant. *See e.g.*, RESTATEMENT SECOND OF TORTS § 939 (1977).

b. Laches as an Equitable Statute of Limitations

At common law, the statute of limitations applied to legal actions, but not to equitable actions. Laches served as the "equitable statute of limitations."

c. Laches Distinguished from the Statute of Limitations

The SOL contains a specified and definite period of time. The focus under laches is on "unreasonable delay" and "prejudice" both of which can occur prior to the expiration of the SOL, or, for that matter, much later.

4. Estoppel

Estoppel applies when defendant makes a promise to plaintiff on which he/she reasonably relies to his/her detriment.

a. The Defaulting Employer

Estoppel might be applied when an employer offers to provide a pension to a long and faithful employee when and if she retires, but reneges on the promise once the employee has retired.

b. The Relationship Between Laches and Estoppel

Laches applies when plaintiff unreasonably delays in pursuing a claim, and defendant reasonably relies on the delay to his detriment.

c. Estoppel Against the Government

Historically, courts have refused to apply the doctrine of estoppel against the government. Some later cases have relaxed this prohibition.

d. Promissory Estoppel Distinguished from Equitable Estoppel

Equitable estoppel is purely a remedial device which, if applicable, precludes equitable relief and relegates plaintiff to his/her legal remedies. Promissory estoppel, on the other hand, is a substantive cause of action which permits foreseeable reliance to substitute for consideration and thereby supply the basis for a breach of contract action.

F. THE RIGHT TO TRIAL BY JURY

Historical distinctions between law and equity are also important because of the right to trial by jury. The Seventh Amendment to the U.S. Constitution guarantees the right to trial by jury "[i]n suits at common law, where the value in controversy shall exceed twenty dollars." Although the Seventh Amendment only applies to federal proceedings, many state constitutions also guarantee the right to trial by jury.

1. "Preservation" of the Right to Trial by Jury

Most jury trial provisions "preserve" the right to jury trial as it existed at the time they were adopted. When the Seventh Amendment was adopted in 1791, equity cases were tried to a judge while legal cases were generally tried to a jury.

2. Difficulties with the Historical Approach

Applied literally, the Seventh Amendment would have required an exclusively historical analysis of the 1791 common law in order to decide whether a party had a right to a jury trial at that time. As the year 1791 became more distant, and as the federal courts and most state courts merged their law and equity courts into a single system, that task became exceedingly difficult.

3. The *Dairy Queen* Rule

In *Dairy Queen, Inc. v. Wood*, 369 U.S. 469 (1962), even though the plaintiff sought an accounting, which would have been an equitable claim at common law, the court held that there was a right to jury trial. In doing so, the Court noted that plaintiff should have brought the claim as a legal action (an action for debt) and therefore the Court concluded that plaintiff could not seek an accounting because he had an adequate remedy at law. Since equitable relief is unavailable except when the legal claim is inadequate, and since the claim could be recharacterized as one for debt, the Court did recharacterize it and held that a jury trial was required. The case is regarded as creating a strong, pro-jury, approach to the right to jury trial.

4. Reassignment of Claims from Equitable to Legal

Of course, as at common law, if legal relief is available, a court will "reassign" a case from equitable to legal and therefore impose a jury trial (as it did in the *Dairy Queen* case).

5. The Historical Approach and Statutory Claims

The historical approach makes it difficult to determine the right to jury trial in actions based on legislation, especially statutory rights and remedies (including administrative remedies) unknown at common law.

6. Congressional Extensions of the Right to Jury Trial

Since there is no constitutional right to a non-jury trial, Congress may expand the right to jury trial to cases which would have been judge-tried in 1791.

7. "Jury Preference?"

In *Ross v. Bernhard*, 396 U.S. 531 (1970), the Court seemed to suggest that cases involving requests for damages (as opposed to *in personam* relief) are subject to the right to trial by jury.

8. Demands for Jury Trial

Even though the Seventh Amendment preserves the right to trial by jury, Rule 38 of the Federal Rules of Civil Procedure requires that a party who seeks a jury trial must demand it in writing. Failure to make the demand constitutes a waiver of the right.

■ CHAPTER TWO: ENFORCEMENT OF EQUITABLE DECREES

A. EQUITABLE DECREES AND THE CONTEMPT SANCTION

Equitable remedies are usually framed as *in personam* decrees that order a defendant to engage in some act (or refrain from engaging in an act). Such decrees are reinforced by the threat of contempt sanctions including fines and jail.

B. CONTEMPT DEFINED

"Contempt" is broadly defined as an offense against the dignity of the court. Contemptuous conduct can include a refusal to obey a court order, as well as a variety of other actions.

1. Contempt Under the Federal Rules

The Federal Rules of Criminal Procedure specifically include two types of conduct within the definition of contempt: failure to obey a judicial subpoena "without adequate excuse", Rule 17, F.R.Cr.P., and violation of the obligation of secrecy by a grand juror. Rule 6, F.R.Cr.P.

2. Recalcitrant Witnesses

Contempt can also occur when a witness refuses to obey a court order requiring him/her to testify.

3. Failure to Comply with a Court Order

Contempt can also occur when a party refuses to comply with a court order.

4. Contempt and Speech

Courts can also impose contempt sanctions for speech (e.g., a defendant or lawyer who speaks disrespectfully to a judge or who suggests that a judge is corrupt). However, there are situations when individuals are entitled to latitude for their comments when they are making valid points.

C. CIVIL CONTEMPT DISTINGUISHED FROM CRIMINAL CONTEMPT

Contempt is divided into "civil contempt" and "criminal contempt." This division has both procedural and remedial consequences. Criminal contempt must be tried by different constitutional and procedural rules than civil contempt.

1. The Nature of the Distinction

Civil contempt is distinguished from criminal contempt, not by the nature of the conduct, but by the purpose of the sanction imposed. Criminal contempt is imposed for purposes of punishment. By contrast, civil contempt is designed to coerce compliance with a court order, or to compensate a party who has suffered injury due to another party's violation of a court order.

2. Examples of Civil Contempt

Civil contempt might arise when a witness refuses to testify in a case, and the judge orders the witness imprisoned until he/she agrees to testify. The sanction is civil because it is coercive and designed to force the witness to testify.

3. Examples of Criminal Contempt

If the contempt sanction is framed for punishment purposes, each of the examples of civil contempt could constitute criminal contempt.

4. Calculating Criminal Contempt Fines

In imposing a criminal contempt fine, courts take various factors into account, including the defendant's financial resources and the consequent seriousness of the burden to that particular defendant. Of course, if the goal is to coerce compliance, these same factors might be relevant.

5. Criminal Contempt for the Recalcitrant Witnesses

When a witness is jailed for civil contempt, it is impermissible to hold the witness in jail after the grand jury's term ends. Since the witness can no longer purge the contempt by testifying, no coercive reason remains for keeping the witness in jail.

6. Civil-Criminal Contempt Combined

In a given case, the contempt sanction can involve both civil and criminal components.

D. CIVIL CONTEMPT DAMAGES

In a civil contempt proceeding, the court may order the contemnor to compensate an injured party for damage that results from violation of a court order. In order for the sanction to remain civil (as opposed to criminal), the amount of damages must correlate to plaintiff's injury rather than to punishment.

1. Calculating Damages

The measure of recoverable civil contempt damages can vary from state-to-state. However, damage calculations can include compensation for the actual loss (e.g., damage caused to plaintiff's real estate by the trespasser), and also attorney's fees. However, some jurisdictions follow the so-called "American Rule" which make attorney's fees unrecoverable.

2. Proof of Damages

In order to recover contempt damages, plaintiff must present proof of loss.

E. PROCEDURAL REQUIREMENTS FOR CIVIL AND CRIMINAL CONTEMPT

Courts try contempt proceedings differently depending on whether the contempt is civil or criminal. Courts also treat "direct" contempt differently than "indirect" contempt.

1. Direct Contempt

Courts tend to distinguish between "direct" contempt and "indirect" contempt. The distinction is important because courts sometimes handle direct contempt differently than civil contempt, and they can try the two types of contempt differently.

2. Distinguishing Direct Contempt from Indirect Contempt

"Direct" contempt is a contempt committed in the court's presence. "Indirect" contempt is contempt that is committed outside the court's presence.

3. Hybrid Contempt

Some cases do not fit easily into either the direct contempt or the indirect contempt category.

4. Procedural Handling of Direct Versus Indirect Contempts

When a direct contempt (one in the presence of the court) occurs, the judge may act summarily without notice or order to show cause. By contrast, when an indirect contempt (one that occurs outside the court's presence) occurs, the judge must act based on notice and an order for arrest or an order to show cause.

5. The Limits of Direct Contempt

Direct contempt usually involves conduct that a judge observes and that tends to obstruct the administration of justice.

6. Summary Punishment of Disruptive Defendants for Direct Contempts

If a defendant is unduly disruptive in a courtroom proceeding, and refuses to desist from disruptive behavior, courts are sometimes forced to take extreme actions (e.g., binding and gagging the defendant or removing defendant from the courtroom) in an effort to maintain order.

7. Summary Punishments and the Confrontation Clause

In *Illinois v. Allen*, 397 U.S. 337 (1970), the Court held that an extremely disruptive defendant could be summarily removed from a courtroom without violating his constitutional right to confront the witnesses against him.

8. Commencement of Contempt Proceedings

A contempt proceeding can be commenced in one of two ways: on the court's own motion, or at the behest of a party. When a party institutes a contempt proceeding, it does so by filing a motion for an "order to show cause" why the defendant should not be held in contempt of court.

9. The Right to Trial by Jury

Some contempts must be tried to a jury.

F. COLLATERAL CHALLENGES TO JUDICIAL ORDERS

A court order can be directly challenged by appealing the order to a higher court. Sometimes, defendants try to challenge orders collaterally.

1. The Duty to Obey Court Orders

In *United States v. United Mine Workers of America*, 330 U.S. 258 (1947), the court held that "an order issued by a court with jurisdiction over the subject matter and person must be obeyed by the parties until it is reversed by orderly and proper proceedings." The Court held that the duty to obey applies even if an allegation is made regarding the constitutionality of the underlying statute.

2. The Duty to Obey and Contempt Remedies

Even though defendants are obligated to comply with validly issued orders that are later found to be invalid, there are limits to the sanctions that can be imposed under such orders. Although a defendant can be subjected to criminal penalties for disobedience, there is no right to compensatory relief if the original order was invalid.

3. Defenses That May Be Raised in a Contempt Proceeding

Several defenses can be raised in a contempt proceeding: defendants can claim that they were not bound by the decree; that they did not receive notice of its requirements; or that it was impossible to comply with the decree.

4. Duty to Obey: Constitutional Claims

In *Walker v. City of Birmingham*, 388 U.S. 307 (1967), because of the collateral bar rule, the court imposed criminal contempt sanctions on defendants for their defiance of an allegedly unconstitutional injunction. Since the collateral bar rule does not apply to civil contempt, a civil sanction would fail if the injunction were invalidated on appeal.

5. State Rules and Constitutional Claims

California provides an exception to the duty to obey. In *In re Berry*, 68 Cal.2d 137, 65 Cal.Rptr. 273, 436 P.2d 273 (1968), the court stated that: "In California [the] rule followed is considerably more consistent with the exercise of First Amendment Freedoms than that adopted in [Alabama]."

6. Transparently Invalid and Void Orders

There is an exception to the collateral bar rule for "transparently invalid" or "void" orders on the one hand, and "merely invalid" or "voidable" orders.

■ CHAPTER THREE: INJUNCTIONS

A. THE NATURE AND PURPOSE OF INJUNCTIVE RELIEF

An injunction is perhaps the most powerful judicial remedy. It is used to order defendants to engage in, or to refrain from engaging a specified act (or acts).

1. Mandatory Injunctions Distinguished from Prohibitory Injunctions

Some injunctions are mandatory while others are prohibitory: an injunction which compels an act is referred to as mandatory, while one which forbids an act is a prohibitory injunction.

2. Categories of Injunctions

Injunctions can be used to accomplish many different objectives: preventative injunctions protect against continuing or threatened harm; reparative injunctions require defendant to restore plaintiff to his/her rights; and structural injunctions apply to organizations (e.g., a prison or school system) and are designed to bring those organizations into compliance with legal requirements, or (a court might order reforms designed to make the punishment constitutionally acceptable).

3. Uses of Injunctive Relief

Historically, injunctions have been used to enjoin both private and public conduct, especially in nuisance and trespass cases.

B. STANDARDS FOR ISSUANCE OF INJUNCTIVE RELIEF

There are different types of injunctions, and each has its own function. Some injunctions are permanent in nature: they are issued after a determination of the merits of a lawsuit and are designed to apply prospectively and permanently unless modified or dissolved.

Other injunctions are temporary in nature including the temporary restraining order (TRO) and the preliminary injunction (a/k/a temporary injunction).

1. Requirements for Provisional Relief

To obtain either a TRO or a preliminary injunction, a plaintiff must show that immediate and irreparable injury will result absent the injunction. When a preliminary injunction is sought, plaintiff must show that this injury will occur during the pendency of the lawsuit. When a TRO is sought, plaintiff must show that it will occur before a hearing can be heard on whether to grant a preliminary injunction.

a. The Five Factor Test

Under Rule 65, Fed. R. Civ. P., in order to obtain a TRO or preliminary injunction, a plaintiff must show: 1) that unless the restraining order issues, they will suffer irreparable harm; 2) that the hardship they will suffer absent the order outweighs any hardship the defendants would suffer if the order were to issue; 3) that they are likely to succeed on the merits of their claims; 4) that the issuance of the order will cause no substantial harm to the public; and 5) that they have no adequate remedy at law.

b. Mandatory Injunctions Distinguished from Prohibitory Injunctions

The distinction between prohibitory and mandatory injunctions has important consequences.

c. Illustration of Preliminary Injunctive Relief

In one case, plaintiff sought to enjoin a nearby shopping center from continuing a concert series that led to high noise levels and litter. The court concluded that the imposition on nearby neighbors was so great as to impose great and irreparable injury.

d. An Additional Illustration

In *Washington Capitols Basketball Club, Inc. v. Barry*, 304 F.Supp. 1193 (N.D.Cal., 1969), a court enjoined a star basketball player from playing for a different club.

2. The Hearing Requirement

In order to obtain either a TRO or a preliminary injunction, plaintiffs must satisfy several procedural requirements. In general, judicial orders should only be issued after a contested hearing. The TRO is unique because it can be granted *ex parte.*

a. Rule 65 and *Ex Parte* Hearings

Rule 65 of the Federal Rules of Civil Procedure allows courts to issue *ex parte* TROs but creates a strong presumption in favor of contested hearings. However, Rule 65(a)(1) prohibits courts from issuing *ex parte* preliminary injunctions. Many state procedural provisions contain comparable provisions.

b. Exceptions to the Hearing Requirement

In re Vuitton et Fils S.A., 606 F.2d 1 (2d Cir. 1979), stated an exception to the hearing requirement when the giving of notice would frustrate Vuitton's ability to protect its rights, and therefore the hearing requirement would not be imposed.

c. **Appeal Rights**

At the federal level, an order "granting, continuing, modifying, refusing or dissolving" an injunction can be immediately appealed. 28 U.S.C. § 1291(a)(1). In general, and subject to some exceptions, TROs do not fall within the scope of § 1291 and are therefore not appealable.

3. **Persons Bound**

Fed. R. Civ. P. 65 provides that a TRO or preliminary injunction "is binding only upon the parties to the action, their officers, agents, servants, employees, and attorneys, and upon those persons in active concert or participation with them who receive actual notice of the order by personal service or otherwise."

a. **Illustration of the Federal Rules Provision**

In one case, a university obtained an injunction prohibiting students from continuing their protest demonstrations. Although there was evidence suggesting that the faculty were "sympathetic" to the students, the faculty were not deemed to be in concert or participation with the students, and therefore could not be held in contempt.

b. **Inapplicability to Others with Different Rights and Interests**

The federal rules make it difficult to apply injunctions to those who do not fit within the category of "parties . . . their officers, agents, servants, employees, and attorneys, and upon those persons in active concert or participation with them. . . ."

c. ***In Rem* Injunctions?**

Although *in rem* injunctions seem to fall outside the parameters of the Federal Rules, courts do issue injunctions that are *in rem* in nature.

d. **More on *In Rem* Injunctions**

In rem injunctions are more likely when a matter involves a particular piece of property that is already under the court's jurisdiction.

e. **Substitution of Parties**

Rule 25, F.R.Civ.P. provides for the substitution of parties.

f. **Joinder of Parties**

Rule 25, F.R.Civ.P., provides for the substitution or joinder of parties.

g. **Successors in Interest**

In some instances, equitable decrees can bind successors in interest.

(1) **General Principles**

Courts have held that persons acquiring an interest in property that is a subject of litigation are bound by, or entitled to the benefit of, a subsequent judgment, despite a lack of knowledge. RESTATEMENT OF JUDGMENTS § 89, and comment c (1942).

(2) **Illustration: The Replacement Company**

In *Golden State Bottling Co., Inc. v. NLRB*, 414 U.S. 168 (1973), a court bound a successor under a decree.

4. **Notice Requirement**

Although the Constitution and various federal statutes generally require that an injunction proceeding be conducted only with notice to opposing parties, and after service of the summons and complaint. TROs can be issued *ex parte*.

a. **General Requirement of Notice**

Fed. R. Civ. P. 65(d) responds to this problem by providing that a TRO or preliminary injunction is binding only on those "who receive actual notice of the order by personal service or otherwise."

b. **The Content of Notice**

A number of courts have held that two requirements must be satisfied in order for notice to be adequate. First, the notice must come from a source that is entitled to credit. Second, it must adequately inform defendant of the act or acts sought to be prohibited.

c. **The Usual Scenario**

In the ordinary case, the defendant will be in court when the order is entered and will hear the judge enter it. From the standpoint of notice, nothing more is required.

d. **Personal Service**

When defendant is not in court but is actually served with a copy of the order, the notice is clearly sufficient.

e. **Telegrams and Messengers**

In *The Cape May & Schellinger's Landing R.R. Co. v. Johnson*, 35 N.J.Eq. Rep. 422 (Ch., 1882), a telegram notice was deemed to be adequate.

f. **Posting**

In *Midland Steel Products Co. v. International Union, United Automobile, Aerospace and Agricultural Implement Workers of America, Local 486*, 61 Ohio St.3d 121, 573 N.E.2d 98 (1991), union members were held to be bound by notices posted at company entrances.

g. **Thwarted Service**

In *Vermont Women's Health Center v. Operation Rescue*, 159 Vt. 141, 617 A.2d 411 (1992), a judge held that defendants were properly served when they blatantly created noise to prevent themselves from hearing the reading of the terms of an injunction.

5. **Bond Requirement**

At both the federal level and the state level, one who obtains a preliminary injunction or a TRO must usually post security to protect the defendant against loss.

a. **Exception for Indigents (and the Rich)**

Although Rule 65 seems to mandate the posting of a bond, courts have created exceptions to the mandate (e.g., for situations when plaintiff is indigent or, sometimes, when plaintiff is rich and can easily afford to pay damages).

b. **Calculating the Bond**

The amount of the bond will vary from case-to-case just as a defendant's potential damages can vary.

c. **Recovery on the Bond**

When an injunction or order is overturned, although most courts tend to assume that damages will be given, recovery on the bond is not automatic.

(1) **Recovery Limited to Proof of Loss**

When recovery is permitted, it is limited by the amount of loss proven by the party subjected to the erroneously issued order.

(2) **Recovery Limited to the Amount of the Bond**

In many states, although not all, recovery will be limited to the amount of the bond.

(3) **Calculating Damages**

The types of damages that are recoverable may vary from state-to-state. In many jurisdictions, the enjoined defendant can recover for those losses that are proved including attorney's fees. In some jurisdictions, attorney's fees are not recoverable.

(4) **Denial of Recovery**

Even when a temporary restraining order is vacated, courts have discretion to deny recovery on the bond.

6. **Stays**

Courts have discretion to stay their injunctions.

a. **Grounds for Stay**

In *Washington Metropolitan Area Transit Commission v. Holiday Tours, Inc.*, 559 F.2d 841 (D.C.Cir.1977), the court articulated the following criteria for the granting of stays: "(1) Has the petitioner made a strong showing that it is likely to prevail on the merits of its appeal? Without such a substantial indication of probable success, there would be no justification for the court's intrusion into the ordinary processes of administration and judicial review. (2) Has the petitioner shown that without such relief, it will be irreparably injured? . . . (3) Would the issuance of a stay substantially harm other parties interested in the proceedings? . . . (4) Where lies the public interest?"

b. **Illustration**

In one case a stay was granted because, otherwise, defendant's business would have been destroyed.

c. **Bond Requirement**

In general, in order to obtain a stay, plaintiff must post a bond or other appropriate security.

C. PERMANENT INJUNCTIONS

Permanent injunctions are subject to the ordinary rules governing equitable relief. And, like other forms of equitable relief, are highly discretionary. In *Weinberger v. Romero-*

Barcelo, 456 U.S. 305 (1982), the Court held that the ordinary rules governing equitable relief apply unless Congress has clearly directed the courts to apply a different standard.

D. FRAMING THE INJUNCTION

Whether a court issues a preliminary injunction or a permanent injunction, the court must be concerned about how the order is worded or "framed."

1. The Constitutional Aspects of Framing

Injunctions which implicate constitutional rights may be scrutinized with greater specificity, especially when they implicate protected activities like free speech.

2. Collateral Challenges Based on Specificity

Defendants can sometimes defeat a contempt charge based on a claim that an injunction is too vague.

3. Non-Constitutional Cases

In cases that do not implicate constitutional rights, courts rarely conclude that an injunction is so vague as to be invalid and unenforceable.

4. Unenforceable Decrees

Even though some orders are framed with specificity, courts may refuse to enforce them because they present practicality or supervision problems.

5. Vagueness Illustration: Vagueness of the "Upbringing" Provision

Other orders, which might otherwise be enforceable, are not framed with sufficient specificity and therefore are not enforceable.

6. Second Illustration: The Cookie Recipe

Another illustration of vagueness is provided by *Peggy Lawton Kitchens, Inc. v. Hogan*, 403 Mass. 732, 532 N.E.2d 54 (1989). In that case, plaintiffs alleged that defendants had stolen a chocolate chip cookie recipe from their business and were using the recipe to make cookies in a competing business. Although the trial court issued an order against defendant, the court concluded that the order was not defined with specificity, and therefore was not enforceable.

7. The *Madsen* Case

In *Madsen v. Women's Health Center, Inc.*, 512 U.S. 753 (1994), the Court articulated specific rules applicable to injunctions affecting free speech. The case involved protests at or near an abortion clinic, and the trial court placed various restrictions on the protestors.

a. Content-Viewpoint Neutrality

In general, the court has tended to apply strict scrutiny to restrictions on speech that are not content-neutral and viewpoint-neutral. However, in *Madsen*, the Court concluded that injunctive restrictions are necessarily content-based and viewpoint-based simply because the trial court issues an injunction against a specific group of protestors (in *Madsen*, anti-abortion protestors).

b. Scope of Review

In *Madsen*, because of the uniqueness of injunctions, the Court chose to impose a lesser standard of review: "when evaluating a content-neutral injunction." The Court concluded that its "standard time, place, and manner analysis is not sufficiently rigorous. We must ask instead whether the challenged provisions of the injunction burden no more speech than necessary to serve a significant government interest."

c. **36 Foot Buffer Zone**

In *Madsen*, the trial court imposed a 36-foot buffer zone around the clinic which prohibited petitioners from "congregating, picketing, patrolling, demonstrating or entering" any portion of the public right-of-way or private property within 36 feet of the property line of the clinic as a way of ensuring access to the clinic. The Court held that the 36-foot buffer zone was valid except as applied to the private property to the north and west of the clinic. As for the private party, the order burdened more speech than necessary to protect access to the clinic.

d. **Restriction on "Singing, Chanting, Whistling, Shouting, Yelling"**

The Court upheld noise restrictions, noting that they "burden no more speech than necessary to ensure the health and well-being of the patients at the clinic. The First Amendment does not demand that patients at a medical facility undertake Herculean efforts to escape the cacophony of political protests."

e. **"Images Observable" Provision**

In *Madsen*, the trial court also imposed a restriction on "images observable to . . . patients inside the clinic" during the hours of 7:30 a.m. through noon on Mondays through Saturdays. However, the Court struck this restriction down noting that it burdened "more speech than necessary to achieve the purpose of limiting threats to clinic patients or their families." Instead, the clinic could simply close its curtains to block out the images.

f. **The Prohibition Against Approaching Persons**

In *Madsen*, the trial court also ordered that petitioners refrain from physically approaching any person seeking services of the clinic "unless such person indicates a desire to communicate" in an area within 300 feet of the clinic. The court expressed concern that clinic patients and staff might be "stalked" or "shadowed" by the petitioners as they approached the clinic. The Court invalidated the restriction:

g. **The Prohibition on Picketing, Demonstrating and Sound Equipment Within 300 Feet**

Finally, the trial court prohibited picketing, demonstrating, or using sound amplification equipment within 300 feet of the residences of clinic staff. The Court concluded that, while the trial court could have prohibited targeted picketing of residences, the 300-foot zone was too large to be sustainable.

E. EXPERIMENTAL AND CONDITIONAL INJUNCTIONS

Since injunctions are equitable decrees, and their grant or denial is inherently discretionary, courts are free to shape their orders as required by the circumstances. Thus, the mere fact that plaintiffs are suffering injury does not mean that they will receive the injunctive relief desired. As the circumstances dictate, the court may choose to issue an "experimental" or "conditional" injunction.

1. The Function of Experimental and Conditional Injunctions

Even when courts decide to grant equitable relief, they try to enter decrees that accommodate both parties' needs, desires and interests. In other words, as the equities dictate, courts may try to mold their decrees by entering partial injunctions (a.k.a., "experimental injunctions") designed to provide relief to the plaintiff, but allowing defendant to continue her conduct as much as possible.

2. *Boomer* and Conditional Injunctions

In *Boomer v. Atlantic Cement Company*, 26 N.Y.2d 219, 257 N.E.2d 870, 309 N.Y.S.2d 312 (1970), the injunction contained a provision vacating its effect if defendant provided specified compensation to plaintiff. In other words, if defendant paid, it could continue its operations. If not, it would be required to shut down.

3. *Boomer* and the Delayed Injunction

Although the *Boomer* court did not grant a delayed injunction, the court thought about whether "to grant the injunction but postpone its effect to a specified future date to give opportunity for technical advances to permit defendant to eliminate the nuisance. . . ."

4. *Boomer* and the Possibility of an Experimental Injunction

One thing that the court could have done was to impose an "experimental" injunction—an injunction that required defendant to modify its operation in important respects in the hope that the modifications will ameliorate the interference.

5. *Spur Industries* and the Compensated Injunction

In some cases, courts decide to enter "compensated" injunctions. For example, in *Spur Industries, Inc. v. Del E. Webb Development Co.*, 108 Ariz. 178, 494 P.2d 700 (In Banc, 1972), the court enjoined defendant's feedlot operation, but ordered plaintiff to pay the cost of moving that operation elsewhere.

F. DECREES AFFECTING THIRD PARTIES

In some instances, a court may find it necessary to enjoin third parties in order to grant complete relief to a plaintiff. In a few instances, these joinders are permissible. In other situations, they are difficult or impermissible.

1. The *Milliken* Rule

Under the holding in *Milliken v. Bradley,* 418 U.S. 717 (1974), the Court has suggested that the federal courts have limited authority to pull third parties into their decrees.

2. The *Hills* Exception

In *Hills v. Gautreaux,* 425 U.S. 284 (1976), the court entered a broad order crossing jurisdictional boundaries, but its order was entered against a federal governmental agency. The Court upheld the decree.

3. The *General Building Contractors Association* Case

In *General Building Contractors Association, Inc. v. Pennsylvania*, 458 U.S. 375 (1982), the Court held that lower courts have limited authority to enjoin third parties when the third parties are not implicated in the misconduct.

G. MODIFICATION OF DECREES

Even though "permanent" injunctions are issued at the conclusion of a lawsuit and are designed to last indefinitely, and in that sense "permanently," they can be modified or dissolved under appropriate circumstances. Rule 60b, F.R. Civ. Pro., provides that "on motion and on such terms as are just, the court may relieve a party [from] a final judgment [for] the following reasons: (5) [it] is no longer equitable that the judgment should have prospective application."

1. General Standards

Perhaps the leading decision is *Agostini v. Felton*, 521 U.S. 203 (1997), in which the Court held that "it is appropriate to grant a Rule 60(b)(5) motion when the party seeking relief from an injunction or consent decree can show 'a significant change either in factual conditions or in law.' "

2. The *Agostini* Case

Agostini v. Felton, 521 U.S. 203 (1997), involves perhaps the most famous example of modification. In that case, the Court abandoned its prior decision in *Aguilar v. Felton*, 473 U.S. 402 (1985), and effectively lifted the injunction imposed in that case.

3. Illustration: Factual Changes

In *Ladner v. Siegel*, 298 Pa. 487, 148 A. 699 (1930), the trial court entered an injunction against a proposed parking garage. Over time, the surrounding area changed from residential to mostly commercial, and Siegel modified his plans in an effort to provide proper ventilation. The court agreed to lift the injunction.

4. The Limited Nature of School Desegregation Decrees

In a number of cases, the Court has recognized that desegregation decrees are not designed to last forever, but instead should eventually be terminated. For example, in *Board of Education v. Dowell*, 498 U.S. 237 (1991), the Court held that desegregation decrees should eventually terminate because of the preference for local control of schools.

5. Partial Releases from Desegregation Decrees

In *Freeman v. Pitts*, 503 U.S. 467 (1992), the Court held that a school district should be released from a desegregation decree in regard to "discrete categories in which the school district has achieved compliance with a court-ordered desegregation plan."

H. INJUNCTIONS AGAINST CRIMINAL ACTIVITY

In general, courts have been reluctant to enjoin the commission of future crimes. As a result, if Jesse James were still alive and robbing banks and trains, courts would be loath to enjoin him from committing future robberies.

1. Justifications for the Restriction

Various justifications have been offered for the reluctance to enjoin crime, including the fact that courts are reluctant to enter futile decrees, and the fact that the criminal laws are "sufficiently effective in deterring similar conduct of these parties, thereby affording plaintiff an adequate legal remedy" And, if the criminal laws are insufficient to deter crimes, there is no reason to believe that an injunction would be more effective.

2. Additional Justifications

"[Four] potential harms are always present when a case involves an injunction against criminal offenses. First, there is a potential harm in the possible conflict with the constitutional guarantee of the right to trial by jury. . . . Second, the proof necessary for a conviction in a criminal court is constitutionally designed to require a high standard of proof, proof beyond a reasonable doubt. . . . Third, a court of equity can issue a show cause order, and the person cited must show why he should not be held in contempt. In a criminal proceeding the accused cannot be compelled to give evidence against himself. . . . Fourth, the person enjoined will suffer some stigma or embarrassment comparable to that suffered by being labeled a habitual offender because, before a court of equity assumes jurisdiction, there must be proof that the person enjoined committed acts of violence with such systematic persistence as to warrant a finding that they would be continued unless restrained."

3. Exceptions to the Rule

Courts will frequently enjoin public nuisances even though the conduct might also be regarded as criminal.

I. INJUNCTIONS AGAINST LITIGATION

In some instances, courts are asked to enjoin litigation pending in other courts. Whether courts will grant injunctive relief against litigation is dependent on a variety of complex factors.

1. Early Equitable Injunctions Against Law Court Litigation

In the early common law, when separate courts of law and equity existed, courts of equity sometimes enjoined litigation in the law courts in order to protect their jurisdiction.

2. Modern Injunctive Contexts

Modern courts are also asked to enjoin pending litigation, but in somewhat different contexts. Three separate and distinct contexts emerge: 1) state courts are asked to enjoin litigation in the courts of other state courts; 2) state courts are asked to enjoin litigation in federal courts; & 3) federal courts are asked to enjoin litigation in state courts. Because different rules apply to each context, we will examine them separately.

3. State Court Injunctions Against Foreign State Litigation

If a state court can obtain personal jurisdiction over the parties, a state court may have the power to enjoin litigation in other states. Of course, as at common law, the court does so by ordering the parties not to proceed with the foreign litigation rather than by issuing an injunction against the foreign court.

a. The *James v. Grand Trunk Western Railroad Company* Deadlock

James v. Grand Trunk Western Railroad Company, 14 Ill.2d 356, 152 N.E.2d 858 (Ill., 1958), provides the classic illustration of what can happen when state courts attempt to enjoin litigation in other states. The case became entangled with conflicting state court injunctions.

b. The *James* Holding

In *James*, the court noted that courts generally decline to issue injunctions against foreign litigation. Even when courts have the power to enjoin the litigation, the better view is that "the exercise of such power by equity courts has been deemed a matter of great delicacy, invoked with great restraint to avoid distressing conflicts and reciprocal interference with jurisdiction."

c. The Doctrine of *Forum Non Conveniens*

In general, cases like *James* should be dealt with under the doctrine of *forum non conveniens* rather than by the issuance of an injunction.

d. **Statutory Approaches to Conflicting Jurisdictional Claims**

The Uniform Child Custody Jurisdiction Act (UCCJA) (L.1978, ch. 493, eff. Sept. 1, 1978), provides an alternate method of dealing with inter-jurisdictional conflicts. The UCCJA triggers a separate inquiry to determine where custody issues should be litigated.

4. **State Court Injunctions Against Federal Litigation**

In general, state courts lack the power to enjoin federal court proceedings.

5. **Federal Court Injunctions Against State Litigation**

Although the federal courts have the power to enjoin state court proceedings, they generally abstain from doing so.

a. **The *Younger* "Our Federalism" Doctrine**

In *Younger v. Harris*, 401 U.S. 37 (1971), the Court stated that "Since the beginning of this country's history, Congress has, subject to few exceptions, manifested a desire to permit state courts to try state cases free from interference by federal courts." *Younger's* so-called abstention doctrine, also known as "Our Federalism," stated a rule of policy rather than a rule of jurisdiction based on the notion that equity should not act when the parties have an adequate remedy at law, as well as on notions of comity.

b. **Application of the "Our Federalism" Doctrine**

Younger itself provides the classic illustration of how the "Our Federalism" doctrine applies. In that case, Harris was charged with violation of California's Criminal Syndicalism Act and filed suit in federal court seeking to enjoin the District Attorney of Los Angeles County from prosecuting him. The Court held that the federal court request for injunctive relief should have been dismissed.

c. **The *Dombrowski* Exception**

Younger recognized that its prior holding in *Dombrowski v. Pfister*, 380 U.S. 479 (1965), would establish a limited exception to the Our Federalism doctrine. In that case, no valid criminal prosecution was pending. Instead, the prosecutor had threatened to enforce statutes, but had done so without any expectation of prosecution or any effort to secure convictions.

d. **Our Federalism and Threatened Prosecutions**

In *Steffel v. Thompson*, 415 U.S. 452 (1974), plaintiff was threatened with criminal prosecution if he continued to protest at a shopping mall. Since no state court prosecution was pending, plaintiff did not have an adequate legal remedy and federal court intervention would not interfere with such proceedings.

e. **Our Federalism and Requests for Declaratory (but Not Injunctive) Relief**

In *Samuels v. Mackell*, 401 U.S. 66 (1971), the Court held that, even though injunctive relief was not requested, Our Federalism precluded the federal court from issuing declaratory relief.

f. **Subsequent Prosecutions and Pending Federal Proceedings**

Our Federalism might also preclude federal courts from hearing a case when a later criminal prosecution is brought.

g. The Anti-Injunction Statute

Younger's Our Federalism doctrine is reinforced by the federal anti-injunction statute.

h. The "Expressly Authorized" Exception

There is also an "expressly authorized" exception to the anti-injunction statute.

J. STRUCTURAL INJUNCTIONS

Some injunction cases involve broad challenges to the operation of a school district or prison system. In these latter cases, litigants sometimes ask a court to enter a "structural injunction" directed at governmental officials. These structural injunctions are designed to eliminate past violations and regulate the way a school, prison, or police department functions in the future.

1. The Justifications for Structural Injunctions

Despite these concerns, federal courts have entered structural relief in an extraordinary array of cases that have dramatically reshaped society, directly regulated state governments, and routinely involved courts in issuing orders that involve continuing supervision problems.

2. The Origins of Structural Relief

The development of structural remedies is generally traced to the United States Supreme Court's holding in *Brown v. Board of Education (Brown I)*, 347 U.S. 483 (1954), in which the Court ordered school desegregation.

3. The Growth of Structural Injunctions Following *Brown II* and *Swann*

Following *Brown v. Board of Education*, in *Swann v. Charlotte-Mecklenburg Bd. of Education*, 402 U.S. 1 (1971), the Court signaled an end to the Court's go slow approach. In *Swann*, although the trial court allowed school officials to submit three separate and distinct desegregation plans, the trial court rejected all three plans as constitutionally inadequate. In frustration, the trial court decided to desegregate the school system itself based on the advice of an outside consultant.

4. The Decline of Structural Remedies

Recent years have witnessed a decline in the use of structural remedies. In many parts of the country, the courts have started terminating their control over local school districts and returning those districts to the control of local officials.

5. *O'Shea* and Limits on Structuralism

In addition, the Court has placed limits on the availability of structural remedies. For example, in *O'Shea v. Littleton*, 414 U.S. 488 (1974), the Court rejected a request to supervise judges and magistrates who were allegedly discriminating.

6. Rizzo v. Goode

In *Rizzo v. Goode,* 423 U.S. 362 (1976), the Court rejected an effort as judicial supervision of a major metropolitan police department.

K. EXTRA-TERRITORIAL DECREES

A number of cases have focused on the permissibility of extra-territorial decrees, and courts have formulated special rules governing the permissibility of such decrees.

1. Decrees Affecting Land

In general, decrees affecting land are regarded as local in character, and it would generally be inappropriate for a court in a foreign country (e.g., Canada) to attempt to transfer property located in New York.

a. *Deschenes* and Coerced Conveyances

In *Deschenes v. Tallman*, 248 N.Y. 33, 161 N.E. 321 (N.Y.App., 1928), although the reaffirmed the general rule, holding that a Canadian court's transfer of property located in New York was valid. However, that case also involved an order that court coerced the company that owned the land into conveying the property. The New York court upheld the conveyance notwithstanding the coercion.

b. *Burnley v. Stevenson*

Although foreign courts are not required to accept out-of-state decrees affecting real property, they can choose to do so.

c. *The Salton Sea Cases:* More on Potential Extra-Territorial Decrees

In the *Salton Sea Cases*, 172 Fed. 792 (9th Cir., 1909), the court held that defendant could be required to remedy a problem (even though part of the problem was in Mexico) because the most effective place to deal with the problem was in California.

2. Decrees Affecting Personal Property

Similar principles apply to personal property located in other states. In other words, a court in another state may not have the power to take control of property located in the other state.

L. NATIONAL SECURITY

Courts are reluctant to sustain injunctions designed to protect national security.

1. *The N.Y. Times* Case

In the Court's landmark decision in *New York Times Company v. United States*, 403 U.S. 713 (1971), a Pentagon employee stole a classified study entitled "History of U.S. Decision-Making Process on Viet Nam Policy" (The Pentagon Papers), and turned it over to the *New York Times* and *Washington Post* newspapers who planned to publish them. In a *per curiam* opinion, the United States Supreme Court rejected the government's attempt to enjoin the publication: "Any system of prior restraints of expression comes to this Court bearing a heavy presumption against its constitutional validity." The Court held that the government "thus carries a heavy burden of showing justification for the imposition of such a restraint." The Court concluded that the government could not satisfy that burden. Despite the holding, the case produced a plethora of concurring and dissenting opinions.

2. *The Progressives* Case and Nuclear Weapons

In *United States v. Progressive, Inc.*, 467 F.Supp. 990 (W.D.Wis., 1979), the courts ultimately lifted an injunction prohibiting publication of an article about how to build a hydrogen bomb

3. The *Snepp* Case

In *Snepp v. United States*, 444 U.S. 507 (1980), when a former CIA employee divulged information in violation of an agreement not to do so, the court ordered restitution of the proceeds from the book.

M. INJUNCTIONS FOR BREACH OF CONTRACT

Injunctions for breach of contract include specific performance (compelling the defendant to perform as promised) and negative injunctions (precluding the defendant from undertaking other duties inconsistent with performance of the contract).

1. Specific Performance

Specific Performance is an injunction ordering a party to perform as promised.

a. Irreparable Injury Rule

Specific performance, like any injunction, is available if the remedy at law is inadequate. Inadequacy sometimes is defined in terms of uniqueness. Thus, the Uniform Commercial Code allows specific performance when the goods are unique, "or in other proper circumstances." U.C.C. § 2–716. Uniqueness is simply one way to prove that the remedy at law is inadequate.

(1) Real Estate Presumed Unique

No two parcels of real estate are completely identical. Thus, courts presume that the buyer of land is entitled specific performance of the contract.

(2) Good Presumed Fungible

Goods often can be replaced with other, nearly identical goods. As such, courts generally presume that damages will protect plaintiff's interest adequately. Shortage—and uniqueness, the extreme case of shortage—offers the most obvious route to proving that damages are inadequate.

(3) Services

No presumption applies either direction to services. Services often will be unique. The reasons for avoiding injunctive relief of personal services contracts generally do not involve the irreparable injury rule, but other policy issues. For example, courts do not want to "foist" unwilling parties on each other or impose orders that will require continuing and ongoing supervision.

b. Other Defenses

Even when the remedy at law is inadequate, difficulties may make specific performance unwise. All equitable defenses apply, but two special problems arise.

(1) Concerns for Practicality

Unless a contract is very specific, a court may be unable to frame an injunction in terms that permit it to supervise performance. Orders may be too general ("Perform as promised") or too specific ("Perform in this way") even if the contract does not specify that manner of performance). Some injunctions might generate constant litigation (usually in contempt proceedings) over whether the defendant intentionally breached or made good faith efforts to perform as ordered, whether compliance with the order was possible, whether the conduct actually complied with the letter of the order but circumvented the goal, etc. In either situation, courts may be reluctant to issue the injunction in the first place—recognizing practical limits on their capacity to achieve a just result.

(2) Concerns for Personal Freedom

Courts refuse to award specific performance of personal service contracts to employers. Ordering an employee to return to work for an employer carries with it an implication of involuntary servitude and problems with enforcement.

(a) Mutuality

In some cases, courts deny specific performance no matter which party seeks it. Thus, employees may be denied specific performance of employment contracts on the basis that a personal service contract cannot be specifically enforced.

(b) Statutory Changes

Modern statutes, especially civil rights laws, often provide for an employee's right to reinstatement or other specific performance of an employment contract. As courts become more comfortable with orders of this type, concerns for mutuality seem likely to recede.

2. Negative Injunctions

When specific performance is not available, courts may order a party to refrain from any conduct inconsistent with performance. For example, an employee might be ordered to refrain from working for any other employer during the period covered by the employment contract. This type of order is referred to as "negative specific performance."

a. Contractual Source of Injunction

Negative injunctions usually have a contractual source, either an explicit promise not to work for a competitor for a period of time after leaving an employer or an inference that working for others would be impossible under the contract.

b. Rationale as a Limit on Injunctive Relief

Courts differ regarding the advisability of negative injunctions. If a negative injunction is sought merely as an attempt to coerce the employee to return to the original employer, courts may decline to issue the order. More realistically, negative injunctions protect employers against part, but not all, of the harm caused by the breach. Working for a competitor may increase the harm to an employer who loses an employee's service. If so, that portion of the harm can be decreased by a negative injunction. This rational suggests negative injunctions should be limited to cases where competitive losses seem likely.

c. Public Policy Concerns

Injunctions that prevent employees from earning a living raise public policy concerns. Thus, courts may refuse a negative injunction unless it is limited to a reasonable geographic area, a reasonable range of jobs, and a reasonable period of time.

N. INJUNCTION-LIKE REMEDIES

Three bodies of law have the feel of injunctions, but do not quite fit into the standard mold described above: ejectment, replevin, and conversion.

1. Ejectment

Ejectment, a legal remedy available in an action for trespass, enables a possessor of land to regain sole possession of her property and recover the fair rental value of the land during the time it was wrongly occupied by the defendant.

2. Replevin

Replevin is a remedy for an action for trespass to chattels, which returns to the plaintiff property wrongfully in the possession of the defendant. Replevin is available in two forms—legal and equitable.

a. Legal Replevin

The procedure for obtaining legal replevin is statutory. Its enforcement mechanism is that the sheriff is directed to seize the property in possession of the defendant and return the property to the plaintiff. Legal replevin is available as pre-trial relief and permanent relief. In most states, a defendant has no right to appeal pre-trial legal replevin. The primary advantage of legal versus equitable replevin is that the enforcement mechanism is faster, particularly where property can be located.

b. Equitable Replevin

Equitable replevin is merely a form of injunction. Due to the availability of legal replevin, the equitable requirement of "inadequate legal remedy" is often difficult to prove. Pretrial equitable replevin may be either mandatory in form or prohibitory: if mandatory, it consists of an order to the defendant to return the property to the plaintiff; if prohibitory, it involves an order prohibiting the defendant from damaging, selling, or hiding the property pending trial. The appealability of pre-trial equitable replevin is governed by the rules applicable to other types of injunctions. Because equitable replevin is an *in personam* order, enforceable by contempt, a defendant is incentivized not to secrete, damage, use, sell, or otherwise dispose of the property.

3. Conversion

Conversion is either a tort in its own right or a legal remedy to an action for trespass to chattels. Its remedy is a "forced sale" of personal property to which the plaintiff gives title to the defendant, in exchange for payment of the property's market value at the time of the conversion (or at resolution of the case, if the property has risen in value). Conversion is limited to cases that require payment for the full value of the chattel. There is some disagreement among courts as to whether conversion is available as against a *bona fide* purchaser.

▪ CHAPTER FOUR: RESTITUTION

A. GENERAL PRINCIPLES

The doctrinal core of restitution is misleadingly simple: "A person who has been unjustly enriched at the expense of another is required to make restitution to the other."

RESTATEMENT OF RESTITUTION § 1 (1937). The purpose of restitution is simply to prevent a defendant from retaining benefits unjustly derived from plaintiff. Despite the simplicity, restitutionary remedies can be extremely powerful and flexible.

1. Quasi-Contract Distinguished

Quasi-contract is perhaps the best-known aspect of restitution.

2. Quasi-Contract Today

Today, quasi-contract extends to many different types of situations.

3. Other Forms of Restitution

As we shall see, restitution extends far beyond quasi-contract. It also includes special restitutionary devices such as constructive trusts, equitable liens tracing, and subrogation.

a. The Mistaken Home Builder

For example, in *Beacon Homes, Inc. v. Holt*, 266 N.C. 467, 146 S.E.2d 434 (1966), defendant's mother contracted with plaintiff to build a house on defendant's land. Once the house was built, the mother refused to pay for it. Defendant also refused to pay for it but claimed ownership of the house and began renting it out. The court ordered defendant to give restitution to the builder.

b. Legal Versus Equitable Restitution

Restitution has roots in both law and equity.

c. The Cheating Bettor

When there is a relative discrepancy in the culpability of parties, a court might overlook a cheating bettor's misconduct and order restitution.

d. "Volunteers" and "Officious Intermeddlers"

Even though defendant receives an enrichment at plaintiff's expense, it may not be "unjust" for defendant to retain that benefit. As a rule, courts are reluctant to permit "volunteers" and "officious intermeddlers" to recover sums expended on behalf of others.

B. MEASURING THE ENRICHMENT

Even when a court finds that defendant has been unjustly enriched, it must decide how to measure the enrichment. In fact, as we shall see, the measurement can vary depending on circumstances.

1. General Principles

The RESTATEMENT OF RESTITUTION, Comment to § 1, at 13, provides for the following measure of recovery in restitution cases: "*d.* Ordinarily the benefit to the one and the loss to the other are coextensive, and the result of the remedies given under the rules stated in the Restatement of this subject is to compel the one to surrender the benefit which he has received and thereby to make restitution to the other for the loss which he has suffered."

2. Alternative Measures

In contrast to damages, which are usually measured by plaintiff's loss, restitution can be measured by defendant's gain.

3. Example #1: The Tree Thief

When a thief steals mahogany trees worth a high amount but uses the wood in ways that do not reflect that value, the thief might still be held responsible for the higher value.

4. The Tree Thief: Redux

If instead of being a tree thief, defendant was an innocent convertor, defendant might still be responsible for the higher value (on the theory that he should bear the loss rather than the innocent owner).

5. The Tree Thief: Third Variant

A different result might obtain if the plaintiff, rather than the defendant, is at fault.

6. The Defaulting Publisher

When a publisher refuses to publish a book, the writer is entitled to restitution based on an hourly rate for the time spent in preparing the manuscript.

C. SPECIAL RESTITUTIONARY REMEDIES

The equitable side of restitution includes several special restitutionary devices, including the constructive trust, equitable lien, tracing, and subrogation. Because each of these devices is powerful and flexible, they can provide a plaintiff with unique advantages.

1. The Constructive Trust

A constructive trust is created and imposed by operation of law, without any reference to the trustee's actual or supposed intent to create a trust, and sometimes in contravention of the "trustee's" intent. It is imposed to prevent unjust enrichment.

a. Distinguished from Express Trusts

A constructive trust does not, like an express trust, arise because of a manifestation of an intention to create it, but it is imposed as a remedy to prevent unjust enrichment.

b. Illustration: The Defaulting Wife

Special restitutionary devices might be applied in an array of contexts. In *Sieger v. Sieger*, 162 Minn. 322, 202 N.W. 742 (1925), a constructive trust was applied against a defaulting wife who inappropriately titled community property in her own name.

c. Second Illustration: The Defaulting Niece

A constructive trust has been applied against a niece who received real property, but failed to follow through on her obligations.

2. Equitable Lien

An equitable lien is similar to a constructive trust, but instead of requiring defendant to hold the property in trust, the court imposes a lien against property as security for plaintiff's interest.

3. Special Advantages of Constructive Trusts and Equitable Liens

Both the constructive trust and equitable lien offer plaintiffs special advantages over other remedies. The two most important advantages are that both devices allow plaintiffs to "trace" their property into other forms and can be used to give plaintiffs priority over other creditors.

a. **Tracing**

"Tracing" is the idea that plaintiffs can trace their property into different forms and impose a constructive trust or equitable lien on the property in those other forms.

(1) **Illustration: The Embezzling Employee**

In *G & M Motor Company v. Thompson*, 567 P.2d 80 (Okla., 1977), a constructive trust was applied against an embezzling employee who invested the embezzled money in an insurance policy.

(2) **Second Illustration: The Bank and the Ex-Wife**

In *In re Allen*, 724 P.2d 651 (Colo., En Banc, 1986), a bank applied a constructive trust against a wife who received embezzled funds in a divorce settlement and invested the money in real estate.

(3) **Third Illustration: The Defrauded Purchasers**

In *Coppinger v. Superior Court of Orange County*, 134 Cal.App.3d 883, 185 Cal.Rptr. 24 (Cal.Ct.App.1982), a constructive trust was applied against real estate purchased by a real property seller who sold a house infested with termites and invested the proceeds in other real estate.

b. **Priority over Other Creditors**

A second advantage of the special restitutionary remedies (e.g., constructive trust and equitable lien) is that they can be used to gain priority over other creditors. In other words, rather than standing in line with other creditors and receiving pennies on the dollar, plaintiff can assert a constructive trust or equitable lien against the property and receive priority over other creditors.

(1) **Illustration: The Defrauded Real Estate Purchaser**

In *In re Radke*, 5 Kan.App.2d 407, 619 P.2d 520 (1980), plaintiff claimed that he was defrauded in the purchase of real estate, and that the money was invested in other real estate. As a result, plaintiff sought to trace his money into the other real estate and impose an equitable lien on it (rather than stand in line as a general creditor). The Court stated that: "Equity permits the tracing of assets and the impression of a trust or equitable lien on them without the showing that a money judgment against the party who precipitated the fraud would be uncollectible. I PALMER, LAW OF RESTITUTION § 3.14(a)(1978)."

(2) **The Rule in *Knatchbull v. Hallett***

In *Knatchbull v. Hallett*, L.R. 13 Ch. D. 696, the court held that "where a fund was composed partly of a defrauded claimant's money and partly of that of the wrongdoer, it would be presumed that in the fluctuations of the fund it was the wrongdoer's purpose to draw out the money he could legally and honestly use rather than that of the claimant, and that the claimant might identify what remained as his *res*, and assert his right to it by way of an equitable lien on the whole fund, or a proper pro rata share of it."

(3) **Lowest Intermediate Balance Theory**

The "lowest intermediate balance theory" is articulated in RESTATEMENT OF RESTITUTION § 212: "Where a person wrongfully mingles money of another with money of his own and makes withdrawals from the mingled fund and dissipates the money so withdrawn, and subsequently adds money of his own to the fund, the other can enforce an equitable lien upon the fund only for the amount of the lowest intermediate balance, unless: (a) the fund or a part of it earns a profit; or (b) the subsequent additions were made by way of restitution."

(4) The Limits of Tracing: Ponzi Schemes and Defrauded Investors

In *Cunningham v. Brown*, 265 U.S. 1 (1924), the Court refused to allow a constructive trust as applied to a so-called "Ponzi Scheme." In *Cunningham*, the Court refused to apply "the fiction of *Knatchbull v. Hallett* [noting that the] rule is useful to work out equity between a wrongdoer and a victim; but, when the fund with which the wrongdoer is dealing is wholly made up of the fruits of the frauds perpetrated against a myriad of victims, the case is different."

c. Circumvention of Debtor Exemptions

An additional advantage of special restitutionary remedies is that they can be used to circumvent debtor exemptions. Each state provides debtors with certain "exemptions" (e.g., the homestead exemption) that allow them to protect assets against creditors. Special restitutionary remedies allow creditors to circumvent the exemptions and assert a claim against the property that is the subject of the exemptions.

d. Subrogation

Subrogation is yet another special restitutionary remedy. The RESTATEMENT OF RESTITUTION § 162 (1937), provides that: "Where property of one person is used in discharging an obligation owed by another or a lien upon the property of another, under such circumstances that the other would be unjustly enriched by the retention of the benefit thus conferred, the former is entitled to be subrogated to the position of the obligee or lien-holder."

(1) Subrogation and Tracing

Tracing can also be combined with the remedy of subrogation.

(2) The Defrauder

In *Wilson v. Todd*, 217 Ind. 183, 26 N.E.2d 1003 (1940), the court applied subrogation to an individual who had been defrauded: "Subrogation is the substitution of another person in the place of a creditor, so that the person in whose favor it is exercised succeeds to the right of the creditor in relation to the debt."

■ CHAPTER 5: DECLARATORY JUDGMENTS

A. GENERALLY

The declaratory judgment is designed to decide disputed rights, obligations or status. Although the declaratory remedy can be combined with other remedies (e.g., injunctive relief), it can function independently.

1. **Development of the Declaratory Remedy**

The declaratory remedy was developed in various states early in the last century. The remedy received recognition on a national level in the Uniform Declaratory Judgments Act (UDJA) and the Federal Declaratory Judgment Act (FDJA).

2. **The Function of Declaratory Relief**

In some instances, individuals may be unsure about what they may or may not do. Rather than risk prosecution in a protest case, or breach of contract in a business case, the individuals might prefer to seek a declaration of their rights before acting.

3. **The Uniform Declaratory Judgment Act**

The Uniform Declaratory Judgment Act (UDJA) contains several provisions.

a. **Scope**

Section 1 of the UDJA provides that "Courts of record within their respective jurisdictions shall have power to declare rights, status, and other legal relations whether or not further relief is or could be claimed. No action or proceeding shall be open to objection on the ground that a declaratory judgment or decree is prayed for. The declaration may be either affirmative or negative in form and effect; and such declarations shall have the force and effect of a final judgment or decree."

b. **Power to Invoke**

Section 2 of the UDJA provides that "[a]ny person interested under a deed, will, written contract or other writings constituting a contract, or whose rights, status or other legal relations are affected by a statute, municipal ordinance, contract or franchise, may have determined any question of construction or validity arising under the instrument, statute, ordinance, contract, or franchise and obtain a declaration of rights, status or other legal relations thereunder."

c. **Discretionary**

The issuance of a declaratory judgment is not mandatory, even where the claimant has established the required elements under the statute.

d. **Jury Trial**

The availability of a trial by jury in a declaratory action is determined according to how a court would have resolved the case had the plaintiff sought substantive relief.

e. **Harmony Between States**

The UDJA provides that it should be interpreted to promote harmony between the states, as well as with "federal laws and regulations on the subject of declaratory judgments and decrees." UDJA, Sec. 15.

4. **Federal Declaratory Judgment Act**

The Federal Declaratory Judgment Act (FDJA) is similar to the UDJA. *See* Federal Declaratory Judgment Act, 28 U.S.C. §§ 2201–02.

a. **Authority to Declare**

Under the FDJA, § 2201, federal courts have the authority to "declare the rights and other legal relations of any interested party seeking such declaration, whether or not further relief is or could be sought." However, such declarations can only be made when a case or controversy exists.

b. Jury Trial

As with the right to jury trial in other contexts, the right to obtain a jury determination depends on whether, at the time the Seventh Amendment was ratified, the relevant issue would have been resolved by a court of law or equity.

c. Adequacy of Legal Remedy

Under Rule 57, the existence of an adequate remedy does not "necessarily" preclude a declaratory judgment.

d. Statute of Limitations and Laches

The applicable statute of limitations (or laches) in a declaratory judgment action depends on the underlying substantive claim.

e. Speedy Resolution

Under Rule 57, the existence of an adequate remedy does not "necessarily" preclude a declaratory judgment.

B. CASE OR CONTROVERSY REQUIREMENT

Under the FDJA, and consistent with Article III of the Constitution, declaratory relief is only available when "a case or actual controversy" exists. 28 U.S.C. § 2201.

1. The Principles of Justiciability

The case or controversy requirement incorporates other principles of justiciability—namely, standing, ripeness, and mootness. Each of these justiciability principles apply in declaratory judgment cases.

2. The *Haworth* Principle

In *Aetna Life Insurance Co. v. Haworth*, 300 U.S. 227 (1937), the Court was confronted by a dispute regarding the meaning of insurance policies. In that case, the Court concluded that the case was justiciable noting that determinations of justiciability are to be made based on the distinction that a " 'controversy' in this sense must be one that is appropriate for judicial determination."

3. The *Mitchell* Decision

In *United Public Workers of America v. Mitchell*, 330 U.S. 75 (1947), employees of the federal government sought declaratory relief regarding the validity of the Hatch Act (which prohibited officers and employees in the executive branch of the Federal Government, with exceptions), from taking "any active part in political management or in political campaigns. . . . " The Court refused to hear the case.

4. The Case or Controversy Requirement in State Courts

The UDJA does not specifically require a case or controversy. Nor are state courts bound to abide by Article III of the federal Constitution. Many state courts nonetheless follow an analysis parallel to that found in federal cases.

C. JURISDICTION

The FDJA cannot be invoked by a court that lacks personal or subject matter jurisdiction over the case in question. In other words, the FDJA is "procedural" and does not create an independent cause of action. As a result, in order to invoke federal jurisdiction, individuals must be able to demonstrate that diversity or a federal question exists.

D. STANDARD OF REVIEW

1. Adequacy of Remedy

As previously noted, declaratory judgments generally are not conditioned upon the inadequacy of remedial alternatives. F.R.Civ.P. 57 specifically provides that "another adequate remedy does not preclude a judgment for declaratory relief in cases where it is appropriate."

2. Judicial Discretion

In deciding whether to grant declaratory relief, courts remain free to exercise discretion.

E. DECLARATORY JUDGMENTS IN CONTEXT

1. Written Instruments

Declaratory relief is frequently sought (and granted) in cases involving wills, trust agreements and other written instruments. In this context, declaratory relief allows the parties to ascertain their rights in advance and avoids the possibility of breach or repudiation.

2. Intellectual Property

Declaratory relief is also sought in some cases involving disputes relating to patents, copyrights and trademarks. Such declarations are frequently necessary to provide the parties adequate information regarding their obligations, and enables them to assure purchasers that they are not infringing patents or copyrights.

3. Constitutional Claims

Declaratory relief is also available in cases involving constitutional claims. In some instances, those requests for declaratory relief will be denied on the basis that the claim involves injury that is too remote or speculative to present a justiciable controversy.

F. THE EFFECT OF DECLARATORY JUDGMENTS

Declaratory judgments bind the parties so that principles of RES JUDICATA and collateral estoppel apply. In addition, both the UDJA and FDJA provide for "further" relief when "necessary and proper" including coercive remedies. UDJA, Sec. 8; FDJA, 28 U.S.C. § 2202.

■ CHAPTER SIX: DAMAGES

A. GENERAL APPROACH TO COMPENSATORY DAMAGES

With some exceptions, compensatory damages seek to place the plaintiff (the victim of a legal wrong) in the position that she would have occupied if the defendant had not committed the wrong, sometimes called the plaintiff's "rightful position."

1. **Clarifying Common Misinterpretations of the Rule**

   a. **Position Today, Not Position Before the Wrong**

   Damages seek to create the position the plaintiff would have occupied today (at the time of judgment) if the wrong had not occurred, including prospective future losses caused by the wrong, not merely the position that existed before the wrong occurred.

   b. **Would Have Occupied, Not Could Have Occupied or Hoped to Occupy**

   The rule here turns on the position the plaintiff *would have occupied* if the wrong had not occurred; not subjective hopes or abstract possibilities.

   c. **Double Recovery**

   Courts attempt to avoid double counting any element of recovery.

2. **Generality of the Rule**

   The basic compensatory damages principle applies throughout the law—tort, contract, and most statutory remedies. While facts differ with each context, the goal remains constant.

3. **Where the Plaintiff's Rightful Position Is Unclear: Expectation, Reliance, and Restitution Damages in Contract**

   Expectation seeks to place the plaintiff in the position she would have occupied if the contract had been performed (that is, no breach occurred). Reliance seeks to put the plaintiff in the position she would have occupied if the contract had never been made (that is, no duty arose). Restitution—not really a measure of damages at all—seeks to put the *defendant* in the position she would have occupied if the contract had never been made.

   a. **Communication as the Wrong**

   When the wrong involves deception, plaintiff often recovers the price paid (out of pocket) minus the value of the property received—a measure resembling reliance. Alternatively, many states award the value the property would have had if the statement had been true (the benefit of the bargain) minus the value of the property received—a measure resembling expectation.

   b. **Problems Proving Expectation Losses**

   Where expectation cannot be proven with sufficient certainty, courts seek to come as close as to expectation damages as the evidence permits. The reliance measure often provides the closest recovery ascertainable.

   c. **Special Contexts**

   If expectation recoveries seem excessive, courts may resort the reliance interest or a similar measure based on plaintiff's expenditures.

   (1) **Problems with Title to Real Estate**

   When a defendant promises to sell real estate, but cannot deliver good title, the English rule limits recovery to expenditures plaintiff made in preparation for the transaction (such as title searches or surveys)—the reliance interest. Many states prefer the American rule, which allows plaintiff to recover the market value of the land minus the contract price of the land (in addition to a refund of any portion of the price already paid)—

the expectation interest. The English Rule does not apply to defendants who know their title is bad at the time they enter the contract, who cause the problem of title (such as by selling to someone else after entering the contract with the plaintiff), or who could deliver good title but choose to breach instead.

(2) Fantastic Promises

If sellers promise a product that does not exist, the value of the nonexistent product may seem very high. Reliance may seem a better alternative, but courts usually award expectation anyway.

(3) Disproportionate Recoveries

When plaintiff expected large gains in return for small payments to defendant, expectation may seem disproportionate. While expectation remains the primary measure, some courts limit remedies in the name of justice.

4. Terminology

Compensatory damages are for the purpose of compensating the plaintiff and to deter the defendant and other potential future wrongdoers.

Punitive damages are for the purpose of punishing a defendant for particularly bad behavior or to deter a defendant and other potential wrongdoers.

Nominal damages are a representative sum awarded in cases in which compensatory damages are difficult to prove or where policy reasons counsel against allowing a jury to award compensatory damages.

Statutory damages are damages provided by statute as a means of (1) limiting jury discretion in issuing damages difficult to prove, (2) to provide predictability, and (3) to deter particularly odious behavior.

Within the category of compensatory damages, courts often break down damages awards into subcategories: general damages, special damages, incidental damages, pre- and post-judgment interest, costs and fees, and attorneys' fees.

General damages are the fundamental damages on which an action is based. In a breach of contract action, general damages are those that are the natural consequence of the breach. In the tort context, general damages are nonpecuniary damages.

Special damages might also be thought of as "ensuing damages," or damages that are one step removed from the immediate harm of a defendant's wrong. In a breach of contract action, special damages, are those that do not flow directly from the breach. In an action for tort, special damages are pecuniary expenses.

Incidental damages are costs incurred in mitigation.

Prejudgment interest is interest on compensatory damages from the time of the defendant's wrong to the final resolution of the case.

Post-judgment interest is interest from the time of final resolution to the actual payment of the judgment.

Costs and fees are expenses required by the court in the course of litigation.

Attorneys' fees are fees charged by the attorneys in representing their clients in litigation.

5. Organization of the Chapter

The chapter starts with the distinction between direct loss to the thing at issue and ensuing losses, often called special, consequential, or remote. It proceeds to address special problems posed by damages for which market measures do not work well: pain, suffering, joy, indignity, distress, consortium and death. It proceeds to limitations on damages, followed by a few special issues: agreements concerning damages, punitive damages, and attorney's fees.

B. DIRECT LOSS

Direct loss refers to the thing injured by the wrong.

1. Reduced Value

When property is damaged, direct loss may be measured by its value immediately before the injury minus its value immediately after the injury. In contract, slightly different language produces the same measure: the value of performance as promised (on the date for delivery) minus the value of the performance as received.

a. Definition of Value

Fair market value is the amount that a willing buyer would give and a willing seller would accept in exchange for the property in an arm's-length transaction, each being reasonably informed and neither being under any compulsion to enter the transaction.

b. Calculating Value

Three different techniques may be used to calculate value: market value, replacement cost less depreciation, and capitalization of earnings. Each should produce about the same result.

(1) Market Value

Market value seeks the amount it would cost a person to buy similar property (or services) in the market. Similar includes similar age, similar condition, similar features, etc.

(2) Replacement Cost Less Depreciation

This measure starts with the cost to buy new property (or services) similar to those lost, then adjusting the cost to reflect differences in age and condition.

(3) Capitalization of Earnings

The value of income-producing property equals the present value of the income stream it will produce over time.

(4) Repairs as Evidence of Value

The cost to repair property is some evidence of the amount of value lost. Subtracting repair costs from the value the property will have once repaired is a reasonable estimate of the value of the property in its injured condition.

c. Problems of Timing

Statements of the rule relying on "before" and "after" assume a relatively sudden accident, as where a car is in good condition one moment, but damaged by impact a moment later. More accurately, damages must reflect the value the property would have had if not injured minus the value of the property does have in its injured condition, measured on the same day. Usually, the date the injury is complete works well, but where property would have appreciated but for the wrong, the date of judgment includes compensation for lost appreciation.

2. **Alternative Measure: Cost of Repair**

The cost of repair (plus any ensuing losses during the time required for repairs) may put plaintiff in the position she would have occupied if the wrong had not occurred.

a. **Market Value of Repairs**

The amount the plaintiff spent on repairs may not be recoverable if plaintiff spent more than the repairs were worth.

b. **Excessive Repair Costs**

When the cost of repair is disproportionate to (that is, greatly exceed) the diminution in value of the property, repair costs are excessive. Other formulations of this rule deny recovery of cost of repair if that cost exceeds: (a) the value of the property before the injury; or (b) the amount of value that repairs will add to the property.

Exception: Environmental Harm to Real Property

For reasons of public policy, in cases in which a defendant's wrong causes environmental damage to a plaintiff's real property, courts frequently award repair costs even where such an award might violate the rules outlined above.

c. **Incomplete Repairs**

If repairs will not restore the property to its original value, the difference between the value the property would have had if never injured and the value the property has as repaired must be added to the award.

3. **Undelivered Value**

Remedies for undelivered value usually equal the value the plaintiff would have received if the contract had been performed (including ensuing gains) minus costs the plaintiff avoided because of the breach. Costs avoided because of the breach typically involve any performance plaintiff would have needed to provide under the contract, but has not yet provided. The same result will follow from the other direction: the costs plaintiff cannot avoid incurring plus any profit plaintiff would have earned had the contract been performed. Recovery of unavoidable costs brings the plaintiff back to the break-even point. Awarding profits on top of that gives the plaintiff the gain it expected on the transaction. (Profit equals total gains minus total costs. Thus, unavoidable costs plus profit always should equal total gains minus avoided costs.) Again, profit may be limited to direct gains or may include ensuing losses.

a. **Sales of Goods**

Article 2 of the Uniform Commercial Code codifies contract remedies for sales of goods.

(1) **Nondelivery by Seller**

Buyer is entitled to receive a refund of any amount paid to seller. U.C.C. § 2–711(1). In addition buyer may recover the cover price (the cost to obtain substitute goods in good faith, without unreasonable delay, in a reasonable transaction) minus the contract price promised to the original seller, U.C.C.

§ 2–712, or the market price of the goods (the amount it would have cost if he had made a reasonable substitute purchase) minus the contract price promised to the original seller. U.C.C. § 2–713.

(2) Nonpayment by Buyer

When a buyer refuses to pay for goods, seller may refuse to deliver the goods—including recovering the goods from a third party, such as a transportation company or warehouse. U.C.C. § 2–703. In addition, buyer may recover the contract price minus the resale price (the amount seller realized in a good faith and commercially reasonable sale of the goods to another buyer), U.C.C. § 2–706, or the contract price minus the market price (the amount she would have received if she had made a reasonable substitute sale). U.C.C. § 2–708(1). If the market value is zero or the seller cannot resell them at any reasonable price, seller may recover the entire contract price, but must hold the goods (if she has them) available for buyer. U.C.C. § 2–709. In each case, any savings to the seller would be subtracted from the recovery. In addition, plaintiff may recover ensuing losses, such as the cost incurred trying to resell the goods and of storing and insuring them pending resale.

Exception: if seller could have made both the original sale and the resale, seller may recover the profit lost on the first sale, without regard to the resale.

(3) Comparing the Remedies

The remedies for buyers and sellers are almost exactly parallel, as can be seen in the chart below.

SUMMARY OF U.C.C. DAMAGE REMEDIES

SELLER	BUYER
Contract Price – Resale Price + Incidental – Savings (2-706) [+ Consequential]	Refund + Cover Price – Contract Price + Incidental + Consequential (2–712)
Unpaid Contract Price – Market Price + Incidental – Savings (2–708) [+ Consequential]	Refund + Market Price – K Price + Incidental + Consequential (2–713)
	Value Warranted – Value Received + Incidental + Consequential (2–714)
Contract Price (2–709) + Incidental – Savings [+ Consequential]	Specific Performance + Damages Not Avoided by SP (2–716)

b. Employment Contracts

Where an employee breaches, the employer may recover the cost to hire a substitute employee (in good faith and reasonably) minus the cost of the original employee. Where an employer breaches, the employee may recover the amount promised by the employer minus the amount received from a new employer. In each case, both wages and fringe benefits should be considered. In either case, if no substitute transaction occurs, the market price may be substituted for cover price (cost of a new employee) or resale price (pay from a new employer):

c. Construction Contracts

As with goods and employment, when the seller (contractor) breaches, the buyer (landowner) may recover the cost to complete the project minus the unpaid portion of the contract price (the savings from not paying the original contractor the rest of what she would have collected had she finished the job). As usual, the substitute transaction must be a reasonable one made in good faith. Ensuing losses may be recoverable, though many construction contracts exclude damages for delay.

When the landowner breaches (dismissing the contractor without cause), the contractor recovers the amount promised for the full job, minus any expenses saved by not needing to complete the job. (This may include salvage value of materials already purchased for the job.) The amount the contractor earned or could have earned on other jobs usually is not subtracted from the award.

d. Real Estate Contracts

The same principles apply to real estate, but with some differences.

(1) Seller Breaches

When seller fails to deliver real estate, buyer normally is entitled to specific performance. Where damages are awarded instead, buyer may recover a refund of any payments, plus the market value of the land minus the contract price of the land (unless the court applies the English rule, *see* A.3.c.(1), *supra*). Because each parcel of real estate is unique, courts almost never award cover price minus contract price, even if plaintiff enters a substitute transaction.

(2) Buyer Breaches

When buyer refuses to take delivery and pay for a parcel, seller can resell the parcel and collect the original contract price minus resale price, minus any savings (*e.g.*, brokerage commissions, if lower because of the resale—and perhaps the value of retaining possession of the land, as where it produces a crop before it is resold). As always, ensuing losses (such as cost of resale, insurance while resale was pending, etc.) may be necessary to fill out the remedy. If buyer does not resell, the contract price minus the market value (on the date of the breach) remains a viable remedy—again, taking account of any savings and any ensuing losses.

(3) Leases

When the estate being sold is less than a fee simple, the same principles apply. If the landlord breaches, plaintiff may recover the fair rental value of the property minus the lease (contract) price of the property—plus ensuing losses. A substitute transaction poses the same problems based on the uniqueness of real estate.

Where the tenant breaches, landlord recovers the lease price (unpaid rent). In some cases, especially commercial real estate, no reduction occurs for the fair rental value of the remaining term of the lease. That was the traditional rule for all property. In some cases, especially residential leases, modern statutes or court decisions reduce the unpaid rent by the amount the landlord does (or should) earn by leasing the property to another.

4. Loss of Intangible Property

Some losses involve intangible property, such as contract rights, patent rights, insurance, stock certificates. Where these rights have a market value, the techniques described above can apply with full force.

a. Insurance Policies

When defendant breaches a promise to obtain insurance for plaintiff, cover price minus contract price will suffice only if plaintiff discovers the problem with enough time to obtain insurance coverage elsewhere before an insured loss occurs. After an insured loss, courts award the full amount of insurance plaintiff would have received under the policy promised by defendant.

b. Contract Rights, Intellectual Property Rights

If buyer fails to pay for intangible rights, seller recovers the promised price, less any savings. If seller fails to deliver promised rights, all losses might be ensuing losses: the profits plaintiff would have made by using the rights. In some cases, rights may have a market value that can be assessed as direct loss under the rules relating to value.

5. Personal Injury

The approaches detailed here can apply with equal force to personal injuries.

a. Physical Injury to a Person

Courts award medical costs plus pain and suffering plus any ensuing losses (such as lost earnings). Medical costs are the cost of repair.

(1) Future Medical Costs and Medical Monitoring

The plaintiff may also recover reasonably certain future medical expenses, such as foreseeably necessary surgeries, physical therapy, nursing care, prostheses, etc. Where the plaintiff has not suffered any initial injury or symptoms, courts are often reluctant to award medical monitoring costs—some courts are willing, some are not. Where the plaintiff has suffered initial injury, however, courts are more willing to award medical monitoring costs.

b. Anguish Accompanying Physical Injury

Pain and suffering caused by the wrong is recoverable.

(1) Emotional Injuries Without Physical Injury

The pain and suffering that accompanies physical injury is typically recoverable. Tort law has imposed stringent limits, however, on plaintiffs' recovery in claims for pure emotional distress—typically couching such limitations in the language of "duty."

(2) Awards for Physical Injuries Without General Damages

In many jurisdictions, as a matter of law a jury may not award special damages without accompanying general damages. The rationale behind this rule is that if a conscious, feeling plaintiff suffered tortious physical injury, pain and suffering must necessarily have accompanied it and ought to be compensated. In other jurisdictions, personal injury awards of special damages alone are not per se invalid, but are merely suspect and subject to the applicable standard of review by the court.

C. ENSUING LOSS (CONSEQUENTIAL DAMAGES, LOSS OF USE)

If awarding plaintiff the direct loss will not place him in the position he would have occupied if the wrong had not occurred, ensuing losses will be awarded to achieve that goal. Ensuing losses frequently face limitation under doctrines discussed below. *See* E, *infra.*

1. Terminology

In contract, the inability to use the goods is called consequential damages or the more specific lost profits. In tort, especially property torts, the ensuing loss is called loss of use. In personal injury actions, courts usually refer to loss of earning potential or loss of income. Lost wages sometimes are called special damages, to distinguish them from general damages (typically, pain and suffering). The distinction between general and special damages differs in different contexts, making the terminology confusing. The glossary lists several of these different meanings.

2. Failure to Pay Money: Interest as Damages

Consequential damages for failure to pay money are limited to interest on the sum that should have been paid.

a. Rationale and Critique

Nonpayment forces plaintiff to find a substitute source of money, usually a loan. Plaintiff then can invest the borrowed money as planned and earn the same profit (or loss) that she would have earned if the wrong had not occurred. The loss caused by defendant is measured by the interest on the loan, not by the return on the investment.

The rationale assumes that plaintiff could have arranged a substitute source of funds in time to pursue the original venture. Some plaintiffs cannot borrow at all, others may be unable to replace the money in time. It also assumes that prejudgment interest rates will reflect the rates plaintiffs would need to (or did) pay to borrow money. Prejudgment interest rates may not equal interest rates on loans.

b. Prejudgment and Post-Judgment Interest

All judgments earn post-judgment interest—interest from the date of judgment to the date of payment. Prejudgment interest covers the period from the date of the injury to the date of judgment. Some courts order recovery of prejudgment interest only if the claim is liquidated, meaning where the amount of plaintiff's loss could be ascertained, either as a sum certain or by application of a simple formula. This approach allows prejudgment interest on claims involving property and in contract cases involving a definite sum of money or good that have a fixed or easily ascertainable value. In tort claims, this approach allows recovery of prejudgment interest on pecuniary damages, but denies interest on pain and suffering, emotional distress, or injury to reputation. A majority of courts have now abandoned the rule limiting prejudgment interest to liquidated claims and pecuniary damages.

c. Exceptions

In the minority of jurisdictions that retain the traditional rule, its shortcomings have produced a number of exceptions.

(1) Bad Faith

When a party who owes money lacks a good faith justification for not paying, courts may award damages that exceed interest. An insurer's bad faith refusal to pay claims often produces consequential damage awards—including emotional distress and punitive damages, despite the rule that these recoveries do not apply to contract actions. The same result applies when liability insurers use bad faith in refusing to settle litigation against the insured. Consequential damages typically include the entire judgment against the insured, even if it exceeds the policy limits specified in the insurance contract. Other cases of bad faith include bad faith by banks that refuse to let depositors withdraw their money.

(2) Lenders

Lenders who refuse to fund specific projects may owe losses plaintiff suffers on that project. The investment opportunity is contemplated by both parties.

(3) Actual Interest Losses

Where the evidence establishes the amount of interest plaintiff actually lost, courts sometimes substitute that amount for interest at the legal rate.

3. Loss of Use

Loss of use usually is measured one of three ways. First, where a temporary substitute can be obtained, the cost of that substitute (typically, rental cost) will be awarded. Second, where a temporary substitute cannot be obtained, the loss of profits plaintiff would have earned with the original may be awarded. Where lost profits are unavailable (usually because uncertain), the lost rental value—the amount plaintiff might have received for renting out the thing, not the amount it would have cost plaintiff to rent a substitute—may be awarded.

a. Cost of a Temporary Substitute

If plaintiff can obtain a temporary substitute for the property, to cover the time between injury and repair or replacement, courts usually award the cost of a reasonable substitute transaction. This rule tends to be the preferred measure.

(1) Reasonable and in Good Faith

The amount recoverable for a substitute must be reasonable and in good faith. A substitute of vastly superior quality may be unreasonable. But even a vastly superior substitute may be reasonable if it is the least expensive substitute that is at least as good as the original.

b. Lost Profits

For any period during which a plaintiff reasonably cannot obtain a temporary substitute, any losses caused by being deprived of the thing are recoverable. Where the thing generated income, lost profit provides a measure of the damage to plaintiff during the interim. Beware of cases where profits are delayed rather than lost.

c. Rental Value

Where no substitute is available and no profits lost—or lost profits cannot be proven—courts may assess loss of use at the amount that plaintiff could have gained by renting the property to another.

d. **Archaic Limitations**

Traditionally, loss of use was available when property was damaged, but not when it was destroyed. Recently, courts begun awarding loss of use for damaged or destroyed property. Similarly, courts traditionally capped recovery for loss of use at the value of the damaged property. Courts are beginning to treat cases individually rather than mechanically apply the traditional cap to all cases.

4. **Lost Profits**

Where defendant deprives plaintiff of a thing she would have used to generate profits, courts award recovery of those lost profits.

a. **Losses to a Project**

Lost profits can be directly related to the asset defendant injured, such as where plaintiff intended to resell the thing at a profit. In other cases, plaintiff may have intended to use the thing as one input into a larger project. For instance, a plaintiff may buy or rent land as part of a business (whether farming, ranching, retail, or manufacturing). If defendant deprives plaintiff of the land, the entire project may suffer, making profits lost on the entire project the appropriate measure of loss.

b. **Limitations Significant**

The legitimacy of awarding lost profits has been recognized in almost every context. The most important issues surround concerns that profits might be exaggerated. Thus, the limitations on remedies, discussed below at E, take on great significance in this content.

(1) **Measurement**

Aside from the limitations, the only issue of lost profits involves accurately measuring them. The issues tend to involve accounting rather than law.

(2) **Present Value and Inflation**

Any profit that would have been earned in the years following judgment must be reduced to present value. On the other hand, any money paid now will be worth less over the course of time due to the likelihood of inflation. This requires an upward adjustment to the verdict.

5. **Lost Earning Potential**

The primary ensuing loss physical injuries produce is lost earning potential. This can include the temporary lost earnings when a wrong prevents work, whether while the body heals or simply because the wrong deprived the plaintiff of time. More significant are the lost earnings from a long-term disability that prevents plaintiff from pursuing her career.

a. **Future Increases**

Earnings are not limited to the plaintiff's current income or even the plaintiff's current job.

b. **Ending Liability**

The period for which defendant is liable will vary with the wrong and the injury.

(1) Permanent Disability

Where plaintiff is permanently disabled from any work, the issue focuses on determining when the plaintiff would have retired.

(2) Temporary Disability

Some injuries leave plaintiff able to resume work—either after rehabilitation or by changing careers to one he can still perform. Recovery will depend on when plaintiff can return to work and how much plaintiff can earn after returning.

(3) Discharge from Employment

Discharge does not disable the plaintiff but deprives her of income from one employer. The period during which defendant remains liable for the loss varies with context. In contract claims, the contract duration term will set the end of liability. In tort claims and discrimination claims, the duration may be fixed by the avoidable consequences doctrine.

c. Present Value and Inflation

As with lost profits, future wages require discount to present value and increase to adjust for inflation.

(1) The Procedure

Each year's income is multiplied by $1/(1 + i)_n$, where i is the interest rate plaintiff can earn by investing the damage award and n is the number of years in the future those wages would have been earned. The sum of all yearly calculations is the damage award. (See the example in the body of the outline. There is no short way to explain this.)

(2) Traditional Method

Traditionally, experts project actual increases in future wages and discount by an actual interest rate at which the plaintiff might invest. Thus, increases in wages include increases for inflation and the interest rate includes an amount believed necessary to account for inflation.

(3) Partial Offset Method

The partial offset method seeks to remove inflation from the calculation of present value. In projecting future income and interest rates, it projects real increases—that is, the extent to which increases in income and long-term interest rates exceed the inflation rate. The calculation procedure is the same.

(4) Total Offset Method

The total offset method assumes that real increases in wages will exactly match real interest rates. If so, it becomes unnecessary to project increases and discount to present value. Instead, just multiplying current wages by the number of years of remaining work will produce a reasonable estimate of future wages. The method is acceptable, if the parties stipulate to it. But it cannot be forced on either party over its objection.

(5) Selecting an Interest Rate

The larger the interest rate, the lower the damage award. Courts normally employ an interest rate that allows plaintiff to invest safely—generally, a lower interest rate.

(a) Issues of Race and Gender

Disparities in income and longevity based on gender and race continue to exist in America. Should such disparities be reflected in jury awards in personal injury cases? For example, in estimating lost wages of an African-American decedent, should the jury be allowed to consider evidence that the average African-American lives four fewer years than the average Caucasian and earns 59 percent of what the average Caucasian is paid? How about evidence that the average woman earns 77 percent of what the average man is paid, a gap that grows with age and also exists for women without children? In calculating future lost wages, courts often provide juries with charts reflecting average wages in specific fields throughout an average worker's career. Some charts are broken down by gender and race; others are not. As a matter of public policy, many courts and the Restatement Third of Torts: Remedies have refused race or gender-specific wage and life-expectancy information, instead requiring an average or upper-end range.

D. INTANGIBLE LOSS

Pain, distress, and indignity are real, but no market sets the price for them. The lack of a market benchmark against which to compare the award, makes it hard to say whether an award is too high, too low, or just right. Yet when plaintiff really did suffer pain, zero must be the wrong amount of compensation.

1. Terminology

Use of terms varies. As used here, pain refers to the unpleasant (or worse) physical sensation felt as a result of a physical injury. Suffering refers to both pain and the unpleasant (or worse) thoughts that accompany a physical injury. Distress refers to unpleasant (or worse) thoughts unaccompanied by a physical injury to the distressed person. Loss of joy (or lost enjoyment of life) refers to the reduced ability to experience joy.

2. Subjective Value

Market value is objective value—the amount a reasonable person would pay. Items that have greater value to one person than to the market have subjective value. When defendant deprives plaintiff of property he values more than the market, compensation at the market rate may not make plaintiff as well off as he would have been but for the wrong.

a. Danger of Overcompensation

When plaintiff alleges that the property had special value to him, the claim is hard to prove or to disprove unless plaintiff recently rejected a bona fide offer for the property. Thus, an award based on subjective value may leave plaintiff better off than if the wrong had not occurred.

b. Measuring Subjective Value

Confronted with claims that property has subjective value, courts try to measure that value in several ways. Techniques include: (a) market value; (b) cost to replace or reproduce; (c) value to the plaintiff; (d) emotional distress.

(1) Market Value

Market value is not a measure of subjective value, but a rejection of it. The effect is to deny subjective value for any good available in the market. This will not apply to unique items, such as photographs, keepsakes, heirlooms, etc.

(2) Cost to Replace or to Reproduce

In some cases, property with sentimental value can be reproduced, such as making new prints of photographs from negatives. Awarding the cost to reproduce the property provides compensation that may satisfy some claims of subjective value.

(3) Value to the Plaintiff

The value to the owner arguably means the amount for which the owner would sell, if anyone else made that offer. Some courts limit value to the plaintiff by awarding personal value, but rejecting sentimental value, at least when sentiment becomes affected or mawkish. Another approach focuses on the cost to obtain the item; having invested a certain amount in the item, plaintiffs must value the item more than the investment. Compensating the cost to obtain the property provides a minimal estimate of sentimental value.

(4) Emotional Distress

In some cases, courts shift from a discussion of subjective value into a discussion of distress. Emotional distress over the loss of property, like distress caused by injuries to other people, often is not compensable. The Restatement Third of Torts: Remedies § 21 provides that emotional distress damages are recoverable for "an intentional tort that is principally directed at property rights or financial interests, committed under circumstances in which emotional harm is especially likely to result"—although it recognizes that the law is not well settled in this area.

3. Pain & Suffering

Juries may award a victim of physical injury an amount intended to compensate a for the pain and suffering incurred as a result of the wrong. Trial courts may reject the award if it is against the great weight of the evidence. If a trial court does not remit the award or order a new trial on damages, an appellate court may intervene only if the award is so excessive that it shocks the conscience. Another formulation of this test asks whether the award is so large that it evinces passion, prejudice, corruption, whim, or caprice on the part of the jury.

a. Consistency with Prior Awards

When an award for pain and suffering seems out of line with prior awards in the same jurisdiction, courts sometimes reject or reduce an award. The analysis must account for changing times. It also assumes, without basis, that the earlier awards were correct.

b. Limit to Consciousness

Plaintiffs in a coma may be unable to recover for pain and suffering because they do not feel pain without some consciousness of their state.

c. Inappropriate Arguments at Trial

Appellate courts have been asked, with limited success, to overturn large awards based on the arguments used to inspire juries to make large awards.

(1) Per Diem Arguments

Plaintiffs often suggest that compensation for pain could be calculated using a relatively small amount per day (or hour or week), then multiplying by the number of days plaintiff will suffer the pain. Arguments of this sort are called per diem arguments. Typically, they result in much larger awards for pain than would result from considering the entire period as a whole. Courts generally allow per diem arguments, although often tempered by an instruction to the jury that they are merely arguments and not evidence.

(2) Golden Rule Arguments

Plaintiffs sometimes suggest that jurors consider how much they would want if they suffered the plaintiff's injuries. This is called the golden rule argument—award unto plaintiff as you would have others award unto you. Courts almost universally hold golden rule arguments improper.

4. Lost Enjoyment of Life (Hedonic Damages)

Some injuries (say, spinal cord injuries) may cause nerve damage that prevents pain. These injuries, however, may reduce the capacity for joy. To put plaintiff in the rightful position requires compensation for the lost joy, but courts have not settled on a way to handle these damages.

a. Separate Element of Damages

Loss of joy is logically distinct from pain and suffering but may be harder to segregate in practice. Juries may confuse lost joy with suffering and double count these losses. Lost enjoyment of life seems most justifiable in cases where pain and suffering are not available, thus eliminating concerns for double counting.

b. Part of Pain and Suffering

Properly instructed juries may include loss of joy in evaluating pain and suffering, eliminating the need for a separate component. Limitations appropriate to pain and suffering (such as the consciousness requirement) may not be appropriate to lost joy.

5. Indignity and Emotional Distress

Some mental harms may result from wrongs that do not cause physical injury, such as defamation, intentional (or negligent) infliction of emotional distress, or deprivation of constitutional rights. Courts allow compensation for indignity and distress. These awards raise many of the same problems discussed under pain and suffering, with the added difficulty that they are more subjective.

a. Torts Involving Indignity

Where torts cause distress or indignity, courts include compensation for this injury in the award. Like pain and suffering, courts allow juries discretion to determine an appropriate amount. Like pain and suffering, courts review the amount for excessiveness. Like pain and suffering, disputes about the propriety of per diem and golden rule arguments arise.

(1) Actual Damages

Where the plaintiff presents evidence of distress or emotional suffering, juries may award an appropriate amount to compensate for these harms. In affirming awards, courts consider the outrageousness of defendant's conduct.

(2) Presumed Damages

In some torts, presumed damages are available as a substitute for actual damages. For instance, if a libel plaintiff cannot prove any loss to business or financial interests, she may nonetheless recover presumed damages. Some statutes, such as the copyright act, allow presumed damages.

b. Contract Actions

Emotional distress in contract actions remains rare and limited. Damages for distress can arise where: (1) the breach also constitutes a tort; (2) the breach causes physical injury; or (3) the breach or the contract are of a type that makes serious emotional distress particularly likely to occur. The last exception has been very limited, with some recent expansion.

c. Constitutional Rights

Deprivation of a constitutional right may not involve much actual loss. This is particularly true of procedural rights, where the denial of a hearing may not affect the outcome. Damages for the abstract value of a right have been rejected. Where loss of the right is the only harm, plaintiff may recover nominal damages. Where loss of the right caused other losses, such as distress or lost income, those losses are awarded. Damages for loss of the right to vote have been upheld.

6. Wrongful Death and Survival Actions

Plaintiff's death can produce two independent causes of action, one on behalf of the victim and another on behalf of her survivors. Survival actions allow the victim's estate to recover for losses suffered between the time of the injury and the time of death—in some cases even if the time is a matter of minutes. Wrongful death statutes allow survivors to recover their losses caused when defendant caused the deceased's death. Most wrongful death statutes limit recovery to pecuniary losses. The wrongful death action measures losses to the survivors, not to the deceased.

a. Out-of-Pocket Costs

Survivors may recover any out-of-pocket costs resulting from the death, such as funeral expenses.

b. Loss of Support

Where the deceased supported the survivors, the amount of support is recoverable. Typically, courts calculate loss of support by assessing the deceased's lost income (for the entire work-life expectancy) and subtracting the amount the deceased would have consumed for purely personal purposes.

c. **Loss of Services**

If the deceased provided services to the survivors, the value of those services is a pecuniary loss in a large majority of states. Whether they pay for those services or give up other activities to perform the services for themselves, they are net worse off than before, requiring compensation.

d. **Loss of Consortium (Society)**

A majority of states allow recovery for loss of consortium, including intangible contributions of the deceased, such as affection, care, comfort, companionship, love, and protection.

e. **Grief and Distress**

Very few states allow recovery for grief and distress caused by the death. Some states, however, have begun to allow recovery for these components.

f. **Survival Actions**

The survival action covers all losses incurred between the time of injury and the time of death, including lost wages, pain and suffering, and occasionally some property damage. It requires that the victim survive the initial impact, at least by a short time.

7. **Loss of Consortium**

Loss of consortium is a cause of action brought by a close relative alleging that injuries to a spouse or parent deprived the plaintiff of services and support.

a. **Recoverable Losses**

Loss of consortium generally includes three components: services, society, and sexual relations. It usually does not encompass grief, distress, or outrage at the injuries caused to another. As with wrongful death, some states have extended consortium to distress.

(1) **Services**

Services represent pecuniary losses to the plaintiff. When injuries to one spouse prevent him from performing household tasks, others must perform those tasks. Hiring others to perform the tasks clarifies (and liquidates) the pecuniary nature of the losses.

(2) **Society**

Loss of society includes affection, solace, comfort, companionship, assistance, and (between spouses) sexual relations.

b. **Permissible Plaintiffs**

Courts limit consortium to a very narrow range of relatives—traditionally, spouses only, but some states (at least 15) now allow consortium claims by children, at least during their minority or while disabled (dependent) adults. Consortium claims by fiancés, domestic partners, roommates, and relatives outside the nuclear family have met with almost no success.

c. **Procedural Aspects**

Some states require that the consortium claim be joined with the victim's suit.

E. LIMITATIONS ON RECOVERY

1. Causation

The general rule on damages builds causation into its formulation by limiting plaintiff to the position she would have occupied if the wrong had not occurred. This rejects damages not caused by defendant's misconduct, losses plaintiff would have suffered even if defendant had not committed the wrong.

a. Mixed Motive

Sometimes the wrong depends on defendant's motivation: conduct motivated by one reason is wrong, but the same conduct motivated by other reasons would be legal. When the action has mixed motivation, causation questions arise.

(1) Multiple Sufficient Causes

Sometimes either of two (or more) reasons, one wrong and one acceptable, would have produced the conduct independently of the other. When the conduct would have been the same even if the wrongful reason did not exist, then the wrongful reason is not a but-for cause of the harm. In the standard torts case, however, but-for causation is not required in such a case—both the legitimate and illegitimate reasons would be held to be causes of the harm. The Supreme Court in Title VII and ADEA employment discrimination cases has not chosen to follow tort law in this respect, however, limiting causation to the but-for requirement.

(2) Multiple Insufficient Causes

Sometimes neither of two (or more) reasons, one wrong and one acceptable, would have produced the conduct independently of the other. If the combination was essential to cause the conduct, the conduct would have been different if the wrongful reason did not exist, thus the harm was caused by the wrongful reason.

b. Loss of Chance

Loss of chance refers to situations where plaintiff has a chance of avoiding a harm, but defendant's wrong reduces the chance. It has thus far been limited to medical cases, where the failure to diagnose a problem earlier may reduce the likelihood of treating the condition. Defendant did not cause the condition and, thus, did not cause the harms attributable to the condition. But defendant's wrong did deprive plaintiff of opportunities that might (or might not) have prevented the harm. Thus, zero recovery seems to underestimate the plaintiff's loss.

(1) Actual Causation

If a court could determine whether the plaintiff would have successfully avoided the harm but for the wrong, plaintiff proves actual causation and need not rely on loss of chance.

(2) Proportional Recovery

Courts typically award proportional damages, calculating the harm plaintiff suffered and multiplying by the percent reduction in chance defendant caused.

(3) Separate Cause of Action

Some courts treat loss of chance as a separate cause of action, requiring separate pleading.

c. Potential Harm

In some cases, defendant's wrong does not immediately cause harm to plaintiff, but subjects plaintiff to a risk of harm. Proof that defendant's wrong caused the harm—or even that plaintiff will suffer the harm—is problematic.

(1) Proportional Recovery After Harm

If the plaintiffs wait and sue after they develop the harm, the issue becomes one of causation. Courts can apportion the loss caused by defendant over the plaintiffs who suffer the harm, including those who might have suffered the harm anyway.

(2) Proportional Recovery After Exposure

When plaintiffs sue at the time of exposure, courts cannot identify which plaintiffs will suffer harm at all. Apportioning losses requires that a share be awarded to people who never will suffer loss, decreasing dramatically recovery by those who will suffer loss. Very few courts allow such recovery.

(3) Risk of Harm Distinguished from Fear of or Testing for Harm

Exposure to a toxic chemical, for example, may cause plaintiff any (or all three) of the following: (1) increased risk of suffering a future disease; (2) fear of the increased risk; and (3) the costs of detecting future illness. The rules governing recovery of each of these harms are different. Most courts prohibit or severely curtail recovery for the increased risk itself. Courts are more amenable to allowing recovery for fear and medical monitoring. Courts' approach to claims for fear of future illness may be summarized as follows: Most courts allow exposure-generated emotional distress claims with a showing of current physical symptoms or harm. In exposure claims without accompanying injury or symptoms, courts typically limit recovery to cases in which the plaintiff was actually exposed to a particularly horrible illness.

(4) Res Judicata vs. Statute of Limitations

The divided harms put plaintiff in a dilemma. If the injury has already begun, the statute of limitations may begin to run, forcing plaintiff to sue after exposure. Yet suing now precludes a later suit concerning the same misconduct, unless courts alter the way they apply res judicata.

d. Harm to Others: Fluid Class Recoveries

In some cases, plaintiffs have proposed that wrongs to some people be remedied by awards to others. Courts may approve settlement agreements that benefit classes similar to those injured. With rare exceptions, courts may not impose remedies to persons who were not injured by the defendant's wrong over defendant's objection.

2. Avoided Consequences

Any loss the plaintiff avoided should not be included in the recovery. More controversially, when a wrong bestows benefits in addition to causing losses, plaintiff should recover her net loss, after offsetting the benefits.

a. Avoided Losses Without Benefits

In many cases, plaintiffs will minimize their own loss. Plaintiffs cannot recover for losses that they do not suffer.

b. Cost of Avoiding Losses

The cost of avoiding a loss is recoverable. These costs sometimes are called incidental damages.

c. Nominal Damages

In some cases, no damages may be recovered unless the plaintiff suffered an actual injury. For example, in a slight majority of jurisdictions, nominal damages are recoverable in negligence actions only if the plaintiff proves harm, but cannot prove compensatory damages with sufficient certainty. In other cases, including actions for breach of contract, courts allow a plaintiff who suffered no actual losses to recover a trivial amount, typically $1, to vindicate their rights.

d. Offsetting Benefits

In some cases, a breach bestows a benefit on the defendant. Even if the breach harms the plaintiff in some ways, the net loss suffered may be reduced by the benefit bestowed. Typically, the benefits will be offset against the harms in calculating damages, to the extent that this is equitable.

(1) Basic Illustrations

The most common operation of the offset the benefits rule is to reduce a plaintiff's recovery by a benefit gained in mitigation. For example, suppose a plaintiff is unable to work as an iron worker for six months due to injuries suffered at the hands of defendant in an auto accident. For three of those months, plaintiff finds replacement work as a janitor. So long as plaintiff could not have done the janitor work while serving as an iron worker, plaintiff's janitor wages should be subtracted from his lost-wages award against defendant.

(2) Benefit to the Interest Injured

The Second Restatement and a minority of courts offset the benefit only if it inures to the same interest injured. Thus, a financial benefit might offset a financial harm. But a financial benefit might not offset pain and suffering or harm to dignitary interests (such as reputation).

(3) To the Extent Equitable

In some cases, plaintiffs do not want the benefits—and even paid to prevent the benefits, as in cases involving negligent sterilizations. The rule aims to limit plaintiffs to their actual losses, not to allow defendants to foist unwanted benefits on the plaintiff.

(4) Calculating the Offset

Courts that limit benefits to the interest injured face unanswered questions about how to offset benefits. For instance, if the emotional benefit exceeds the emotional harm, should the excess benefit also offset pecuniary harms? Or, once the emotional harm has been reduced to zero, do the emotional benefits cease to apply? Such difficulties explain why a majority of courts have abandoned the same-interest rule.

e. Collateral Source Exception

Benefits bestowed by sources other than the defendant do not offset the plaintiff's recovery. This may include insurance payments, Charitable aid, and government benefits plaintiff received. Tort reform proponents have attacked the collateral source rule, sometimes with success.

3. Avoidable Consequences

Often called mitigation of damages, the avoidable consequences doctrine limits the amount of damage a plaintiff may recover to the amount she could not have avoided by reasonable conduct undertaken after the defendant's wrong.

a. Rationale

If plaintiff could have avoided the loss, it is harder to say defendant caused the loss. A policy to avoid waste also urges courts to provide an incentive to prevent losses, when reasonable. The rule treats avoidable consequences the same way courts treat avoided consequences. In effect, it treats plaintiff as if she did avoid the losses that she should have avoided.

b. The Rule

If the plaintiff fails to make reasonable post-injury efforts to minimize the loss, the losses she could have avoided by reasonable efforts will be denied. The rule applies in tort and contract. In the tort context, the avoidable consequences doctrine is distinguished from comparative fault by the fact that the avoidable consequences doctrine considers conduct *after* the defendant's tort, whereas the comparative fault occurs *before or simultaneous with* it. Whereas avoidable consequences complete bars the recovery of damages the plaintiff might have avoided. Comparative fault merely reduces plaintiff's recovery according to the percentage of responsibility the jury assigns to the plaintiff.

(1) Defendant's Burden

This is an affirmative defense that defendant must plead and prove. Defendant must show not only that plaintiff's efforts were unreasonable, but also the amount of loss that reasonable efforts would have prevented.

(2) Reasonable Efforts, Not Successful Efforts

If a plaintiff makes reasonable efforts to minimize the loss, no reduction in damages occurs even if those efforts failed. In effect, where plaintiff's reasonable efforts fail, courts conclude that reasonable efforts would not have prevented the loss.

(3) Reasonable Efforts, Not the Best Choices

Faced with several different ways to minimize the loss, plaintiff may choose any reasonable way. Even if 20–20 hindsight shows that a different choice might have reduced damages more, plaintiff recovers the damages he actually suffered.

(4) Reasonable Efforts, Not Extraordinary Efforts

Sometimes damages can be reduced by exceptional efforts. Where minimizing the loss requires undue risk, burden, or humiliation, no reduction of damages results.

(5) **Reasonable Efforts vs. Good Faith Efforts**

The rule requires reasonable efforts, but some courts are slow to hold that a plaintiff acted unreasonably. When courts take into account factors that explain why the plaintiff acted unreasonably, they border on requiring only good faith efforts.

c. **Exceptions, Real and Imagined**

(1) **Lost Volume Seller**

In some cases, transactions that appear to reduce the loss are not really substitute transactions. Where plaintiff could have entered two transactions—both the one defendant precluded and the one claimed in mitigation—the second transaction does not offset the harm of the first.

(2) **Mitigation Before the Breach**

If the plaintiff anticipates a breach, he can take precautions (such as fastening seat belts) to minimize the harm the breach will cause. Most courts do not apply avoidable consequences to pre-breach precautions.

(3) **Defendant's Equal Opportunity to Mitigate**

Some courts have said that plaintiff's recovery should not be reduced if defendant had an equal opportunity to mitigate the loss and failed to do so. In most cases, the holding is dicta, following a conclusion that plaintiff did act reasonably. The exception makes no sense and probably will disappear even from dicta.

(4) **Intentional and Reckless Torts**

Damages against an intentional or reckless defendant will only be reduced if the plaintiff has intentionally or recklessly failed to mitigate their damages.

4. **Foreseeability**

Foreseeability can affect several issues. Here we discuss foreseeability as a limit on damages, especially lost profits, especially in contract actions.

a. **The Rule**

Plaintiff cannot recover damages for loss that the defendant did not have reason to foresee at the time of contract formation as a probable result of the breach. Where damages flow naturally from the breach in the ordinary course of events, the rule is satisfied. Where consequences are less ordinary, other circumstances—such as notice from the plaintiff—may give defendant reason to know of these probable losses.

(1) **Reason to Know**

The rule requires that defendant have reason to know, not necessarily actual knowledge. A particularly dense defendant remains liable for the damages he should have foreseen.

(2) **Time of Contract Formation**

Foreseeability applies to the time of contract formation. This protects a defendant's ability to bargain for a different allocation of risk.

(3) **Breach Need Not Be Foreseeable**

The rule governs the foreseeability of losses if the contract is breached. The fact that the defendant had no reason to know she would breach the contract has no bearing on the inquiry.

(4) **Probable Result of Breach**

The fact that loss was possible will not satisfy the rule. Parties to a contract need not bargain over every remote possibility that might follow a breach. But if the loss was a probable consequence of breach, defendant should either bargain over the loss or pay damages for the loss.

(5) **Amount of Loss vs. Type of Loss**

On one reading, defendant must have reason to know that plaintiff probably would suffer losses of the type she now claims. More commonly, the amount of profits must be foreseeable as a probable result of the breach.

b. **Consequential Damages vs. Market Value**

The foreseeability rule applies to consequential damages—typically lost profits. Its application to other losses has not been as consistent.

5. **Reasonable Certainty**

A plaintiff must prove that the defendant's wrong caused harm to the plaintiff pursuant to the preponderance standard. By contrast, the *amount* of damages need only be determined with "reasonable certainty," a less demanding standard. The rule merely precludes juries from speculating about the amount of damages, leaving juries the freedom to make a reasonable estimate.

a. **Applicable to Each Component Separately**

The rule applies to each component of a damage award. Thus, if plaintiff can show one component (say, cost to repair a building) with reasonable certainty, but cannot show other elements (say, the profit plaintiff would have earned from operating a business from the building) with reasonable certainty, plaintiff can recover the components proven.

b. **The Standard Varies with the Wrong**

The degree of certainty required with regard to the amount of damages varies with the nature of the wrong. Damages such as pain and suffering, emotional distress, dignitary harm are so inherently uncertain that courts do not generally curb them by application of the reasonable certainty rule. Rather, such damages are typically reversed only if "grossly excessive" or "grossly inadequate."

c. **Wrongdoer Exception**

Where the defendant's wrongful conduct created plaintiff's inability to prove damages with sufficient certainty, courts usually permit the jury to estimate the amount of the loss without even the reasonable certainty limitation. Courts applying the exception generally limit it to uncertainty concerning the amount of damages, not uncertainty concerning the existence of damages.

d. **Proving Damages with Reasonable Certainty**

The rule may not preclude damages very often, but it does force plaintiffs to prepare their damage evidence carefully. The increasing willingness of courts to accept the testimony of accountants and appraisers, however, gives most plaintiffs room to satisfy the rule. New businesses still occasionally fall prey to the rule.

e. **Reducing Damages Awarded**

Even if the court allows the jury to estimate the amount of damages, courts retain the ability to reject or reduce any particular award as excessive under the certainty doctrine, via remittitur.

6. **The Economic Loss Doctrine**

With some exceptions, tort defendants are not liable unless their misconduct physically injures the person or property of plaintiff. The rule is typically expressed as a limitation on defendants' duty. If a tort injures the person or property of plaintiff, all losses, including economic losses, may be recoverable.

a. **Rationale**

The rule maintains the division between tort and contract law for warranty claims forcing plaintiff to sue in contract if the only injury was to the property defendant provided. It also limits which plaintiffs may sue, denying recovery to plaintiffs who suffer economic consequences but no damage to property.

b. **Exceptions**

If a tort is inherently economic—or, at least, inherently unrelated to physical injury—courts generally allow economic losses without proof of physical injury. Fraud, attorney malpractice, defamation, invasion of privacy, and intentional (or negligent) infliction of emotional distress might have no damages if subjected to the physical injury requirement. Of course, fraud, invasion of privacy, and interference with contractual relations are intentional torts—and the economic loss rule only limits negligence claims (and certain strict liability claims, like product liability, that resemble negligence).

A second exception exists for negligence claims against a defendant who has provided a service for a third party for the specific benefit of the plaintiff. Classic examples are (1) an attorney who negligently drafts a will for client X that was meant to benefit the plaintiff, and (2) an accountant who performs an audit of its client company, knowing that the audit was going to be relied upon by the plaintiff (and not the general public) in considering whether to pursue a private stock offering.

Still other courts have created ad hoc exceptions that expand liability to remote plaintiffs, especially when no other plaintiff could bring a suit.

7. **Public Policy**

In some cases, strict application of damage rules may produce results that undermine the substantive policy objectives of one or more laws. When this happens, courts may reject or limit damages in a way that protects the policy objectives.

a. **Undermining Policy Goals**

Laws ban misconduct in order to prevent certain harms. In unusual cases, the rule may in fact promote the harm instead of preventing it. When damages would undermine the policy goals of a rule intended to promote those goals, courts may decide to reject or limit damages.

b. Conflicting Goals

In some cases, awarding damages may undermine one policy goal, but denying them may undermine a different policy goal. In these cases, courts may decide to reject or limit damages in order to prevent undermining one of the policies at issue. No rules govern which of the conflicting policies a court should protect. In most cases of conflicting policies, both parties are wrongdoers.

c. Unanticipated Implications of Rules

Some cases confront courts with unanticipated implications of otherwise good rules. Courts sometimes invoke public policy to avoid results they find unsavory.

8. The Mechanism for Judicial Limitations on Damages

a. Additur and Remittitur

Courts in many states reserve the power alter a jury's damages award by order of additur (an increase in damages) or remittitur (a reduction of damages). In other states, courts have decided that such alterations are an unconstitutional abridgment of the jury's power under state constitutional provisions similar to the Seventh Amendment to the federal Constitution. In states in which additur and remittitur are allowed, courts yet give strong deference to jury awards via the standard of review. In addition, most states and the federal courts require courts to offer the affected party the option of either accepting the adjustment or a retrial on the damages issue, either with the same or a different jury.

b. Standard of Review

In some jurisdictions, a court may only alter a jury's damages verdict if it "shocks the conscience" or "suggests passion, prejudice, or corruption" on the part of the jury. In other jurisdictions, alterations are permitted only where the award falls "as a matter of law, outside the scope of the evidence." In still others, the standard of review is framed as "abuse of discretion."

F. AGREED REMEDIES

Parties to a contract may include terms intended to limit or to augment the remedies courts normally award. After early hostility to such provisions, courts have begun to enforce these contractual terms relating to remedies, within limits.

1. Limitations on Remedy

Limitations on remedy usually take one of two forms: (1) terms precluding recovery of some element of damages, such as consequential damages; or (2) terms substituting a different remedy for the ones provided in the code, such as the cost to repair or replace promised property.

a. Excluding Consequential Damages

A term precluding recovery of consequential damages is valid unless unconscionable. The U.C.C. includes a rebuttable presumption that a clause is unconscionable if it limits consequential damages when consumer goods cause personal injury. Clauses limiting commercial consequential losses are expressly authorized. Unconscionability probably means the same thing in this section that it means in section 2–302: (1) **unfair surprise**; and (2) **oppression**, sometimes stated as terms unreasonably favorable to the person who proposed them.

(1) **Unfair Surprise**

Unfair surprise implies that one party: (1) was unaware of the existence or effect of the terms; and (2) that party had no fair chance to determine the existence or effect of the terms before entering the contract.

(2) **Oppression**

Oppression (or unreasonably favorable terms) implies that one party: (1) receives an advantage from having the terms in the contract; and (2) the advantage is unreasonable. Commercially justifiable terms often survive this test.

(3) **Alternative Formulations of Unconscionability**

The definition of unconscionability here is relatively strict. Some courts require only one element instead of both. Other courts state the elements differently. Unfair surprise sometimes becomes lack of reasonable choice, which may encompass disparities in bargaining power. Oppression may focus on the harmful effects to the plaintiff rather than the reasonableness of the term.

b. **Substituted Remedies**

The U.C.C. allows parties to substitute remedies for those provided in the code. The remedies may expand recovery (perhaps adding attorneys' fees) or limit recovery (perhaps limiting plaintiff to repairs). If the substitute remedy does not specify that it is exclusive, then it is optional. U.C.C. § 2–719(1)(b). An exclusive remedy precludes recourse to remedies under the code, unless the exclusive remedy fails of its essential purpose.

c. **Double Limitations**

When contracts both limit the remedy (e.g., to repairs) and exclude consequential damages, some courts award consequential damages if the limited remedy fails of its essential purpose, without finding that excluding consequential damages is unconscionable. Others hold that the two clauses are independent: if the express term excluding consequential damages is not unconscionable, it is enforceable, without regard to the fate of the substituted remedy.

2. **Liquidated Damages**

Some contracts specify an amount of damages, either as a fixed amount or by a formula. These liquidated damage clauses have achieved general acceptance, but penalty clauses remain void as against public policy. The substance of the clause determines its classification: merely calling a clause liquidated damages (or a penalty) will not ensure that the courts will treat it as such.

a. **Liquidated Damages Clauses**

A liquidated damages clause is enforceable if it is reasonable. Factors considered in determining the reasonableness of a clause include the anticipated or actual harm caused by the breach, the difficulties of proof of loss, and the inconvenience or infeasibility of otherwise obtaining an adequate remedy (say, through injunctive relief or restitution). Amendments to the UCC, not yet widely adopted, propose to limit the second two factors to consumer contracts.

(1) **Anticipated or Actual Harm**

Clauses are enforceable if the amount "is reasonable in light of the anticipated or actual harm caused by the breach." Thus, a clause may be valid even if it wildly exceeds the actual harm, as long as it is reasonable in light of the anticipated harm, and vice versa.

(2) **Difficulty of Proof of Loss**

Difficulty of proof of loss is one (probably secondary) factor to discuss in evaluating reasonableness. It primarily effects the degree of accuracy a court will require. Where damages are relatively difficult to assess after a breach, a clause may be enforceable even if it seems relatively large in comparison to the actual loss the court believes occurred. If damages are relatively easy to calculate, the tolerable margin of error decreases.

(3) **Inconvenience or Infeasibility of Other Remedies**

Where a plaintiff foregoes other remedies in favor of a liquidated damage clause, the court may suspect that the liquidated damage clause is excessive. Thus, a court may be tempted to call the clause a penalty unless the decision to forego other remedies is reasonable.

b. **Bonuses**

In some situations, parties can achieve the same effect by writing a bonus clause instead of a liquidated damage clause. Bonuses typically do not specify damages for breach at all, falling outside these restrictions. Still, some authorities urge that the rules governing penalties here should be applied to contract provisions that seek to circumvent the limitations.

c. **Alternative Performance**

Some contracts specify alternative performances: that is, they allow one party to perform in either of two ways, one of which may be more onerous than the other. Alternative performance is not a breach and, hence, not a liquidated damage clause. Similarly, courts have not employed penalty analysis to take-or-pay clauses in oil and gas contracts.

3. **Agreements Regarding Equitable Remedies**

Agreements sometimes provide that specific performance or other equitable relief should be awarded in the event of breach. Because equity is discretionary relief, courts generally do not give these clauses binding effect. Rather, courts view these clauses as invitations to use their discretion that way and maybe as a waiver of some objections a party might raise.

G. PUNITIVE OR EXEMPLARY DAMAGES

Punitive Damages are not damages in the usual sense. They are a monetary recovery, but they are not based on the loss or damage the plaintiff suffered. Rather, they seek to impose an additional burden on defendant over and above the cost of compensating the plaintiff.

1. **Rationale**

Punitive damages may be justified by retribution or deterrence. The choice of theory may have some implications for how these damages are implemented.

2. **Standard for Awarding**

Punitive damages are not limited by the cause of action brought by the plaintiff, but by the level of culpability of the defendant. Thus, for example, although intentional torts are the quintessential actions in which punitive damages are available, punitives might also be available for actions in restitution, replevin, ejectment, quiet title, or even negligence if defendant's conduct constitutes recklessness.

Generally, intentional or malicious misconduct justifies punitive damages, while mere negligence or strict liability (including breach of contract) do not. The exact boundary varies among the states. All states that allow punitive damages allow them for actual malice, where defendant intends the harm. Most allow punitive damages where defendant's conduct implies malice—conduct so outrageous that it seems likely defendant knew harm would result. Many states also allow punitive damages for reckless disregard of a known risk, at least where the risk of harm is great.

In most jurisdictions, a plaintiff must establish the relevant state of mind by clear-and-convincing evidence.

3. **Measuring the Amount**

No precise standard for measuring punitive damages has achieved general acceptance. Instead, states tend to list a number of factors juries may consider, including: (1) reprehensibility of the conduct; (2) defendant's wealth (*but see* G.4, *infra*); (3) amount of compensatory damages; (4) amount likely to deter similar conduct by defendant and others; and (5) the aggregate amount of all civil and criminal sanctions awarded against the defendant for the conduct at issue.

A court may review the amount of punitive damages for gross excessiveness or inadequacy, so long as there is a strong basis in the record for so concluding.

4. **Limitations**

Punitive damages have come under attack both in legislatures and in courts. As a result, a number of limitations have been imposed on the availability and amount of punitive damages.

a. **Contract**

Punitive damages cannot be recovered for breach of contract. Litigants sometimes find ways around this limitation.

b. **Actual Damages**

Some states refuse to award punitive damages unless the plaintiff can prove some actual damages resulted from the misconduct. Most states allow punitive damages even if plaintiff receives only nominal damages.

c. **Statutory Limitations**

Statutes may limit two aspects of punitive damages: (1) how much may be awarded; and (2) who receives the award. Limits on the amount of punitive damages may resemble limits on the amount of pain and suffering or other nonpecuniary damages recoverable in litigation. Statutes sometimes specify that some portion of any punitive award be paid to the state.

d. **Constitutional Limitations**

An award of punitive damages may be so excessive that it violates the due process clause of the fourteenth amendment. Due process requires that defendant receive fair notice of the conduct subject to punishment and the severity of the penalty. To determine whether an award satisfies that standard, courts consider three factors: (1) the reprehensibility of the misconduct; (2) the relation between the harm and the punitive damages award; and (3) the difference between the punitive damages and similar penalties. Courts must review the constitutionality of a punitive award de novo, rather than applying an abuse of discretion test.

(1) Reprehensibility

Courts consider the nature of the harm (physical injury vs. economic loss), the defendant's state of mind (malice or indifference to the safety of others vs. mere accident), the financial vulnerability of the plaintiff, and the frequency of the misconduct (repeated actions vs. isolated incident). The Supreme Court in *Philip Morris USA v. Williams*, 549 U.S. 346, 127 S.Ct. 1057 (2007), held that reprehensible conduct by a defendant against anyone other than the plaintiff may not be considered by the jury in assigning punitive damages. Evidence of general reprehensible conduct may, however, be admissible to show that the conduct that harmed the plaintiff also posed a risk to the general public and was therefore particularly reprehensible. It seems unlikely that a jury will find it easy to parse such a distinction.

(2) Proportionality

Courts consider the relationship between the compensatory damages and the punitive damages. Where punitive damages exceed nine times compensatory damages, they may be excessive. On the other hand, the larger the compensatory award, the more likely it is that compensatory damages alone will deter the misconduct adequately, making punitive damages unnecessary.

(3) Other Sanctions

Courts consider other sanctions that might apply to the misconduct. The larger the other sanctions, the more likely a large punitive damage award will survive. Where penalties are smaller, the defendant lacks warning of the severity of the penalty that a state may impose.

5. Punitive Damages in Arbitration

Courts disagree about the circumstances under which arbitrators may award punitive damages.

a. Federal Arbitration Act

The Federal Arbitration Act (FAA) governs arbitration clauses in contracts involved in interstate commerce. Under federal law, courts seem to enforce arbitration awards that include punitive damages if a court could have considered punitive damages had the case been litigated.

b. State Laws

Contracts not governed by the FAA may include arbitration clauses permitted under state arbitration acts. Many state courts have affirmed arbitration awards including punitive damages. As with the FAA, most of these cases include some allegation of tort.

(1) Authorizing the Arbiter

Courts sometimes focus on whether the clause allows arbiters to award punitive damages. Several approaches emerge: (1) a broad clause authorizes punitive damages unless it expressly excludes them; (2) a clause authorizes punitive damages only if it expressly includes them; (3) any indication that the parties intended to authorize arbitration of punitive damages will suffice—for instance, where one party submits a request for punitive damages and the other party does not contest the request in the arbitration proceeding.

(2) Public Policy

One famous New York case appears to hold that public policy precludes any arbitration award including punitive damages, even if the parties expressly authorized the arbiter to do so.

H. ATTORNEYS' FEES

The American Rule rejects recovery of attorneys' fees, leaving each party to pay their own counsel. Numerous exceptions to the American Rule allow prevailing parties to recover their attorneys' fees.

1. Statutory Exceptions

State and federal statutes permit the prevailing plaintiff to recover attorneys' fees. Some apply to all cases, some to contract cases, others to civil rights cases.

a. Asymmetrical Fee Shifting

Most fee-shifting statutes allow the prevailing plaintiff to recover fees as a matter of course. Denying fees to a prevailing plaintiff would be an abuse of discretion, barring unusual circumstances. Prevailing defendants, however, often face a stricter standard: they may recover their fees only if the plaintiff's action was frivolous.

b. Prevailing Party

Most statutes provide fees to the prevailing party. When a party wins a judgment in court on all counts, no problem arises. Difficulties arise whenever a lesser success occurs.

(1) Partial Success

When plaintiffs succeed on some but not all of their claims or against some but not all of the defendants named, courts must decide whether to reject fees associated with the unsuccessful claims. Sometimes all hours spent on the case deserve compensation, as where defendants' conduct prevented plaintiff from discovering which of them was liable or where the unsuccessful claims were necessary to cover contingencies that otherwise might allow defendants to escape liability. In other cases, plaintiff may be limited to the fees incurred pursuing the successful claims, especially where the other claims bordered on the frivolous.

(2) Settlement vs. Consent Decrees

A consent decree is a judgment of the court, thus qualifying the plaintiff as a prevailing party. A settlement agreement, however, does not permit attorneys' fees. Settling parties may include fees in the settlement agreement.

(3) Catalyst

Filing a suit may cause defendant to change its ways. When the relief requested is injunctive, the change may moot the suit. In these situations, plaintiffs have sought fees, alleging that their suit obtained the relief sought, even though no court order was entered. The U.S. Supreme Court has ruled that catalysts are not prevailing parties under federal fee-shifting statutes.

c. Lodestar

Courts interpreting fee-shifting statutes start by calculating a number called the lodestar: the number of hours reasonably spent on the action times the reasonable hourly fee. This makes accurate time records important even for attorneys who do not generally charge by the hour. Enhancement for contingency under federal statutes has been rejected. States remain free to interpret their own statutes.

2. Common Funds

The American Rule allows plaintiffs to collect attorneys' fees when their litigation created a fund that benefits a group of persons. The exception does not actually allow fee shifting to the defendant. Rather, the fee comes from the award; the portion each claimant receives is reduced to account for the fees of the attorneys who created the fund. In common fund cases, courts sometimes award a percentage of the fund rather than applying lodestar.

3. Other Exceptions

a. Contract

If the parties to a contract agree that the prevailing party may recover attorneys' fees, courts will honor those provisions.

b. Contempt

When a party's violation of a court order forces the opponent to bring contempt proceedings, courts allow recovery of the fees incurred in connection with the contempt.

c. Family Law

In family law cases, courts often order the party with greater means to pay the other's attorney. In effect, orders of this nature simply distribute family resources among the parties, much the way the division of property distributes assets from one spouse to another.

d. Collateral Litigation

In some cases, defendant's wrong forces plaintiff to incur expenses in litigating against third parties. In these situations, expenses incurred in the collateral litigation are recoverable as an ensuing loss, like medical expenses or any other consequential damage.

e. Litigation Misconduct

When a party conducts litigation without a good faith belief that it has merit, courts may award the other party fees for opposing the move. This can be a tort, such as malicious prosecution or abuse of process. In other cases, court rules provide sanctions for bad-faith litigation. The wrong can involve the entire suit, or it might involve a single motion filed in bad faith.

f. Bad Faith Conduct by an Insurer

Attorneys' fees are commonly awarded in suits alleging the tort of bad-faith conduct by an insurer.

Perspectives

APPROACH TO THE SUBJECT

The course in Remedies studies the array of things a court can do for the prevailing party in litigation. The prevailing party usually refers to the plaintiff (or counter plaintiff). For the prevailing defendant, no remedy at all usually is enough—though the course occasionally discusses ways a defendant might be made whole, as through awards of attorneys' fees or collecting on an injunction bond.

The course surveys several different remedial approaches. A good deal of the course focuses on the details of each remedy. To some extent these details are no more than a prelude to the real problem of remedies: deciding which remedy to seek. Knowing the alternatives is essential to choosing among them. Choosing the wrong remedy may lead you to file the wrong cause of action in the wrong jurisdiction—or even to sue the wrong defendant. In some ways, the remedy should be the first thing an attorney considers when contemplating how to help a client. The remedy often is foremost in the client's mind. Focusing on the remedies at the outset of litigation may prevent a number of poor litigation choices.

The course focuses on one primary lesson: courts seek to place the prevailing plaintiff as nearly as possible in the position she would have occupied if the wrong had not occurred—as one casebook author puts it, the plaintiff's "rightful position." *See* DOUGLAS LAYCOCK, MODERN AMERICAN REMEDIES 16 (3d ed. 2002). This fundamental principle supports a limit on remedies—no more than plaintiff would have obtained but for the wrong—as well as a standard by which we can assess the adequacy of remedies—no less than the plaintiff would have obtained but for the wrong. At a doctrinal level, the course focuses on the rules by which courts implement (and occasionally deviate from) this goal. At a societal (or policy) level, the course explores the reasons for implementing or deviating from this goal. Each deviation teaches something about the policy choices society makes. Punitive damages and restitution, by allowing recoveries to exceed the rightful position, probe the rationale for this goal, while limitations on remedies, such as foreseeability and certainty probe the effectiveness of the goal.

The focus on the rightful position emphasizes the inextricable link between the remedy and the wrong. Plaintiff has no entitlement to any remedy unless defendant committed a wrong. Equally important, the extent of the wrong determines the extent of the remedy. Wrongs that cause less harm produce less remedy and vice versa.

Most of this volume will explore the doctrines. Much of the value of the course, however, stems from introducing you to the arguments that will shape the future evolution of remedies. A moment exploring the justification for this framework seems appropriate. Interestingly, both of the primary approaches to remedies both support the basic rule, which may explain its widespread application.

Corrective justice theories focus on the plaintiff. Plaintiff should not bear the cost of another's wrong. If remedies fall short of the plaintiff's rightful position, plaintiff bears part of the cost. On the other hand, to award more than the harm suffered would be a windfall to plaintiff. Compensation (or compensation plus prevention) must leave the plaintiff as close as possible to the rightful position. Fairness for the defendant also dictates this goal. The defendant should not be forced to pay for harms it did not cause. Limiting plaintiff's recovery to the harm defendant caused is fair to both parties.

Law and economics proposes the same result, but for different reasons. The theory posits that the law should encourage efficient conduct. Remedies provide the incentive to obey the law. The incentive should encourage legal conduct when the harm caused by illegal conduct exceeds the cost of obeying the law (preventing the harm). On the other hand, if the cost of preventing the harm exceeds the harm prevented, prevention is inefficient. As long as remedies assess defendant with the cost of the harm, the incentive will match this goal. But if the remedy awards plaintiff more than the harm defendant caused, it may encourage defendants to overinvest in prevention—in effect, wasting money preventing harms that should not be prevented. (If that seems counterintuitive, consider whether you would pay more for collision coverage than it would cost to replace your car in the event of an accident.) On the other hand, if remedies do not assess the full harm of the wrong, defendants may have too little incentive to invest in prevention. As long as defendant pays the full cost, the incentive is correct—even if defendant pays the cost to someone other than the plaintiff. The reason to give the money to the plaintiff is to encourage her to come forward and prove the wrong. Without that incentive, the wrong may go unremedied, again producing too little incentive for defendants to prevent harms.

Challenges to these theories often are *ad hoc*, rather than global. For instance, many justify punitive damages (which intentionally exceed the harm to the plaintiff) as a way to make up for shortcomings in other remedial doctrines or in the way procedures impede some suits. Others suggest that remedies in excess of harm are justified as a deterrent—that no violations of law are appropriate (at least in some causes of action), so that remedies should be high enough to discourage any harms, not just the inefficient harms. Along the same lines, restitution in excess of plaintiff's loss has been justified by the need to remove any gain defendant received from the wrong. This will deter the wrong, even if it is efficient (that is, the benefit to defendant exceeds the harm to plaintiff). Criminal law embodies this approach, for those wrongs society has codified and decided to penalize. Even law and economics does not propose efficient theft—though in part as a way to encourage people to agree on a price. Theft bypasses the market, risking the possibility that the property is more valuable to the original owner than to the new owner.

As indicated above, these principles have application throughout the course. Each limitation on recovery faces the challenge that it undercompensates the plaintiff and underdeters the defendant. Each remedy in excess of harm faces the opposite challenge. As remedies evolve—and they are evolving—these arguments will shape the ways in which they expand and contract.

In the meantime, we will explore the ways in which the law approaches or deviates from the rightful position. Sometimes courts can achieve the rightful position precisely, giving the plaintiff exactly what she deserved. Injunctions often seek to provide such specific relief, by preventing the defendant from committing the wrong or compelling the defendant to undo the damage. Damages more commonly provide substitute relief, compensating the plaintiff for any difference between his current position and the position he would have occupied if the wrong had not occurred. Occasionally, money will equate to specific relief—say, where the seller of goods was owed money and nothing more.

Within injunctive relief, the same debate rages about the extent to which relief should be limited to the plaintiff's rightful position. Injunctive relief emerged from a tradition of judicial discretion. In effect, judges sitting in equity seek to do the right thing. Occasionally, judges claim the right to do more or less than the rightful position requires—

to deny injunctions or limit them in ways that leave plaintiff short of the rightful position or to grant injunctions that leave plaintiff better off than if the wrong had not occurred. The extent to which judicial discretion should be limited by the rightful position remains open to debate.

When money substitutes are used, the debate splits along a different fault line. In restitution, the stated goal is to put the defendant in the position she would have occupied if the wrong had not occurred. In effect, the defendant's gains from misconduct should be disgorged. By contrast, damage rules always start with the plaintiff's rightful position, regardless of defendant's gain. Often, defendant's gain will be far less than plaintiff's loss. For instance, in most accidents, defendant gains nothing from having harmed plaintiff. Plaintiffs in these cases always ask for their loss, not defendant's gain. But in some cases defendant's gain exceeds the plaintiff's loss—that is, the benefit of the breach exceeds the harm it causes. In these situations, restitution urges disgorgement to deter the efficient conduct that damages seek to encourage.

While these general approaches will help keep the material in context, understanding remedies requires considerable attention to detail. The general rule states the goal, but identifying all the differences between plaintiff's current position and the rightful position (let alone quantifying them) requires some detailed thought. The rule requires attention to the specific harms plaintiff suffers.

APPROACH TO THE BOOK

This book can contribute to your study of remedies in several ways. One thing it cannot do, however, is replace a careful reading of the cases. Remedies are inherently case-specific. Each wrong causes different effects, which in turn produce a different measure. The guidelines for remedies can be stated generally. But understanding their application requires some attention to the detailed facts of each case. This book cannot provide those details. To explore remedies intelligently, you will need to read the cases in your casebook with some care.

At all stages of the course, this book may help you get the most from a course. Before the class begins, you can get a useful overview of remedies from this Perspectives chapter and from the Capsule Summary. Reading the body of the outline would allow you to appreciate the way remedies interrelate as you study each remedy in class.

As you prepare for class, this book can help in several ways. First, the glossary may help you understand some of the terms in your casebook. Second, the body of the outline can serve as a check on your understanding of the cases you read for class. In effect, it can reassure you that you understood the way courts assess remedies. Third, the criticisms or alternatives noted in the outline may enrich classroom discussion or discussion in study groups. They can help you probe the inner workings of remedies.

As the semester ends, this book offers a useful resource as you synthesize what you learned during the term. Naturally, this book will not reflect exactly the same emphasis as your course. Casebooks and professors vary in their approach, spending more time on some portions of the course than others, supplementing casebooks with additional materials of particular interest to them. You will want to create your own outline, which can include these materials and reflect the different emphasis of your course. This book offers one way to understand the structure of remedies, perhaps a way that makes remedies a little easier to understand than the structure of your casebook or class. In addition, the doctrines and critiques here should help you review each remedy individually.

You may find the practice questions among the most useful features. Not only will they help you identify areas in which you may need more thorough review, they also may help you prepare for the examination.

APPROACH TO THE EXAM

Examinations vary enormously among professors. Professors use different mixes of objective, short answer, and essay questions. But that is just the tip of the iceberg. Professors differ in the extent to which they ask about policy, about standard remedies, and about cutting edge issues. Even when presenting a standard set of facts, professors differ in whether they expect a detailed discussion of the most important issues or a quick analysis of all the issues raised by the facts (or something in between these extremes). In short, you will need to alter any advice offered here to fit the way your professor tests remedies.

Thus, the most important advice we can offer is to read the questions carefully. Rarely will professors ask you to tell them everything you learned during the term, so rarely should your answer be that indiscriminate. Professors will pose questions that resemble the cases you may confront in practice. Clients will have a problem—perhaps a big one with lots of facets, but still one problem. They will want you to help them solve it, not just recite a lot of things you know about remedies. Most questions will contain clues to the topics or approach your professor believes will be most productive. In some cases, professors will offer you smaller questions to help guide your answer. By all means, pay attention to these suggestions. Your professors will not intentionally mislead you. They enjoy the holidays much better if your answers are clearly organized and interesting to read.

Another clue professors often provide is to give you a role. You may be a judge asked to decide a case, but you may be an advocate asked to evaluate the chances of success and outline the best legal strategy. Or you may be a legislative analyst asked to advise a legislator whether to enact a particular amendment to existing rules. In any event, pay attention to your role and write accordingly. If you are a lawyer, don't write as if you are judging the case. And if you are a judge, be a careful judge, not one who makes a minimal argument in favor of the result and stops.

Unless you are using this book in a first-year course, such as contracts or torts, you already have considerable experience in taking law school exams. Perhaps the suggestions here will seem like old news; perhaps they will seem like odd notions. But perhaps a few thoughts will help you prepare for and write a remedies exam.

Remedies involves strategic choices. That point is critical on the exam. The exam questions, at least the essays, are likely to offer facts where you could choose to pursue different remedies. Maybe the choice is between an injunction and damages, maybe between damages and restitution, maybe a declaratory judgment will seem useful. In any event, you are likely to face a question where you must explore two or more remedial options and explain why one is better than the other(s). While some questions may ask you to explore in depth a single remedial choice, it will pay to consider whether an alternative remedy might be available on these facts.

Detailed analysis will be important. Whether the question asks you to explore a single remedy or compare alternative remedies, the comparison will require you to analyze the remedy in detail. Each remedy is likely to include more than one element of recovery, plus an issue of affirmative defense or limitation. Avoid the temptation to short circuit the analysis and simply justify the result. Most professors give some credit if you recite the rule, but unless you can link the rule to the facts of the case in a way that justifies the conclusion you reach, you are likely to miss the vast majority of points available.

This may be among the most important lessons, so it bears repeating. Good lawyers use facts—more than one, when possible—to demonstrate that their client satisfies each component of a rule. The conclusion is justified by thorough, systematic use of the facts (and occasionally policy arguments), not by a recitation of a rule and a conclusory suggestion that the your client satisfies the rule.

Where the law as it exists presents a hurdle, find a way over or around it. Don't be afraid to make creative suggestions on an exam—just as you may need to make creative suggestions in practice. You might explore a different remedy that doesn't confront this obstacle. You might urge the court to create an exception or new rule based on the policies that guide remedial decisions. Some questions practically invite a policy discussion.

Where time allocation is left to you, stick to a schedule. Don't spend so much time on one question that you barely answer or ignore the others. Almost invariably, you will score worse on the exam if any part of it is at or near the bottom of the class than if each part is at least competent. Don't assume that one more point on question 1 is the same as one more point on question 2, even if they are evenly weighted. Barring statistical errors by the professor, that is extremely unlikely. Remember, too, the law of diminishing returns. Usually, the first few sentences on an issue produce several points. At some point, however, it may take several sentences to make the next point. If you reach that point (and know it), you might be better served to move to the next issue, where the same number of sentences may earn more points.

Normally, the smaller the question, the smaller the answer. Short answer questions usually focus on a single remedy and often a single aspect of that remedy. Your answer should be as focused as the question. This does not mean it should be superficial. Better analysis still pays off. But it does suggest that straying into side issues is less likely to be productive.

Chapter One

Equity and Equitable Remedies

A. Historical Perspective on the Development of "Law" and "Equity"

At common law, there existed a dual court system that included "law" courts and "equity" courts. The King's Courts were in place early on. Later, "equity" courts (a/k/a, chancery courts) developed from the King's power to dispense justice. Basically, rather than going to the King's Courts, individuals could directly petition the king for relief. Over time, as the number of cases brought to the King grew, the King eventually delegated his power to the King's Chancellor, authorizing the Chancellor to dispense justice on his behalf. Over time, as the number of cases brought to the Chancellor grew, he began delegating his power to his subordinates, and there developed a new system of courts referred to as "equity courts" or "chancery courts." The King's courts, a/k/a "law courts," dispensed "legal remedies." By contrast, equity courts granted "equitable remedies."

Today, most states have merged "law" and "equity" into a single, unified, court system. However, the merger of law and equity did not eliminate the distinction between legal remedies and equitable remedies, or the limitations and conditions applicable to those remedies.

1. The King and the Law Courts

In Early England, although people could seek recourse in the King's Courts (which we refer to today as the "Law Courts"), they also could petition the King directly, and ask him to grant them justice. In cases brought to him, the King exercised virtually unbridled discretion to grant or withhold relief.

2. The Medieval Chancellor

The Chancellor was a minister of the king who also served as a high church official. As a minister, the Chancellor functioned more like a prime minister who performed various functions for the King. One of the Chancellor's functions was to issue "writs" authorizing litigants to bring suit in the King's Courts. When a given set of facts did not fit within the scope of an existing writ, the Chancellor sometimes created new forms of writs which the courts could accept or reject.

3. The Provisions of Oxford

Over time, the English Lords objected to the creation of new writs as an infringement of their rights and prerogatives, and as adding to the scope of federal power. As a result, in 1258, they prompted adoption of the Provisions of Oxford that prohibited the creation of new forms of writs absent the consent of the King and the King's Council (composed of Lords). A later statute relaxed this rule by authorizing new writs that were factually similar to existing writs. Statute of Westminster II (1285).

4. The King's Residual Authority

Even though the Provisions of Oxford limited the Chancellor's power to issue new writs, the King retained his equitable power to grant "justice." As the Provisions of Oxford began to limit the ability of the King's Courts to respond to new types of problems, more and more people began to petition the King directly for relief (justice).

5. Development of the Chancellor's Equitable Power

As the quantity of petitions to the King grew in number, the King asked the Chancellor to hear and decide these matters. Because of his dual function, as a high governmental minister and an official of the church, the Chancellor seemed particularly well suited to hear petitions for "justice." Not infrequently, the Chancellor would listen to the parties in a sort of fact-finding exercise and would make decisions somewhat like decisions made by a judge. When the Chancellor rendered his decision, he usually grounded it in pious sounding words like "justice," "equity" and "conscience." Like the King, the Chancellor had broad discretion about whether to grant or deny relief, as well as regarding the scope of the relief to be granted.

6. The Growth of Chancery

Over time, the petitions became too much for even the Chancellor to hear and he began delegating his authority to subordinate officials who functioned like judges in the sense that they developed facts, applied the law to facts, and began to develop and apply legal precedent. Over time, a separate and coordinate system of justice developed. Consistent with its origins, the Chancery Court system (a/k/a equity) continued to dispense justice according to principles of equity, justice and conscience.

B. Distinctions Between Law and Equity

At common law, there were fundamental differences between law courts and equity courts. These differences included the governing principles applied by the courts and extended to the way that they framed their judgments or decisions.

1. The Relationship of Equity Courts to Law Courts

Since equity courts were not bound by the Provisions of Oxford, they could hear new forms of action. However, true to their roots, equity courts refused to act except when the common law courts could not provide the plaintiff with an adequate remedy. When the legal remedy was available and adequate, an equity court would dismiss the case, thereby forcing plaintiff to pursue his legal remedies. Necessarily, since equity courts focused on principles of "equity" and "conscience," they did not apply the same substantive rules as the law courts.

2. Equitable Relief Distinguished from Legal Relief

Equity courts also differed from law courts regarding how they rendered their judgments. In general, a law court would render its judgment as an award of monetary damages. By contrast, courts of equity usually rendered *in personam* judgments. In other words, rather than making a monetary award, a court of equity would issue an order in the name of the King telling the plaintiff to do, or refrain from doing, a specific act. Those who failed to comply could be held in contempt of court.

3. Governing Principles of Equity

True to their religious roots, equity courts were referred to as "courts of conscience," and were supposed to use their powers to bring about "justice" and "equity." As a result, equity judges or chancellors could deny relief on equitable or moral grounds. The chancellor could also withhold relief on practical grounds. Over time, as equity courts heard more petitions, they began to develop "rules" or "maxims" that took on the character of precedent. Although these "maxims" were generalizations of experience based on the results of prior cases, they eventually developed into a loose set of "rules" designed to bring some coherency to the body of decided cases and some consistency to future decisions.

4. Equitable Maxims

"Equitable maxims" included the following principles: He who comes into equity must come with clean hands; He who seeks equity must do equity; Equity is a court of conscience; Equity does not suffer a wrong to go without a remedy; Equity abhors a forfeiture; Equity regards as done that which ought to have been done; Equity delights to do justice and not by halves; Equitable relief is not available to one who has an adequate remedy at law; Equitable relief is discretionary; Equity aids the vigilant, not those who slumber on their rights; Equity regards substance rather than form; Equity acts in personam; Equity is equality; Equity follows the law; Equity will not aid a volunteer; Where the equities are equal, the law will prevail; Equity imputes an intent to fulfill an obligation; Where the equities are equal, the first in time will prevail.

C. The Development of Equity in the United States

Just as the English common law was transplanted to the United States, equity and equitable principles were transplanted as well. All thirteen colonies had chancery courts (in one form or another), as well as law courts, and these chancery courts continued to function after the Revolution. But, as the Nineteenth Century progressed, a movement to abolish equity courts emerged, and states began to merge their law courts with their equity courts.

1. The Field Code and Early Attempts to Abolish Equity Courts

In 1848, the State of New York adopted the Field Code, a civil procedure code, which abolished the distinction between law and equity. Other states followed suit. As a result, most civil procedure codes now create one form of action known as the "civil action" and these actions are heard by courts that hear both legal and equitable claims.

2. Merger in Other States

Since the adoption of the Field Code, many other states have eliminated the distinction between law courts and equity courts, and the distinction remains in less than a handful of states.

3. Variations on Merger

In the United States, merger has taken a number of different forms. Most states, following the Field Code model, merged their law courts with their equity courts. A few states maintained separate equity courts in the common law mode with some variation (e.g., some of these states provided for more liberal transfer of cases between law courts and equity courts). At the federal level, law courts were merged with equity courts. Rule 2 of the Federal Rules of Civil Procedure is illustrative since it provides that "there shall be one form of action known as the 'civil action.' "

D. Equitable Remedies Today

Even though law courts and equity courts have been merged in the overwhelming majority of states, distinctions between law and equity have not completely disappeared. Indeed, although courts no longer draw formal distinctions between "legal actions" and "equitable actions," they do distinguish between "legal remedies" and "equitable remedies." Equitable remedies continue to be subject to many of the same distinctions and limitations that have historically applied to such remedies.

1. Equitable Remedies Are Based on "Conscience" and "Equity"

As we have seen, equity courts developed as "courts of conscience." Equity's roots continue to govern the granting of equitable relief.

a. Equity and Conscience Today

Even though equity courts no longer exist, equitable remedies continue to be available today only when their issuance would be consistent with "equity" and "conscience." Courts apply various rules of conscience. For example, they may apply the doctrine of laches to deny equitable relief to plaintiffs who unduly delay in asserting their rights (even though the statute of limitations has not expired), or who come to court with unclean hands (even though plaintiff's misconduct might not preclude legal relief).

b. Equity Versus Law on Conscience Principles

The description of equity as a "court of conscience" was always somewhat misleading. Courts of law had their own "rules of conscience" although they did not necessarily label their rules as such. For example, just as a court of equity might refuse to specifically enforce a contract when the plaintiff's hands are unclean, a court of law might refuse to enforce a contract which violates the court's conception of public policy.

c. The Difficulty in Defining Terms like "Equity" and "Conscience"

In deciding whether a particular result is "conscionable" or "equitable," equity courts rely on the equitable maxims discussed earlier, as well as on the chancellor's own sense of morality or justice. Many modern courts still use the equitable maxims. However, questions remain regarding whether the maxims are consistent with each other, and whether they really provide the basis for judicial decisions, or whether they are simply used to justify decisions made on other grounds.

2. Equitable Remedies Are Granted in Personam

Another historical distinction that has survived is the rule that "equity acts *in personam*."

a. *In Personam* Remedies Defined

When a court renders an *in personam* judgment, it orders the defendant to do, or refrain from doing, some act. A defendant who refuses to comply can be held in contempt of court and subjected to prison or fine.

b. Legal Remedies Contrasted

By contrast, a law court usually renders a monetary judgment. In other words, it enters a decree stating that defendant owes plaintiff a sum of money. This judgment is not automatically enforcing and defendant cannot be held in contempt for refusal to pay. If defendant refuses to pay the judgment, plaintiff must bring an enforcement action in order to attach defendant's personal property, or place liens on defendant's real property, in order to force satisfaction of the judgment.

3. Inadequacy of Legal Remedy/Irreparable Harm

Another equitable maxim that survives today is the principle that equitable relief is not available except when plaintiff's legal remedy is inadequate. This principle is also known as the "irreparable harm" requirement.

a. Example of an Adequate Legal Remedy

The classic example of an "adequate legal remedy" involves an attempt to seek specific performance of a contract for the sale of an item that is readily available on the open market. For example, in *Fortner v. Wilson*, 202 Okla. 563, 216 P.2d 299 (1950), plaintiff agreed to purchase an automobile from a car dealership. When the dealer breached, the buyer sued seeking specific performance. The Court denied relief on the basis that Chevrolet automobiles were readily available on the open market. As a result, if plaintiff received damages (calculated by taking the difference between the contract price and the fair market price), he could purchase another Chevrolet on the open market. As the Court stated, a court of equity will not "specifically enforce a contract for the sale of ordinary articles of commerce, which can be bought in the open market, such as barroom fixtures, cattle, coal, corn, cotton, logs or lumber, pianos, sauerkraut, whisky, used cars, or an existing business and stock in trade, since the remedy at law for a breach of such contract is regarded as complete and adequate." Plaintiff can be forced to accept damages, in lieu of injunctive relief, and can then use those damages to purchase an equivalent item on the open market.

b. Examples of Inadequacy

The concept of "inadequacy of the legal remedy" and the "requirement of irreparable injury" are extremely important. As a general rule, harm is irreparable when the legal remedy of damages is inadequate to provide relief. Examples of adequacy include the following situations: when property is "unique" so that plaintiff cannot readily purchase a substitute; when damages are difficult or impossible to calculate; when defendant is insolvent or it is otherwise impossible to collect a monetary judgment; when plaintiff will be required to bring multiple proceedings to vindicate his rights; and when the plaintiff's injury is of such a nature (e.g., deprivation of civil rights) that the remedy of damages is substitutionary and ineffective.

c. The Adequacy Requirement Today

The common law requirement of irreparable injury survives today, albeit in somewhat more flexible form. In contracts for the sale of goods, *Fortner's* rule was codified in the Uniform Commercial Code, § 2–716: "specific performance may be decreed where the goods are unique or in other proper circumstances." This provision has been interpreted to permit specific performance even though the goods are not unique in the strict sense but are very scarce or cannot be replaced through alternative sources. *Copylease Corp. of America v. Memorex Corp.*, 408 F.Supp. 758 (S.D.N.Y.1976).

d. The Wisdom of Retaining the Adequacy Requirement

Today, commentators debate whether it makes sense to maintain the historical requirement of inadequacy as a predicate to equitable relief. One reason for maintaining the requirement is illustrated by the *Fortner* case. If the car buyer can purchase an equivalent vehicle on the open market, a court might justifiably be reluctant to order specific performance. The parties are already at odds with each other. If they are ordered to do business with each other, continuing problems are possible, indeed likely, to develop. It is easier and cleaner for courts to simply make an award of damages and thereby let the parties go their separate ways,

4. Equitable Relief Is Discretionary

Another fundamental principle of equity is the notion that equitable relief is discretionary. Even if the plaintiff is suffering irreparable injury, a court has discretion to deny equitable relief.

a. Discretion May Be Exercised to Deny Relief When an Injunction Would Involve the Court in Continuing Supervision Problems

Courts are generally reluctant to issue injunctions which enmesh them in continuing supervision of the parties. For example, in *Grossman v. Wegman's Food Markets, Inc.*, 43 A.D.2d 813, 350 N.Y.S.2d 484 (Sup.Ct., App.Div.1973), plaintiff sought an injunction requiring defendant to occupy leased premises and to operate it as a retail grocery store. The court denied the relief, noting that "courts of equity are reluctant to grant specific performance in situations where such performance would require judicial supervision over a long period of time." What if defendant operates the store, but plaintiff believes that defendant should offer more goods or have more employees. Will the court be expected to micromanage defendant's decisions on those issues? If the court enters such an order, what happens if the store owner refuses to employ sufficient staff or to retain sufficient merchandise? Is a court going to then direct the store owner regarding how to run its business?

b. Discretion May Be Exercised Against Relief Based on Public Policy Considerations

Equitable relief may also be denied when public policy considerations demand it. For example, in one case, a court refused to enjoin defendant from operating an animal shelter even though animals at the shelter caused noise and annoyance that bothered the shelter's neighbors. The court acknowledged the societal need for dog shelters, and noted the absence of a suitable alternative site that would not irritate others. In another case, plaintiff, who lived close to a city's airport, sued claiming that the airport's operation (in particular, the takeoffs and landings) interfered with the use and enjoyment of her home. Given the importance of the airport to the city, the court did not order the airport to shut down.

E. Equitable Defenses

A number of common law equitable defenses might be used by modern courts as a basis for refusing to grant equitable relief. The major defenses are "unclean hands", unconscionability, laches, and estoppel. All of these doctrines are grounded in equitable principles.

1. Clean Hands Doctrine

The "unclean hands" (or "clean hands") doctrine states that "he who comes to equity must come with clean hands." Equitable principles suggest plaintiffs who come with "unclean hands" should be denied relief.

a. The Classic Example: The *Highwayman's Case*

In the *Highwaymen's Case,* perhaps the most famous unclean hands case, two bandits agreed to rob travelers and split the profits. When one of the partners refused to share the profits on the agreed basis, the other sued for an accounting. The Chancellor, after invoking the unclean hands doctrine and dismissing the case, fined plaintiff's solicitors for contempt of court. *See Everet v. Williams*, Ex. (1725), 9 L.Q.Rev. 197 (1893).

b. The Unclean Hands Can Apply to Many Types of Misconduct

"Unclean hands," includes all types of misconduct and wrongdoing that are sufficiently related to the plaintiff's claim. Indeed, almost any conduct that can be considered to be unfair, unethical, improper, or illegal, can provide a basis for denying equitable relief. Courts can also raise the issue, *sua sponte*. However, courts impose a nexus requirement in the sense that plaintiff's conduct must be sufficiently related to the case before the court. In addition, the misconduct must be serious enough to justify withholding an equitable remedy, that might otherwise be available, and relegating plaintiff instead to her legal remedies.

c. Potential Inequities Caused by the Clean Hands Doctrine

Of course, when the clean hands doctrine is strictly applied, the doctrine can lead to potential inequities. For example, in the *Highwayman's Case*, if the court leaves the parties where it found them, then one of the robbers is left with all of the loot. Of course, many judges will notify the police or prosecutors about the parties' conduct and let the police or prosecutors try to find a solution.

d. Unrelated Transactions Exception

As noted, courts will generally refuse to apply the clean hands doctrine when the plaintiff's misconduct is unrelated to the transaction at hand. For example, even a convicted felon can obtain equitable relief when his criminal conduct is unrelated to the matter before the court (e.g., one who is convicted of embezzlement from his employer can, at a later point, seek injunctive relief preventing a neighbor (unrelated to the employer) from trespassing on his property).

2. Unconscionability

Since equity developed as a "court of conscience," courts have always felt free to deny equitable relief on the grounds of conscience. Or, to state it differently, courts may deny relief to a party who obtains a bargain that can be regarded as "unconscionable."

a. Classic Example

The classic example of unconscionability is provided by the case of *Campbell Soup Co. v. Wentz*, 172 F.2d 80 (3d Cir.1948). In that case, the Campbell Soup Co. contracted to purchase all of the Chantenay red cored carrots grown on a fifteen-acre farm. The contract contained a clause prohibiting the farmer from selling the carrots to others even if they were rejected by Campbell Soup Co. In refusing to enforce the contract, the court stated that "We [think] that a party who has offered and succeeded in getting an agreement as tough as this one is, should not come to a chancellor and ask the court for help in the enforcement of its terms."

b. U.C.C. § 2–302

U.C.C. § 2–302 contains an unconscionability provision which states as follows:

> (1) If a court as a matter of law finds the contract or any term of the contract to have been unconscionable at the time it was made the court may refuse to enforce the contract, or it may enforce the remainder of the contract without the unconscionable term, or it may so limit the application of any unconscionable terms as to avoid any unconscionable result.
>
> (2) [If] any term [may] be unconscionable [the] parties shall be afforded a reasonable opportunity to present evidence as to its commercial setting, purpose and effect to aid the court in making the determination. U.C.C. § 2–302 (May 2001 proposed revision). Although the term "unconscionable" is not defined, the U.C.C.s comments offer some clarification: "The principle is one of the prevention of oppression and unfair surprise (*Cf. Campbell Soup Co. v. Wentz*) and not of disturbance of allocation of risks because of superior bargaining power." U.C.C. § 2–302 comment 1.

3. Laches

A third defense that can be used to defeat an equitable claim is the defense of "laches." That defense is associated with the maxim: "Equity aids the vigilant, not those who slander on their right," and is applied today in many different types of cases, particularly tort and contract cases.

a. Laches Defined

Broadly defined, laches involves any unreasonable delay by the plaintiff in instituting or prosecuting an action under circumstances where the delay causes prejudice to the defendant. *See e.g.*, RESTATEMENT SECOND OF TORTS § 939 (1977).

b. Laches as an Equitable Statute of Limitations

At common law, the statute of limitations applied to legal actions, but not to equitable actions. Effectively, laches served as the "equitable statute of limitations."

c. Laches Distinguished from the Statute of Limitations

The defense of laches functions quite differently than the statute of limitations (SOL). The SOL involves a specified and definite period of time (e.g., an action for breach of contract must be brought within five years). Once that time period has elapsed, the suit is barred. The doctrine of laches is not tied to a specific time frame but rather is tied to unreasonable delay and prejudice. As a result, the doctrine of laches can bar a suit either earlier or later than the period specified in the SOL.

d. Examples of Laches

What constitutes laches (and, therefore, unreasonable delay) can vary depending on the circumstances. For example, laches may run much more quickly for a perishable item (*e.g.*, fruits or vegetables), than for something that has more stable value (e.g., sometimes, but not always, real estate). However, even with real estate, laches may apply more quickly in a volatile market.

4. Estoppel

Estoppel, a doctrine that prevents a party from asserting a claim, can be applied in many different contexts. As a rule, estoppel applies when defendant makes a promise to plaintiff on which the latter reasonably relies to his/her detriment.

a. The Defaulting Employer

Estoppel might be applied when an employer offers to provide a pension to a long and faithful employee when and if she retires, but reneges on the promise once the employee (in reliance on the promise) has retired. In *Feinberg v. Pfeiffer Co.*, 322 S.W.2d 163 (Mo.App.1959), the court estopped the employer from denying plaintiff the pension because plaintiff retired "from a lucrative position in reliance upon defendant's promise to pay her an annuity or pension."

b. The Relationship Between Laches and Estoppel

Laches and estoppel are similar, but function differently. Laches applies when plaintiff unreasonably delays in pursuing a claim, and defendant reasonably relies on the delay to his detriment. By contrast, estoppel assumes that plaintiff (or defendant depending on whether the estoppel is offensive or defensive) made misrepresentations on which the other party relied. Although both defenses require a showing of prejudice, estoppel does not necessarily require the passage of time.

c. Estoppel Against the Government

Historically, courts have refused to apply the doctrine of estoppel against the government. Some later cases have relaxed this prohibition and suggested a greater inclination to apply estoppel principles to the government.

d. Promissory Estoppel Distinguished from Equitable Estoppel

The doctrines of promissory estoppel and equitable estoppel are very different. Equitable estoppel is purely a remedial device which, if applicable, precludes equitable relief and relegates plaintiff to legal remedies. Normally, plaintiff's cause of action is still alive. Promissory estoppel, on the other hand, is a substantive cause of action that permits foreseeable reliance to substitute for consideration and thereby supplies the basis for a breach of contract action.

F. The Right to Trial by Jury

Historical distinctions between law and equity are also important because of the right to trial by jury. The Seventh Amendment to the United States Constitution guarantees the right to trial by jury "[i]n suits at common law, where the value in controversy shall exceed twenty dollars." The Seventh Amendment is reinforced by Rule 38 of the Federal Rules of Civil Procedure which provides that: "The right of trial by jury as declared by the Seventh Amendment to the Constitution or as given by a statute of the United States shall be preserved to the parties inviolate." Although the Seventh Amendment only applies to federal proceedings, many state constitutions also guarantee the right to trial by jury.

1. "Preservation" of the Right to Trial by Jury

Most jury trial provisions "preserve" the right to jury trial as it existed at the time they were adopted. When the Seventh Amendment was adopted in 1791, equity cases were not tried by a judge while legal cases were tried by a jury. However, the dividing line between law and equity was not clear-cut regarding the right to a jury trial. Equity courts sometimes exercised "equitable clean-up" jurisdiction which provided that when legal and equitable issues were combined in the same case, and the legal issues were incidental to the equitable issues, the equity court could resolve both the legal and equitable issues. Moreover, equity courts sometimes empaneled advisory juries.

2. Difficulties with the Historical Approach

Applied literally, the Seventh Amendment would have required an exclusively historical analysis of 1791 English common law to decide whether a party had a right to a jury trial at that time. As the year 1791 became more distant, and as the federal courts and most state courts merged their law and equity courts into a single system, that task became increasingly difficult. Few judges or lawyers were conversant in the practices of the common law and equity courts. Accordingly, the U.S. Supreme Court has adopted a more pragmatic approach in recent years.

3. The *Dairy Queen* Rule

In *Dairy Queen, Inc. v. Wood*, 369 U.S. 469 (1962), even though the plaintiff sought an accounting, which would have been an equitable claim at common law, the court held that there was a right to jury trial. In doing so, the Court noted that plaintiff should have brought the claim as a legal action (an action for debt) and therefore the Court held that plaintiff could not seek an accounting because he had an adequate remedy at law. Since equitable relief is unavailable except when the legal claim is inadequate, and since the claim could be recharacterized as one for debt, the Court did recharacterize it and held that a jury trial was required. The case is regarded as creating a strong, pro-jury, approach to the right to jury trial.

4. The Historical Approach and Statutory Claims

The historical approach makes it difficult to determine whether the right to jury trial applies in actions based on legislation, especially when the legislation involves statutory rights and remedies (including administrative remedies) unknown at common law. *Curtis v. Loether*, 415 U.S. 189 (1974), involved section 812 of the Civil Rights Act of 1968 which allowed private plaintiffs to bring civil suits seeking redress for violations of the Civil Rights Act of 1968. The Act authorized the trial court to award various types of relief including damages and injunctive relief. In *Curtis*, the plaintiff sought compensatory and punitive damages, as well as injunctive relief. The U.S. Supreme Court overruled the trial court's denial of respondent's demand for a jury trial. The Court held that "although the thrust of the Amendment was to preserve the right to jury trial as it existed in 1791, it has long been settled that the right extends beyond the common-law forms of action recognized at that time." The Court rejected petitioner's argument that the Seventh Amendment is inapplicable "to new causes of action created by congressional enactment," noting that the Seventh Amendment applies "to actions enforcing statutory rights, and requires a jury trial upon demand, if the statute creates legal rights and remedies, enforceable in an action for damages in the ordinary courts of law." The Court concluded that § 812 created "legal rights" because it sounded basically in tort.

5. Congressional Extensions of the Right to Jury Trial

Since there is no constitutional right to a non-jury trial, Congress may expand the right to jury trial to cases that would have been judge-tried in 1791. In deciding whether a statute does, in fact, expand the right to jury trial, courts usually focus on congressional intent. *Lorillard v. Pons*, 434 U.S. 575 (1978). However, there are limits to Congress' power. In *Lehman v. Nakshian*, 453 U.S. 156 (1981), the Court held that a jury trial was not available under the Age Discrimination in Employment Act (ADEA) in a suit against the U.S. government even though the Act authorized suits for "such legal or equitable relief as will effectuate the purposes of this Act." *United States v. Mitchell*, 445 U.S. 535, 538 (1980), *quoting United States v. King*, 395 U.S. 1, 4 (1969).

6. "Jury Preference?"

In *Ross v. Bernhard*, 396 U.S. 531 (1970), the Court seemed to suggest that cases involving requests for damages (as opposed to *in personam* relief) were subject to the right to trial by jury. In that case, petitioners brought a shareholder's derivative action. At common law, this action would have been purely equitable and would have been tried before a judge. Nevertheless, because the underlying claims were legal and there would have been a right to jury trial had the corporation itself brought those claims, the Court held that the right to jury trial applied. Some have construed *Ross* as creating a broad right to trial by jury for any claim involving damages as opposed to *in personam* relief.

7. Demands for Jury Trial

Even though the Seventh Amendment preserves the right to trial by jury, Rule 38 of the Federal Rules of Civil Procedure requires that a party who seeks a jury trial must demand it in writing. Failure to make the demand constitutes a waiver of the right. The demand must be made no later than 10 days after the service of the last pleading directed to such issue. In the demand, a party may specify the issues which the party wishes so tried; otherwise the party shall be deemed to have demanded trial by jury for all the issues so triable.

TRUE-FALSE QUESTIONS

Please answer the following questions "true" or "false":

1. Although the common law distinguished between so-called "legal actions" and "equitable actions," there is no need to distinguish between "law" and "equity" today.
2. Notions of "equity" and "conscience" are quaint historical relics that have no application today.
3. In most modern jurisdictions, law and equity have been combined and there is "one form of action known as the civil action."
4. Modern courts continue to invoke equitable principles like "laches," "unclean hands" and "unconscionability."
5. The laches doctrine applies when a lengthy period of time has elapsed without regard to whether the plaintiff has suffered prejudice.
6. Today, all cases are tried to a jury if one of the parties makes a timely request for jury trial.
7. The "clean hands" doctrine is rigorously applied to prevent bad actors (e.g., mafia types) from ever obtaining equitable relief.

MULTIPLE CHOICE QUESTION

The medieval chancellor was guided by a number of rules. Which of the following was ***not*** one of those rules:

A. Equitable relief is discretionary.

B. Equitable relief is based on principles of "equity" and "conscience."

C. Equitable relief is freely available to anyone who needs or desires it.

D. Equitable relief is denied to those who come to court with unclean hands.

SHORT ANSWER QUESTION

Please draft a short answer explaining the equitable principle which states that "equitable relief is not available except when plaintiff's legal remedy is inadequate," and explain whether it makes sense to retain that rule today.

TRUE-FALSE ANSWERS

Of the true-false questions, the answers are as follows:

1.	False	There remains a need to distinguish between "law" and "equity" today.
2.	False	Notions of "equity" and "conscience" are not quaint historical relics. They continue to have application today.
3.	True	In most modern jurisdictions, law and equity have been combined and there is "one form of action known as the civil action."
4.	True	Modern courts continue to invoke equitable principles like "laches," "unclean hands" and "unconscionability."
5.	False	The laches doctrine does not depend solely on the passage of time. Plaintiff must also show prejudice.
6.	False	Although the courts have liberally applied the right to jury trial, it is simply not correct to state that all cases are tried to a jury today if one of the parties makes a timely request for jury trial.
7.	False	The "clean hands" doctrine is not rigorously applied to prevent bad actors (e.g., mafia types) from ever obtaining equitable relief. On the contrary, it is only applied when the misconduct is related to the matter before the court.

MULTIPLE CHOICE ANSWER

Answer (C) is correct. Of the available answers, it is the only one that does not state a rule applied by the medieval Chancellor. Answer (A) (equitable relief is discretionary), Answer (B) (equitable relief should be based on principles of equity and conscience), and Answer (D) (equitable relief should be denied to those who come to court with unclean hands) are all correct. These rules were applied by the medieval Chancellor.

SHORT ANSWER

The notion that equitable relief is only available when plaintiff's legal remedy is inadequate was based in history, and was directly related to the development of the Chancellor's jurisdiction. However, it retains vitality today because it reflects the notion that equitable relief is discretionary. If plaintiff in the *Fortner* case (the case in which the buyer of an automobile tried to force the defaulting seller to perform) is given equitable relief (in that case, specific performance), there is a greater risk of future problems that will result in further litigation. For example, suppose that the seller is forced to sell by the courts rather than to pay damages, and suppose that a warranty issue arises after the sale. Will the previously existing bad blood between the buyer and the seller make the seller less cooperative in terms of performing the warranty work? As a result, is the case more likely to end up back in court? On the other hand, if the buyer receives damages and purchases the car from a willing seller, hopefully, the new seller will be more accommodating.

Chapter Two

Enforcement of Equitable Decrees

A. Equitable Decrees and the Contempt Sanction

Equitable remedies are usually framed as *in personam* decrees that order a defendant to engage in some act, or refrain from engaging in an act. Such decrees are enforced by the threat of contempt sanctions, including fines and jail. Contempt sanctions can also be used to punish other offenses against the dignity of the court.

B. Contempt Defined

"Contempt" is broadly defined as an offense against the dignity of a court. Contemptuous conduct can include a refusal to obey a court order, as well as a variety of other actions such as one of the following: filing a spurious will in probate; a physical attack on court officials; the lynching of a prisoner by a sheriff who had been ordered to hold the witness pending the outcome of further proceedings.

1. Contempt Under the Federal Rules

The Federal Rules of Criminal Procedure specifically include two types of conduct within the definition of contempt: failure to obey a judicial subpoena "without adequate excuse", Rule 17, F.R.Cr.P., and violation of the obligation of secrecy by a grand juror. Rule 6, F.R.Cr.P.

2. Recalcitrant Witnesses

Contempt can also occur when a witness refuses to obey a court order requiring him/her to testify in a court proceeding. For example, in a grand jury investigation of organized crime, a witness to a crime is ordered to testify and refuses. The witness can be held in contempt unless he has a legitimate excuse (the Fifth Amendment privilege against self-incrimination because of the potential for self-incrimination).

3. Failure to Comply with a Court Order

Contempt can also occur when a party refuses to comply with a court order. For example, defendant repeatedly trespasses onto plaintiff's property, and plaintiff obtains a court order prohibiting future trespasses. If defendant continues to trespass, his conduct constitutes contempt.

4. Contempt and Speech

Courts might also be able to impose contempt sanctions for speech (e.g., a defendant or lawyer speaks disrespectfully to a judge or suggests that a judge is corrupt). However, there are situations when individuals will have First Amendment or due process protections for their speech (e.g., a lawyer was entitled to send a letter to a judge complaining about the court's reimbursement rates). .

C. Civil Contempt Distinguished from Criminal Contempt

Contempt is divided into "civil contempt" and "criminal contempt." This division has both procedural and remedial consequences. Criminal contempt must be tried differently, in terms of constitutional and procedural rules, than civil contempt.

1. The Nature of the Distinction

Civil contempt is distinguished from criminal contempt, not by the nature of the conduct, but by the *purpose* of the sanction imposed. In other words, the same conduct (e.g., refusal to comply with a court order) can give rise to either civil contempt or criminal contempt (or, for that matter, both). Criminal contempt is imposed for the purpose of punishment. By contrast, civil contempt is designed to coerce compliance with a court order, or to compensate a party who has suffered injury due to another party's violation of a court order. In a given case, a court may be trying to achieve both criminal and civil purposes by, for example, punishing a party for past misconduct and trying to coerce future compliance.

2. Examples of Civil Contempt

Civil contempt sanctions might be imposed when a witness refuses to testify in a case, and the judge orders the witness imprisoned until he/she agrees to testify. The sanction is civil because it is coercive and designed to force the witness to testify. In this context, it is frequently said that the witness "holds the keys to his/her cell." Civil contempt sanctions might also be imposed when defendant violates a court order (e.g., precluding him from trespassing on plaintiff's property), and the court orders defendant to compensate plaintiff for damage caused.

3. Examples of Criminal Contempt

When the contempt sanction is designed to punish, each of the examples of civil contempt provided above could constitute criminal contempt. For example, in the case of the recalcitrant witness, the judge can order that the witness be imprisoned for thirty days rather than until he testifies. Since the sanction appears to be designed to punish rather than to coerce compliance (because the witness does not "hold the keys to his cell"), it is probably criminal rather than civil. Likewise, in the case of the trespassing defendant, if the court orders defendant to be imprisoned for thirty days or to pay a fine that is unrelated to the amount of damage caused (rather than assessing an amount that correlates to the injury), the sanction may be criminal rather than civil.

4. Calculating Criminal Contempt Fines

In imposing a criminal contempt fine, courts might take various factors into account, including the defendant's financial resources and the consequent impact of the size of the fine on that defendant's willingness to comply. Of course, if the goal is to coerce compliance, these same factors might be relevant.

5. Criminal Contempt for the Recalcitrant Witnesses

When a witness is jailed for civil contempt for refusal to testify in a trial or a grand jury proceeding, it is impermissible to hold the witness in jail after conclusion of the trial or the grand jury term in which the witness was ordered to testify Since the witness can no longer purge the contempt by testifying, no coercive reason remains for keeping the witness in jail. At that point, the judge may hold the witness in criminal contempt, and impose a criminal punishment for the prior refusal to testify (as well as because of its impact on the trial or grand jury proceeding).

6. Civil-Criminal Contempt Combined

The contempt sanction can involve both civil and criminal components. For example, in the case of the trespasser referred to above, the judge might order the trespasser to jail for 30 days and also order him/her to compensate plaintiff for any losses. The monetary damages portion of the award would be regarded as civil because they are compensatory. By contrast, the imprisonment is punitive, and therefore criminal, because the imprisoned trespasser does not hold the keys to his cell.

D. Civil Contempt Damages

In a civil contempt proceeding, the court may order the contemnor to compensate an injured party for damage that results from the violation of a court order. In order for the sanction to remain civil (as opposed to criminal), the amount of damages must be designed to compensate plaintiff for injury rather than to punish defendant.

1. Calculating Damages

The measure of recoverable civil contempt damages can vary from state-to-state. However, damage calculations can include compensation for the actual loss (e.g., damage caused to plaintiff's real estate by the trespasser), and also attorney's fees. However, some jurisdictions follow the so-called "American Rule" which makes attorney's fees unrecoverable.

2. Proof of Damages

In order to recover contempt damages, plaintiff must be able to present proof of loss. While the proof of loss might take any number of forms (e.g., plaintiff's testimony regarding the loss, or receipts for repairs), damage awards cannot be based on mere speculation.

E. Procedural Requirements for Civil and Criminal Contempt

Courts try contempt differently depending on whether the contempt is civil or criminal. Courts also treat "direct" contempt differently than "indirect" contempt.

1. Direct Contempt

The distinction between "direct" contempt and "indirect" contempt is important because courts handle direct contempt differently than indirect contempt, and they try the two types of contempt differently.

2. Distinguishing Direct Contempt from Indirect Contempt

"Direct" contempt is a contempt committed in the court's presence. "Indirect" contempt is contempt that is committed outside the court's presence. Two examples illustrate the difference. Suppose that, during the course of a trial, the defendant assaults the plaintiff in front of the judge. The assault would be regarded as direct contempt because it occurred in front of the court. By contrast, suppose that a court orders defendant not to enter plaintiff's property, but the defendant trespasses. Since the trespass occurred outside the court's presence, it constitutes indirect contempt.

3. Hybrid Contempt

Some cases do not fit easily into either the direct contempt or the indirect contempt category. For example, suppose that a judge orders the attorneys in a case to be present for an important trial, but one of the attorneys is absent on the second day of trial. Although the attorney's absence is obvious to the court (and therefore could be construed as direct contempt), the reasons for the absence are not obvious (and therefore, arguably, the case should be regarded as indirect contempt). One court treated this type of situation as a hybrid contempt, involving both direct and indirect components, and therefore as requiring some hearing or explanation before contempt sanctions are imposed. *See, e.g., In re Yengo*, 84 N.J. 111, 417 A.2d 533 (1980). Suppose, for example, that the attorney was absent because he had a heart attack and was rushed to the intensive care unit of a hospital. In such circumstances, it is reasonable to assume that the explanation would be adequate to avoid contempt sanctions. Without a hearing, the attorney would have no chance to offer the excuse.

4. Procedural Handling of Direct Versus Indirect Contempts

When a direct contempt (one in the presence of the court) occurs, the judge may act summarily without notice or order to show cause. In other words, a judge can deal with a direct contempt immediately and on the spot (although not always), and judges will frequently exercise that authority when confronted by courtroom disruptions. And, if the judge has observed the contemptuous contempt (e.g., defendant assaults the plaintiff in front of the judge), there may be no need for a hearing to flesh out the facts. By contrast, when an indirect contempt (one that occurs outside the court's presence) occurs, the judge must act based on notice and either an order for arrest or an order for the defendant to show cause why he/she should not be held in contempt. In that situation, a hearing is needed in order to ascertain the facts and listen to any explanation or excuse that defendant might offer.

5. The Limits of Direct Contempt

Direct contempt usually involves conduct that a judge observes and that tends to obstruct the administration of justice. However, courts have treated a number of other situations as involving direct contempt: when an attorney sends a threatening letter to a court clerk, when a party assaults a witness, or when threats are made against the parties to a proceeding.

6. Summary Punishment of Disruptive Defendants for Direct Contempts

If a defendant is unduly disruptive in a courtroom proceeding, and refuses to desist from disruptive behavior, judges are sometimes forced to take extreme actions in order to maintain order. The U.S. Supreme Court has held that trial judges can take a variety of actions in this situation, including the following, depending on the circumstances: (1) binding and gaging the defendant; (2) citing him for contempt; or (3) taking him out of the courtroom until he promises to conduct himself properly.

7. Summary Punishments and the Confrontation Clause

In *Illinois v. Allen*, 397 U.S. 337 (1970), the Court held that an extremely disruptive defendant could be summarily removed from a courtroom. The Court rejected Allen's claim that the removal violated his Sixth Amendment right to confront the witnesses against him.

8. Commencement of Contempt Proceedings

A contempt proceeding can be commenced in one of two ways: on the court's own motion, or at the behest of a party. When a party institutes a contempt proceeding, it does so by filing a motion for an "order to show cause" why the defendant should not be held in contempt. A judge can also issue an "order to show cause" on his or her own motion.

9. The Right to Trial by Jury

In *Bloom v. Illinois*, 391 U.S. 194 (1968), the Court held that serious contempt proceedings (serious being defined as a contempt carrying a punishment of more than six months in jail) are subject to the constitutional provision for trial by jury. There is no jury requirement for direct contempt committed in the presence of the court. Direct contempt may be punished summarily because, otherwise, it would be difficult for judges to maintain control over their courtrooms. In *United States v. Twentieth Century Fox Film Corp.*, 882 F.2d 656 (2d Cir.1989), the court held that a corporation is entitled to a jury trial in a prosecution for criminal contempt that results in a substantial fine, in that case, $500,000.

F. Collateral Challenges to Judicial Orders

A court order can be directly challenged by appealing the order to a higher court. Sometimes, defendants try to challenge orders collaterally.

1. The Duty to Obey Court Orders

In *United States v. United Mine Workers of America*, 330 U.S. 258 (1947), the court held that "an order issued by a court with jurisdiction over the subject matter and person must be obeyed by the parties until it is reversed by orderly and proper proceedings." The Court held that the duty to obey applies even if there is a challenge to the constitutionality of the underlying statute. Under such circumstances, "violations of an order are punishable as criminal contempt even if the order is set aside on appeal, and even though the basic action has become moot."

2. The Duty to Obey and Contempt Remedies

Even though defendants are obligated to comply with validly issued orders, even ones that are later found to be invalid, there are limits to the sanctions that can be imposed under such orders. Although a defendant can be subjected to criminal penalties for disobedience, the opposing party has no right to compensatory relief if the original order was invalid.

3. Defenses That May Be Raised in a Contempt Proceeding

Several defenses can be raised in contempt proceedings: defendants can claim that they were not bound by the decree; that they did not receive notice of its requirements; that the court lacked personal jurisdiction; or that it was impossible to comply with the decree.

4. Duty to Obey: Constitutional Claims

In *Walker v. City of Birmingham*, 388 U.S. 307 (1967), a state court enjoined civil rights protestors from engaging in demonstrations, parades and picketing. Petitioners, believing that the injunction was constitutionally invalid, chose to violate it. The U.S. Supreme Court held that the constitutional questions, and potential invalidity, did not insulate defendants against contempt sanctions: "The way to raise that question was to apply to the Alabama courts to have the injunction modified or dissolved. The injunction in all events clearly prohibited mass parading without a permit, and the evidence shows that the petitioners fully understood that prohibition when they violated it." In *Shuttlesworth v. City of Birmingham*, 394 U.S. 147 (1969), the Court struck down the ordinance at issue in *Walker*. Since the *Walker* injunction imposed a broader prior restraint than the ordinance, the injunction was also unconstitutional. Nonetheless, because of the collateral bar rule, the court still imposed criminal contempt sanctions on defendants for their defiance of the unconstitutional injunction. Since the collateral bar rule does not apply in civil contempt proceedings, a civil sanction would fail if the injunction were invalidated on appeal.

5. State Rules and Constitutional Claims

California provides an exception to the duty to obey. In *In re Berry*, 68 Cal.2d 137, 65 Cal.Rptr. 273, 436 P.2d 273 (1968), defendants deliberately disobeyed an *ex parte* TRO prohibiting a threatened strike by the Social Worker's Union. Through a writ of habeas corpus (a collateral attack), defendants successfully challenged the constitutionality of the TRO. The California Supreme Court invalidated the TRO and vacated the criminal contempt sanctions: "In California [the] rule followed is considerably more consistent with the exercise of First Amendment Freedoms than that adopted in [Alabama]."

6. Transparently Invalid and Void Orders

There is an exception to the collateral bar rule for "transparently invalid" or "void" orders, on the one hand, and "merely invalid" or "voidable" orders, on the other hand. There is no duty to obey a transparently invalid or void decree. Accordingly, criminal contempt sanctions for deliberate violation of such a decree cannot stand. But it is difficult to know for sure whether an order is "transparently invalid" as opposed to voidable, and therefore it is usually risky to violate an order, or to advise a client to do so.

TRUE-FALSE QUESTIONS

Please answer the following questions "true" or "false":

1. Contempt of court occurs only when a defendant violates a court order.
2. A variety of conduct can constitute contempt including (among other things) the violation of a court order, assaulting a court clerk, perjury, or the filing of a spurious will.
3. Contempt is divided into civil contempt and criminal contempt.
4. Contempt is also divided into direct contempt and indirect contempt
5. Criminal contempt is defined as conduct which is offensive to the dignity of the court.

6. Indirect contempt can occur in the courtroom, in front of the judge, provided that the contemnor is not speaking directly to the judge.
7. Because of its historical roots, contempt can always be tried by a judge without the benefit of a jury.
8. All contempt fines, be they civil or be they criminal, are paid directly to the court itself.

MULTIPLE CHOICE QUESTION

A court enters an order prohibiting defendant from trespassing on plaintiff's land, but defendant repeatedly violates the order. Plaintiff seeks an order designed to coerce future compliance. Which of the following orders would constitute criminal rather than civil contempt?

(A) An order of damages compensating plaintiff for defendant's violation of a court order.

(B) An order sentencing defendant to 10 days in jail.

(C) An order imposing a daily fine of $100 a day for future violations.

(D) An order awarding defendant $100 for damage to a fence during the trespass.

ESSAY QUESTION

Plaintiff runs an abortion clinic in Louisville, Kentucky. Defendants are antiabortion protestors who regularly picket outside the clinic. The court enters an order requiring defendants to remain at least 50 feet away from the clinic, but defendants repeatedly violate the order. Indeed, they frequently hold sit-in demonstrations in front of the clinic door (thereby obstructing the ingress and egress of patients). What sanctions might the trial court impose to coerce future compliance with the order?

ANSWERS TO TRUE-FALSE QUESTIONS

Please answer the following questions "true" or "false":

1. False — Although violation of a court order can constitute contempt other conduct can constitute contempt as well (e.g. filing of a spurious will).
2. True — A variety of conduct can constitute contempt including (among other things) the violation of a court order, assaulting a court clerk, perjury, or the filing of a spurious will.
3. True — Contempt is divided into civil contempt and criminal contempt.
4. True — Contempt is also divided into direct contempt and indirect contempt.
5. False — Criminal contempt is defined as conduct which is offensive to the dignity of the court. In defining criminal contempt, a court does not focus on the nature of the plaintiff's conduct as much as it focuses on the purpose of the sanction. If the sanction is remedial rather than punitive, the contempt is civil. On the contrary, when it is imposed for the purpose of punishment, the contempt is criminal.
6. False — Indirect contempt is conduct that occurs outside the judge's presence. Conduct that occurs in the courtroom, in front of the judge, can be treated as direct contempt whether or not the contemnor is speaking directly to the judge.

7. False Historically, contempt was tried by a judge without the benefit of a jury. However, today, it must be tried to a judge if the punishment involves more than six months in jail.

8. False Civil contempt fines, especially if they are compensatory, are payable to an injured party.

ANSWER TO MULTIPLE CHOICE QUESTION

Answer (B) is correct because this order appears to be punitive rather than compensatory, and therefore is criminal rather than civil. Answer (A), Answer (C) and Answer (D) all involve permissible civil sanctions. Answer (A) provides compensation to the plaintiff and therefore fits directly within the intended scope of compensatory relief. The same is true for Answer (D). Answer (C) might appear to be punitive and therefore criminal because it imposes a daily dollar fine. However, this order is remedial because it is designed to apply in the future, and therefore functions as a remedial deterrent to future violations.

ANSWER TO ESSAY QUESTION

To the extent that the court is seeking to coerce future compliance, it's order would be civil rather than criminal. Any number of orders might be imposed. For example, the court could enter an order requiring defendant to pay a set amount (e.g., $10,000 per violation). If defendants are openly defiant, and clearly statie their intent to disobey the order, the court might order them imprisoned until they agree to comply.

Chapter Three

Injunctions

A. The Nature and Purpose of Injunctive Relief

The injunctive remedy is perhaps the most powerful judicial remedy. It is used to order defendants to engage in, or to refrain from engaging in, a specified act (or acts).

1. Mandatory Injunctions Distinguished from Prohibitory Injunctions

Some injunctions are mandatory while others are prohibitory: an injunction that compels an act is referred to as mandatory, while one that forbids an act is referred to as prohibitory.

2. Categories of Injunctions

Injunctions can be used to accomplish many different objectives: preventative injunctions protect against continuing or threatened harm; reparative injunctions require defendant to restore plaintiff to his/her rights; and structural injunctions apply to organizations (e.g. a prison or school system) and are designed to bring those organizations into compliance with legal requirements (i.e., if prison conditions violate the Eighth Amendment to the United States Constitution (which prohibits "cruel and unusual punishment"), a court might order the prison to make reforms designed to make the punishment constitutionally acceptable). In a given case, the court might issue an injunction designed to achieve more than one objective (i.e., preventative and reparative).

3. Uses of Injunctive Relief

Historically, injunctions have been used to enjoin both private and public conduct, especially in nuisance and trespass cases. The following cases are illustrative: a suit to prevent the operation of a cattle feedlot as a nuisance; a suit to prevent a radio-controlled model airplane club from interfering with the use and enjoyment of nearby residences; a suit to prevent construction of a house in violation of building restrictions; an injunction requiring removal of a trespassing wall; an action to enjoin a public nuisance; an injunction requiring removal of junk tires prohibited by local zoning ordinances; a suit to prevent the owner of a dirt race track from creating excessive levels of dust; an injunction to prohibit a rock concert with loud music and large crowds; an injunction seeking removal of a spite fence; and a suit to prevent construction of an animal shelter designed to house 200 animals injunctive relief has also been sought in suits against federal, state and local governments.

B. Standards for Issuance of Injunctive Relief

There are different types of injunctions and each has its own function and requirements. Some injunctions are permanent in nature: they are issued at the conclusion of a lawsuit, after a determination of the merits, and are designed to apply prospectively and permanently unless modified or dissolved. Other injunctions are temporary in nature, including the temporary restraining order (TRO) and the preliminary injunction (a/k/a temporary injunction). A preliminary injunction is issued at the beginning of litigation and is designed to prevent irreparable harm from occurring during the pendency of a suit (*i.e.*, before the merits can be decided). A TRO can be issued *ex parte* and is designed to maintain the status quo only until a hearing can be held on whether to grant a preliminary injunction. As equitable remedies, injunctions are subject to the ordinary rules governing equitable relief (*e.g.*, the requirement that the legal remedy be inadequate & equitable discretion), but they are also subject to their own special rules.

1. Requirements for Provisional Relief

Preliminary injunctions and TROs are subject to specific requirements imposed by rule and case law. In order to obtain either a TRO or a preliminary injunction, a plaintiff must show that immediate and irreparable injury will result absent the injunction. When a preliminary injunction is sought, plaintiff must show that this injury will occur during the pendency of the lawsuit. When a TRO is sought, plaintiff must show that it will occur before a hearing can be heard on whether to grant a preliminary injunction.

a. The Five Factor Test

Under Rule 65, Fed. R. Civ. P., in order to obtain a TRO or preliminary injunction, plaintiffs must show: 1) that unless the restraining order issues, they will suffer irreparable harm; 2) that the hardship they will suffer absent the order outweighs any hardship the defendants would suffer if the order were to issue; 3) that they are likely to succeed on the merits of their claims; 4) that the issuance of the order will cause no substantial harm to the public; and 5) that they have no adequate remedy at law.

b. Mandatory Injunctions Distinguished from Prohibitory Injunctions

The distinction between prohibitory and mandatory injunctions has important consequences. In many jurisdictions, temporary restraining orders (TROs) can only be prohibitory and not mandatory. Consider, for example, Kentucky Rule of Civil Procedure 65.01: "A restraining order shall only restrict the doing of an act. An injunction may restrict or mandatorily direct the doing of an act." The distinction between mandatory and prohibitory injunctions is based on substance rather than form. Thus, even though a TRO is stated in prohibitory form (*e.g.*, defendant is prohibited from permitting a wall to remain on plaintiff's property), it may in fact be regarded as mandatory (because it requires removal of the wall).

c. Illustration of Preliminary Injunctive Relief

In a number of contexts, plaintiffs have been able to satisfy the requirements for preliminary injunctive relief. In one case, plaintiff sought to enjoin a nearby shopping center from hosting a concert series that created high noise levels and litter. The court concluded that the concert imposed great and irreparable injury on nearby neighbors.

d. An Additional Illustration

Washington Capitols Basketball Club, Inc. v. Barry, 304 F.Supp. 1193 (N.D.Cal.1969), involved a classic example of preliminary injunctive relief. In that case, when a basketball player refused to play for the team to which his contract had been assigned, the team sued to prevent him from playing for any other team. The court granted injunctive relief, noting that the player had unique abilities, and the team would suffer great and irreparable injury absent injunctive relief. Even if the team could obtain damages from the player, it would be unable to hire a player of equivalent quality.

2. The Hearing Requirement

In order to obtain either a TRO or a preliminary injunction, plaintiffs must satisfy several procedural requirements. In general, judicial orders should only be issued after a contested hearing. A TRO is unique because it can sometimes be granted *ex parte*. As a general rule, the due process clause of the U.S. Constitution requires that all affected individuals be given notice of an injunction hearing and an opportunity to participate in the hearing. When a TRO is sought, there is not always time for a contested hearing because plaintiff may suffer serious and irreparable injury before notice can be given and a hearing can be held. Under such circumstances, an *ex parte* hearing might be permissible.

a. Rule 65 and *Ex Parte* Hearings

Rule 65 of the Federal Rules of Civil Procedure allows courts to issue *ex parte* TROs but creates a strong presumption in favor of contested hearings. However, Rule 65(a)(1) prohibits courts from issuing *ex parte* preliminary injunctions. Many state procedural provisions also prohibit *ex parte* hearings.

b. Exceptions to the Hearing Requirement

In re Vuitton et Fils S.A., 606 F.2d 1 (2d Cir.1979), stated an exception to the hearing requirement. In that case, Vuitton claimed that defendants were selling and distributing counterfeit versions of its expensive leather goods. When Vuitton tried to enjoin a counterfeiter from continuing his illegal enterprise, the counterfeiter would immediately transfer his inventory to another counterfeit seller, whose identity would be unknown to Vuitton. As the court explained, "the now too familiar refrain from a 'caught counterfeiter' is 'I bought only a few pieces from a man I never saw before and whom I have never seen again. All my business was in cash. I do not know how to locate the man from whom I bought and I cannot remember the identity of the persons to whom I sold.' " The court concluded that the giving of notice would frustrate Vuitton's ability to protect its rights, and therefore the hearing requirement would be waived.

c. Appeal Rights

At the federal level, an order "granting, continuing, modifying, refusing or dissolving" an injunction can be immediately appealed. 28 U.S.C. § 1291(a)(1). In general, and subject to some exceptions, TROs do not fall within the scope of

§ 1291 and are therefore not appealable. *See Sampson v. Murray*, 415 U.S. 61 (1974).

3. Persons Bound

Fed. R. Civ. P. 65 provides that a TRO or preliminary injunction "is binding only upon the parties to the action, their officers, agents, servants, employees, and attorneys, and upon those persons in active concert or participation with them who receive actual notice of the order by personal service or otherwise."

a. Illustration of the Federal Rules Provision

In one case, a university obtained an injunction prohibiting students from continuing their protest demonstrations. While the injunction was in effect, various faculty decided to stage a sit-in at the university administration building. Although the faculty was "sympathetic" to the students, the faculty was not deemed to be in concert or participation with the students, and therefore was not bound by the order and could not be held in contempt.

b. Inapplicability to Others with Different Rights and Interests

The federal rules make it difficult to apply injunctions to those who do not fit within the category of "parties . . . their officers, agents, servants, employees, and attorneys, and upon those persons in active concert or participation with them. . . . " These "others" may, in fact, have different rights and expectations, and may be entitled to have those rights separately adjudicated. For example, suppose that plaintiff has a boundary dispute with one neighbor and obtains injunctive relief preventing the neighbor from trespassing on his land. The injunction will not necessarily bind a different neighbor, who lives on the opposite side of the property, and who may have different rights and interests and no connection to defendant.

c. *In rem* Injunctions?

Although *in rem* injunctions seem to fall outside the parameters of the Federal Rules, courts do issue injunctions that are *in rem* in nature. For example, in *United States v. Hall*, 472 F.2d 261 (5th Cir.1972), the court held an individual in contempt who was not a party to a suit and had no legal relationship to the suit. The case involved school desegregation, and the court entered an order providing, among other things, that all students and anyone acting in concert or participation with the students, as well as anyone acting independently, was prohibited from engaging in various acts that would undercut the desegregation decree. When Hall violated the decree, the court rejected his argument that he could not be held in contempt because he was not a party to the case: "[T]he plaintiffs were found to have a constitutional right to attend an integrated school. The defendant school board had a corresponding constitutional obligation to provide integrated schools and a right to be free from interference with the performance of that duty. Disruption of the orderly operation of the school system, in the form of a racial dispute, would thus negate the plaintiffs' constitutional right and the defendant's constitutional duty. In short, the activities of persons contributing to racial disorder at Ribault imperiled the court's fundamental power to make a binding adjudication between the parties properly before it." The court concluded that courts "of equity have inherent jurisdiction to preserve their ability to render judgment in a case such as this."

d. More on *In rem* Injunctions

In *Hall*, the court went on to note the possibility of a purely *in rem* injunction: "The principle that courts have jurisdiction to punish for contempt in order to protect their ability to render judgment is also found in the use of *in rem* injunctions. Federal courts have issued injunctions binding all persons, regardless of notice, who come into contact with property which is the subject of a judicial decree. A court entering a decree binding on a particular piece of property is necessarily faced with the danger that its judgment may be disrupted in the future by members of an undefinable class—those who may come into contact with the property." These types of injunctions are the exception rather than the rule.

e. Substitution of Parties

During the civil rights era, it was common for school board members in segregated school systems to resign their offices in an attempt to avoid the dictates of a desegregation decree. They hoped that their successors would be outside the decrees. Rule 25, F.R.Civ.P., deals with this problem by allowing for the substitution of parties. It provides that "When a public officer is a party to an action in his official capacity and during its pendency dies, resigns, or otherwise ceases to hold office, the action does not abate and the officer's successor is automatically substituted as a party. Proceedings following the substitution shall be in the name of the substituted party, but any misnomer not affecting the substantial rights of the parties shall be disregarded. An order of substitution may be entered at any time, but the omission to enter such an order shall not affect the substitution."

f. Joinder of Parties

Of course, if a party needs to be joined in litigation in order to give the plaintiff complete relief, Rule 25, F.R.Civ.P., provides for the substitution or joinder of necessary parties: "A person who is subject to service of process and whose joinder will not deprive the court of jurisdiction over the subject matter of the action shall be joined as a party in the action if (1) in the person's absence complete relief cannot be accorded among those already parties. . . . "

g. Successors in Interest

In some instances, equitable decrees can bind successors in interest. Successors can be bound notwithstanding the provisions of Rule 65(d) which provides that injunctions and restraining orders shall be "binding only upon the parties to the action, their officers, agents, servants, employees, and attorneys, and upon those persons in active concert or participation with them who receive actual notice of the order by personal service or otherwise."

(1) General Principles

Courts have held that persons acquiring an interest in property that is the subject of litigation are bound by, or entitled to the benefit of, a subsequent judgment, despite a lack of knowledge. RESTATEMENT OF JUDGMENTS § 89, and comment c (1942). "Courts of equity may, and frequently do, go much farther both to give and withhold relief in furtherance of the public interest than they are accustomed to go when only private interests are involved." *Virginia Ry. Co. v. System Federation*, 300 U.S. 515, 552 (1937).

(2) Illustration: The Replacement Company

In *Golden State Bottling Co., Inc. v. NLRB*, 414 U.S. 168 (1973), a company bought another company's soft drink bottling and distribution business after the National Labor Relations Board had ordered the selling company to reinstate an employee with backpay. The Court held that "[when] a new employer, such as All American, has acquired substantial assets of its predecessor and continued, without interruption or substantial change, the predecessor's business operations, those employees who have been retained will understandably view their job situations as essentially unaltered. Under these circumstances, the employees may well perceive the successor's failure to remedy the predecessor employer's unfair labor practices arising out of an unlawful discharge as a continuation of the predecessor's labor policies. To the extent that the employees' legitimate expectation is that the unfair labor practices will be remedied, a successor's failure to do so may result in labor unrest as the employees engage in collective activity to force remedial action."

4. Notice Requirement

Although the Constitution and various federal statutes generally require that an injunction proceeding be conducted only with notice to opposing parties (and after service of the summons and complaint), as noted, TROs can sometimes be issued *ex parte*. As a result, some interested parties may not be present (or represented) at the hearing. Thus, they may not know that an injunction has been issued and must be given notice.

a. General Requirement of Notice

Fed. R. Civ. P. 65(d) responds to this problem by providing that a TRO or preliminary injunction is binding only on those "who receive actual notice of the order by personal service or otherwise."

b. The Content of Notice

A number of courts have held that two requirements must be satisfied in order for notice to be adequate: the notice must come from a source that is entitled to credit, and it must adequately inform defendant of the act or acts sought to be prohibited.

c. The Usual Scenario

In the ordinary case, the defendant will be in court when the order is entered, and will hear the judge enter it. From the standpoint of notice, nothing more is required.

d. Personal Service

When defendant is not in court, but is actually served with a copy of the order, the notice is sufficient. In *Hsu v. United States*, 392 A.2d 972, 976

(D.C.App.1978), plaintiff's attorney saw defendant in the courthouse (defendant was there on another matter), and told him about the TRO hearing that was about to take place. Defendant failed to appear at the hearing. After obtaining the order, plaintiff's attorney sought out defendant and personally served him with a copy of the order. The attorney took a city housing inspector along to serve as a witness. The notice was upheld as sufficient.

e. Telegrams and Messengers

In *The Cape May & Schellinger's Landing R.R. Co. v. Johnson*, 35 N.J.Eq. Rep. 422 (Ch.1882), a court entered an injunction against a city council on the day of a council meeting. Because of the distance between the court and the council meeting, it was impossible to physically deliver the order that day. Instead, a telegram was sent to the council and read at the meeting. In addition, a special messenger was sent to the meeting. The court concluded that the notice was sufficient because it "was sent by the counsel who obtained the order, and it not only informed the defendants what act the order prohibited, but warned them, if they disregarded the order, their disobedience would be a contempt of the authority of the court. There is nothing in the conduct of the defendants indicating that they had the least doubt concerning the authenticity of the notice or the truth of its contents."

f. Posting

In *Midland Steel Products Co. v. International Union, United Automobile, Aerospace and Agricultural Implement Workers of America, Local 486*, 61 Ohio St.3d 121, 573 N.E.2d 98 (1991), an injunction prohibited picketing by Union members at a factory. The company tried to serve all Union members by posting copies of the injunction on the factory gates. Although the protestors were not given direct and unambiguous notice, the court refused to accept the unserved Union members' protestations of ignorance as lacking credibility. Regarding some of the Union members, the court emphasized that they served picket duty prior to their misconduct, and the court believed that their presence raised an inference that they had seen copies of the TRO that were posted at the facility's entrances. As a result, the court found "evidence sufficient to support the criminal contempt convictions of each of the appellants." The dissent objected that some of those held in contempt might not have actually received notice of the order.

g. Thwarted Service

In *Vermont Women's Health Center v. Operation Rescue*, 159 Vt. 141, 617 A.2d 411 (1992), a judge entered an order prohibiting protesting at an abortion clinic. When a policeman tried to read the order to protestors at the clinic, the protestors sang and chanted in order to thwart receipt of the notice. The court concluded that the notice was adequate: "We [concur] with the [trial] court that it could consider the actions of defendants in attempting to drown out the reading of the injunction. Such conduct is probative that they were already aware of the content of the order and were trying to prevent the formality of notice. In any event, we do not accept that the concerted actions to defeat notice can be effective for that purpose."

5. Bond Requirement

At both the federal level and the state level, one who obtains a preliminary injunction or a TRO must usually post security to protect the defendant against loss. Rule 65(c) of the Federal Rules of Civil Procedure provides as follows: "No restraining order or preliminary injunction shall issue except upon the giving of security by the applicant, in such sum as the court deems proper, for the payment of such costs and damages as may be incurred or suffered by any party who is found to have been wrongfully enjoined or restrained. No such security shall be required of the United States or of an officer or agency thereof."

a. Exception for Indigents (and the Rich)

Although Rule 65 seems to mandate the posting of a bond, courts have created exceptions to the mandate (e.g., for situations when plaintiff is indigent or, sometimes, when plaintiff is rich and can easily afford to pay damages).

b. Calculating the Bond

The amount of the bond will vary from case-to-case just as a defendant's potential damages can vary. For example, if a business owner seeks to enjoin enforcement of a municipal ordinance, the bond *might* be quite small if the city is unable to show that it will suffer much economic damage. By contrast, if the city seeks to enjoin a business from operating in violation of an ordinance, and there is evidence of significant potential monetary loss, the bond might be substantial. However, as the court indicated in *Coyne-Delany Co., Inc. v. Capital Development Board*, 717 F.2d 385 (7th Cir.1983), courts do not require plaintiff to pay for all losses sustained by defendant.

c. Recovery on the Bond

When an injunction or order is overturned, although most courts tend to assume that damages will be given, recovery on the bond is not automatic. As the court stated in *Coyne-Delany Co., Inc. v. Capital Development Board*, 717 F.2d 385 (7th Cir.1983), "[m]ost cases hold [that] a prevailing defendant is entitled to damages on the injunction bond unless there is a good reason for not requiring the plaintiff to pay in the particular case. . . . Not only is it implied by the text of Rule 65(c) but it makes the law more predictable and discourages the seeking of preliminary injunctions on flimsy (though not necessarily frivolous) grounds." A good reason for not awarding damages is that defendant has failed to mitigate losses.

(1) Recovery Limited to Proof of Loss

When recovery is permitted, it is limited to the amount of loss proven by the party subjected to the erroneously issued order.

(2) Recovery Limited to the Amount of the Bond

In many states, although not all, recovery will be limited to the amount of the bond. For example, in *Coyne-Delany Co., Inc. v. Capital Development Board*, 717 F.2d 385 (7th Cir.1983), the court concluded that it had discretion to grant recovery in excess of the bond, but refused to do so. However, some courts disagree. In *Smith v. Coronado Foothills Estates*

Homeowners Ass'n, Inc., 117 Ariz. 171, 571 P.2d 668 (In Banc., 1977), the court held that recovery should not be limited to the amount of the bond. Additional liability may be imposed by statute, or by other source such as Rule 11 of the Fed. R. Civ. P. Also, when a plaintiff seeks and obtains an exemption from the bond requirement, plaintiff faces additional liability.

(3) Calculating Damages

The types of damages that are recoverable for a wrongfully issued injunction may vary from state-to-state. In many jurisdictions, the enjoined defendant can recover for those losses that are provable, including attorney's fees. In some jurisdictions, attorney's fees are not recoverable.

(4) Denial of Recovery

Even when a temporary restraining order is vacated, courts have discretion to deny recovery on the bond. In *Kansas ex rel. Stephan v. Adams*, 705 F.2d 1267 (10th Cir.1983), plaintiff obtained a temporary restraining order requiring defendants to continue operating passenger trains on certain routes. After Congress enacted a law authorizing the discontinuation of passenger service on the routes in question, the temporary injunction was vacated. Thereafter, defendants sought to recoup the costs incurred in operating trains subject to the TRO. The trial court denied the request noting that "[t]he decision whether to award damages, and the extent thereof, is in the discretion of the district court and is based upon considerations of equity and justice. [Rule 65] did not make judgment automatic upon a showing that damages were suffered. Rather, a court, in considering the matter of damages, must exercise its equity power and must effect justice between the parties, avoiding an inequitable result. [The] end result is that a defendant who is wrongfully enjoined will not always be made whole by recovery of damages."

6. Stays

The party against whom injunctive relief is granted can seek a stay from an appellate court. However, under Rule 8, F.R.App.P., an applicant for a stay is ordinarily required to initially seek relief from the court that issued the order. Such relief is possible under F.R.Civ.P. 65(b): "On 2 days notice to the party who obtained the temporary restraining order without notice or on such shorter notice as the court may prescribe, the adverse party may appear and move its dissolution or modification and in that event the court shall proceed to hear and determine such motion as expeditiously as the ends of justice require."

a. Grounds for Stay

In *Washington Metropolitan Area Transit Commission v. Holiday Tours, Inc.*, 559 F.2d 841 (D.C.Cir.1977), the court articulated the following criteria for the granting of stays: "(1) Has the petitioner made a strong showing that it is likely to prevail on the merits of its appeal? Without such a substantial indication of probable success, there would be no justification for the court's intrusion into the ordinary processes of administration and judicial review. (2) Has the petitioner shown that without such relief, it will be irreparably injured? . . . (3) Would the issuance of a stay substantially harm other parties interested in the proceedings? . . . (4) Where lies the public interest?"

b. Illustration

In *Washington Metropolitan Area Transit Commission v. Holiday Tours, Inc.*, 559 F.2d 841 (D.C.Cir.1977), the Washington Metropolitan Area Transit Commission obtained a permanent injunction restraining Holiday Tours from operating a motor coach sightseeing service without a certificate of public convenience and necessity. The District Court granted a motion staying its injunction pending appeal and the Commission sought to challenge the stay. The court of appeals upheld the stay, concluding that the harm to Holiday Tours absent the granting of a stay would be the destruction of its business and that the public interest favored the stay.

c. Bond Requirement

In general, in order to obtain a stay, plaintiff must post a bond or other appropriate security.

C. Permanent Injunctions

Permanent injunctions are subject to the ordinary rules governing equitable relief. Like other forms of equitable relief, they are highly discretionary. In *Weinberger v. Romero-Barcelo*, 456 U.S. 305 (1982), the Court held that the rules governing equitable relief apply unless Congress clearly directs the courts to apply a different standard.

D. Framing the Injunction

Whether a court issues a preliminary injunction or a permanent injunction, the court must be concerned about how the order is worded or "framed." Fed. R. Civ. P. 65(d) imposes limits on the form, scope and content of injunctions: "Every order granting an injunction and every restraining order shall set forth the reasons for its issuance; shall be specific in terms; shall describe in reasonable detail, and not by reference to the complaint or other document, the act or acts sought to be restrained."

1. The Constitutional Aspects of Framing

Injunctions that implicate constitutional rights may be scrutinized with greater specificity, especially when they implicate free speech. For example, in *Murray v. Lawson*, 136 N.J. 32, 642 A.2d 338 (1994), a court order prohibited abortion protestors from picketing in the "immediate vicinity" of an abortion provider's residence. When the provider sought to hold the protestors in contempt for violating the injunction, the court refused because the injunction lacked specificity: "The description 'within the immediate vicinity of' [is] neither specific nor reasonably detailed. [N]either the parties nor the police can determine with any certainty how close to plaintiffs' residence 'within the immediate vicinity of' can legitimately take one." In general, such injunctions must be framed in terms of a specified number of feet (e.g., "Defendant protestors may not come any closer to plaintiff's home than 200 feet").

2. Collateral Challenges Based on Specificity

As the *Murray* case suggests, defendants can sometimes defeat a contempt charge based on a claim that an injunction was too vague. This challenge can be raised directly or collaterally. However, as *Walker v. City of Birmingham*, discussed in the last chapter, illustrates, collateral challenges can be risky.

3. Non-Constitutional Cases

In cases that do not implicate constitutional rights, courts rarely conclude that an injunction is so vague as to be invalid and unenforceable. In most cases, even when an injunction suffers from some vagueness, the court finds that it is sufficiently precise so that defendants knew that their conduct was prohibited. Illustrative is *People v. Evans*, 165 Ill.App.3d 942, 117 Ill.Dec. 513, 520 N.E.2d 864 (1988), in which plaintiff was prohibited "from providing mortgages or any other financing" of whatever kind in the State of Illinois. The order also required Evans to notify, in writing, all consumers who had pending loan applications that defendants were so restrained. Thereafter, she cashed a mortgage check and provided mortgage information. The trial court held her in contempt. The order was upheld on appeal.

4. Unenforceable Decrees

Even though some orders are framed with sufficient specificity, courts will refuse to enforce them. For example, in *Kilgrow v. Kilgrow*, 268 Ala. 475, 107 So.2d 885 (1958), a husband and wife (who were not separated, but instead were living together in the same house) were of different religious faiths, and agreed that their child would attend a parochial school. When the mother refused to send the child to the agreed-upon school, and instead enrolled her in a public school, the husband sued to enforce the agreement. The trial court entered a decree requiring the mother to take the child to the parochial school. The appellate court refused to enforce the order: "It would be anomalous to hold that a court of equity may sit in constant supervision over a household and see that either parent's will and determination in the upbringing of a child is obeyed, even though the parents' dispute might involve what is best for the child. Every difference of opinion between parents concerning their child's upbringing necessarily involves the question of the child's best interest."

5. Vagueness Illustration: Vagueness of the "Upbringing" Provision

Some orders, which might otherwise be enforceable, are not framed with sufficient specificity. For example, in *Lynch v. Uhlenhopp*, 248 Iowa 68, 78 N.W.2d 491 (1956), a divorced mother and father agreed that the mother would have custody of the children and that the father would provide child support, but that the children would be "reared in the Roman Catholic religion." The agreement was incorporated into a final divorce decree and reflected in a court order. Although the father was Catholic, the mother was not. The evidence revealed that the mother never took the children to the Catholic church, and sometimes took them to a Protestant church. The father sometimes took the children to the Catholic church. The court refused to hold the mother in contempt for violating the order, concluding that the order was unduly vague because it was unclear what the mother was required to do. For example, was she required to regularly take the children to the Catholic church, to instruct them in the doctrine of the church, to observe Catholic rituals at home, or to never take them to Protestant churches?

6. Second Illustration: The Cookie Recipe

Another illustration of vagueness is provided by *Peggy Lawton Kitchens, Inc. v. Hogan*, 403 Mass. 732, 532 N.E.2d 54 (1989). In that case, plaintiffs alleged that defendants had stolen a chocolate chip cookie recipe from their business and were using the recipe to make cookies in a competing business. Plaintiff's recipe involved "a distinctive twist" that incorporated walnut shavings (essentially, "chaff, nut meal, nut dust, and nut crunch") into the cookie mix. The trial court entered an order precluding defendant from using the recipe. After the injunction was issued, even though defendants did not use nut meal in their cookies, and added vanilla in its place, plaintiffs argued that the product was "substantially equivalent" to plaintiff's product. The court concluded that the injunction did not preclude the altered recipe: "While perhaps the injunction reasonably could be construed as forbidding the Hogans to manufacture, bake, and sell chocolate chip cookies made from a formula 'substantially derived' from Kitchens' formula, the injunction does not 'clearly and unequivocally' do so. Furthermore, even if the injunction had expressly prohibited the Hogans from producing cookies according to a formula 'substantially derived' from Kitchens' formula, those terms are too imprecise to justify, let alone require, a finding of contempt in the circumstances of this case."

7. The *Madsen* Case

In *Madsen v. Women's Health Center, Inc.*, 512 U.S. 753 (1994), the Court articulated specific rules applicable to injunctions affecting free speech. The case involved protests at or near an abortion clinic, and the trial court decided to impose various restrictions on the protestors.

a. Content-Viewpoint Neutrality

In general, the court has tended to apply strict scrutiny to restrictions on free expression that are not content-neutral and viewpoint-neutral. As a result, when government singles out speech because of its content or viewpoint, the restrictions are more likely to be struck down. However, in *Madsen*, the Court concluded that injunctive restrictions are necessarily content-based and viewpoint-based simply because the trial court issues an injunction against a specific group of protestors (in *Madsen*, anti-abortion protestors). As the Court stated, "An injunction, by its very nature, applies only to particular individuals or group of individuals, and regulates the activities, and perhaps the speech, of that individual or group. It does so, however, because of the group's past actions in the context of a specific dispute between real parties. The parties seeking the injunction assert a violation of their rights; the court hearing the action is charged with fashioning a remedy for a specific deprivation, not with the drafting of a statute addressed to the general public."

b. Scope of Review

In *Madsen*, because of the uniqueness of injunctions, the Court chose to impose a lesser standard of review. The Court concluded that its "standard time, place, and manner analysis was not sufficiently rigorous in this context, and the Court instead applied an intermediate standard of review: "whether the challenged provisions of the injunction burden no more speech than necessary to serve a significant government interest."

c. 36 Foot Buffer Zone

In *Madsen*, the trial court imposed a 36-foot buffer zone around an abortion clinic that prohibited petitioners from "congregating, picketing, patrolling, demonstrating or entering" any portion of the public right-of-way or private property within 36 feet of the property line of the clinic as a way of ensuring access to the clinic. The Court generally upheld the restriction: "The failure of the first order to accomplish its purpose may be taken into consideration in evaluating the constitutionality of the broader order. On balance, we hold that the 36-foot buffer zone around the clinic entrances and driveway burdens no more speech than necessary to accomplish the governmental interest at stake." However, the Court struck down the buffer zone as applied to private property around the clinic. "The accepted purpose of the buffer zone is to protect access to the clinic and to facilitate the orderly flow of traffic on Dixie Way. . . . Absent evidence that petitioners standing on the private property have obstructed access to the clinic, blocked vehicular traffic, or otherwise unlawfully interfered with the clinic's operation, this portion of the buffer zone fails to serve the significant government interests relied on by the Florida Supreme Court. We hold that on the record before us the 36-foot buffer zone as applied to the private property to the north and west of the clinic burdens more speech than necessary to protect access to the clinic."

d. Restriction on "Singing, Chanting, Whistling, Shouting, Yelling"

In *Madsen,* the trial court also imposed restrictions on "singing, chanting, whistling, shouting, yelling, use of bullhorns, auto horns, sound amplification equipment or other sounds . . . within earshot of the patients inside the clinic" during the hours of 7:30 a.m. through noon on Mondays through Saturdays (the time when abortions were performed). The Court upheld the noise restrictions, noting that they "burden no more speech than necessary to ensure the health and well-being of patients at the clinic. The First Amendment does not demand that patients at a medical facility undertake Herculean efforts to escape the cacophony of political protests."

e. "Images Observable" Provision

In *Madsen,* the trial court also imposed a restriction that prohibited the protestors from displaying "images observable to . . . patients inside the [c]linic" during the hours of 7:30 a.m. through noon on Mondays through Saturdays. The Court struck this restriction down, noting that it burdened "more speech than necessary to achieve the purpose of limiting threats to clinic patients or their families." The Court concluded that the "only plausible reason a patient would be bothered by 'images observable' inside the clinic would be if the patient found the expression contained in such images disagreeable. But it is much easier for the clinic to pull its curtains than for a patient to stop up her ears, and no more is required to avoid seeing placards through the windows of the clinic. This provision of the injunction violates the First Amendment."

f. The Prohibition Against Approaching Persons

In *Madsen,* the trial court also ordered that petitioners refrain from physically approaching any person seeking services at the clinic "unless such person indicates a desire to communicate" in an area within 300 feet of the clinic. The court expressed concern that clinic patients and staff might be "stalked" or "shadowed" by the petitioners as they approached the clinic. The Court invalidated this restriction: "[I]t is difficult, indeed, to justify a prohibition on all uninvited approaches of persons seeking the services of the clinic, regardless of how peaceful the contact may be, without burdening more speech than necessary to prevent intimidation and to ensure access to the clinic. Absent evidence that the protesters' speech is independently proscribable (i.e., "fighting words" or threats), or is so infused with violence as to be indistinguishable from a threat of physical harm, this provision cannot stand. 'As a general matter, we have indicated that in public debate our own citizens must tolerate insulting, and even outrageous, speech in order to provide adequate breathing space to the freedoms protected by the First Amendment.' *Boos v. Barry*, 485 U.S., at 322. The 'consent' requirement alone invalidates this provision; it burdens more speech than is necessary to prevent intimidation and to ensure access to the clinic."

g. The Prohibition on Picketing, Demonstrating and Sound Equipment Within 300 Feet

Finally, the trial court prohibited picketing, demonstrating, or using sound amplification equipment within 300 feet of the residences of clinic staff. The prohibition also precluded impeding access to streets that provide the sole access to streets on which those residences are located. The Court concluded that, while the trial court could have prohibited targeted picketing of residences, the 300-foot zone was too large to be sustainable. "The record before us does not contain sufficient justification for this broad a ban on picketing; it appears that a limitation on the time, duration of picketing, and number of pickets outside a smaller zone could have accomplished the desired result."

E. Experimental and Conditional Injunctions

Since injunctions are equitable decrees, and their grant or denial is inherently discretionary, courts are free to shape their orders as required by the circumstances of a particular case. Thus, the mere fact that plaintiffs are suffering injury does not mean that they will receive the desired injunctive relief. As the circumstances dictate, courts may decide to issue "experimental" or "conditional" injunctions.

1. The Function of Experimental and Conditional Injunctions

Even when courts decide to grant equitable relief, they may try to accommodate both parties' needs, desires and interests. In other words, as the equities dictate, courts may try to mold their decrees by entering partial injunctions (a.k.a., "experimental injunctions") designed to provide relief to the plaintiff, but allowing defendant to continue his conduct as much as possible. In other instances, courts can enter conditional injunctions (a/k/a compensated injunctions). *See* Jeff L. Lewin, *Compensated Injunctions and the Evolution of Nuisance Law*, 71 Iowa L. Rev. 775 (1986); Calabresi & Melamed, *Property Rules, Liability Rules, and Inalienability: One View of the Cathedral*, 85 Harv. L. Rev. 1089 (1972).

2. *Boomer* and Conditional Injunctions

Compensated injunctions allow defendants, if they compensate plaintiffs for their injury, to have the injunction lifted. Once they do, defendants can continue the offending conduct. In *Boomer v. Atlantic Cement Company*, 26 N.Y.2d 219, 257 N.E.2d 870, 309 N.Y.S.2d 312 (1970), defendant owned a large cement plant that caused a nuisance in the form of dirt, smoke and vibration. When a nearby homeowner sought injunctive relief against the plant, the court was reluctant to grant the relief because of the adverse economic impact that would result from a plant closing. As a result, the injunction contained a provision vacating its provisions if defendant paid specified compensation to plaintiff. In other words, if defendant paid, it could continue its operations. If not, it would be required to shut down.

3. *Boomer* and the Compensated Injunction

Although the *Boomer* court did not grant a delayed injunction, the court entertained that possibility. The court emphasized that the technology available at that time was insufficient to allow the plant to continue operating, but nevertheless to abate the nuisance. Nevertheless, the court considered the possibility of granting "the injunction but postponing its effect to a specified future date to give opportunity for technical advances to permit defendant to eliminate the nuisance. . . ." The court decided against this option because it concluded that "techniques to eliminate dust and other annoying by-products of cement making are unlikely to be developed by any research the defendant can undertake within any short period, but will depend on the total resources of the cement industry nationwide and throughout the world. The problem is universal wherever cement is made. For obvious reasons the rate of the research is beyond control of defendant. If at the end of 18 months the whole industry has not found a technical solution a court would be hard put to close down this one cement plant if due regard be given to equitable principles."

4. *Boomer* and the Possibility of an Experimental Injunction

One thing that the court could have done was to impose an "experimental" injunction—an injunction that required defendant to modify its operation in important respects in the hope that the modifications would sufficiently ameliorate the interference. After the modifications had been in effect for some time, the court could evaluate their effectiveness and decide whether to order further modifications.

5. *Spur Industries* and Compensated Injunctions

In some cases, courts enter "compensated" injunctions. For example, in *Spur Industries, Inc. v. Del E. Webb Development Co.*, 108 Ariz. 178, 494 P.2d 700 (In Banc, 1972), plaintiff sought to enjoin defendant's feedlot operation. The evidence revealed that plaintiff "came to the nuisance" and did so because the surrounding land was cheap, and he hoped to make a profit from of developing residential subdivisions on cheap land. Although "coming to the nuisance" is not ordinarily a defense to a nuisance action, and even though the court felt compelled to issue the injunction to protect the senior citizens who now lived in the nearby subdivisions, the court required the developer to compensate the feedlot owner for the cost of the move: "Having brought people to the nuisance to the foreseeable detriment of Spur, Webb must indemnify Spur for a reasonable amount of the cost of moving or shutting down. It should be noted that this relief to Spur is limited to a case wherein a developer has, with foreseeability, brought into a previously agricultural or industrial area the population which makes necessary the granting of an injunction against a lawful business and for which the business has no adequate relief."

F. Decrees Affecting Third Parties

In some instances, a court may find it necessary to enjoin third parties in order to grant complete relief to a plaintiff. In a few instances, these joinders are permissible. In some situations, they are impermissible.

1. The *Milliken* Rule

Under the holding in *Milliken v. Bradley,* 418 U.S. 717 (1974), the Court has suggested that the federal courts have limited authority to bind third parties with their decrees. In that case, plaintiffs sought a decree desegregating the Detroit public school system. Even though there was no evidence that neighboring school districts had participated in the segregative behavior, the trial court ordered a remedial plan that swept in both the Detroit schools and 53 independent suburban school districts. The U.S. Supreme Court reversed on the basis that the suburban school districts were not implicated in the constitutional violation and therefore could not be forced to participate in the remedial decree: "Once a constitutional violation is found, a federal court is required to tailor 'the scope of the remedy' to fit 'the nature and extent of the constitutional violation.' " As a result, the Court held that the desegregation order unconstitutionally extended to the suburban districts.

2. The *Hills* Exception

In *Hills v. Gautreaux*, 425 U.S. 284 (1976), the court concluded that the United States Department of Housing and Urban Development (HUD) violated the Fifth Amendment and the Civil Rights Act of 1964 by selecting sites for public housing in the city of Chicago on the basis of race. Respondents claimed that metropolitan-wide relief was inappropriate because "the wrongs were committed within the limits of Chicago and solely against residents of the City" and there were no allegations that "CHA and HUD discriminated or fostered racial discrimination in the suburbs." The Court of Appeals for the Seventh Circuit disagreed, mandating "the adoption of a comprehensive metropolitan area plan that will not only disestablish the segregated public housing system in the City of Chicago [but] will increase the supply of dwelling units as rapidly as possible." The U.S. Supreme Court upheld the appellate order holding that "nothing in the *Milliken* decision suggests a *per se* rule that federal courts lack authority to order parties found to have violated the Constitution to undertake remedial efforts beyond the municipal boundaries of the city where the violation occurred. "Here, unlike the desegregation remedy found erroneous in *Milliken*, a judicial order directing relief beyond the boundary lines of Chicago will not necessarily entail coercion of uninvolved governmental units, because both CHA and HUD have the authority to operate outside the Chicago city limits." "An order directed solely to HUD would not force unwilling localities to apply for assistance under these programs but would merely reinforce the regulations guiding HUD's determination of which of the locally authorized projects to assist with federal funds."

3. The *General Building Contractors Association* Case

In *General Building Contractors Association, Inc. v. Pennsylvania*, 458 U.S. 375 (1982), a union entered into a collective-bargaining agreement with four construction trade associations that obligated employers to hire operating engineers only from among those referred by the Union. However, in order to gain access to the union lists, an engineer-aspirant was forced to go through the union's apprenticeship program. Plaintiffs brought suit alleging that defendants had violated numerous state and federal laws prohibiting employment discrimination by engaging in a pattern and practice of racial discrimination, by systematically denying access to the Union's referral lists, and by arbitrarily skewing referrals in favor of white workers, and limiting most minority workers who did gain access to the hiring hall to jobs of short hours and low pay. Plaintiffs sought to bring the employers into the remedial decree even though the contracts contained explicit non-discrimination provisions and even though there was no evidence that they had discriminated. The Court held that the employers could not be included: "Absent a supportable finding of liability, we see no basis for requiring the employers or the associations to aid either in paying for the cost of the remedial program as a whole or in establishing and administering the training program. Nor is the imposition of minority hiring quotas directly upon petitioners the sort of remedy that may be imposed without regard to a finding of liability."

G. Modification of Decrees

Even though "permanent" injunctions are issued at the conclusion of a lawsuit and are designed to last indefinitely, and in that sense "permanently," they can be modified or dissolved in appropriate circumstances. Rule 60b, F.R. Civ. Pro., provides that "on motion and on such terms as are just, the court may relieve a party [from] a final judgment [for] the following reasons: . . . (5) [it] is no longer equitable that the judgment should have prospective application."

1. General Standards

Perhaps the leading decision is *Agostini v. Felton*, 521 U.S. 203 (1997), in which the Court held that "it is appropriate to grant a Rule 60(b)(5) motion when the party seeking relief from an injunction or consent decree can show 'a significant change either in factual conditions or in law.' " The court concluded that a change in law could involve either a change in the statutory law or in the decisional law.

2. The *Agostini* Case

In *Agostini* the Court overruled its prior holding in *Aguilar v. Felton*, 473 U.S. 402 (1985). In *Aguilar*, the U.S. Supreme Court had held that the Establishment Clause prohibited New York City from having public school teachers provide remedial education to disadvantaged children in parochial schools Following remand, the trial court entered a permanent injunction. Twelve years later, NYC sought modification, arguing that the Court's subsequent decisions had undermined *Aguilar's* validity. The Court agreed and modified its prior holding: "[O]ur Establishment Clause jurisprudence has changed significantly since we decided *Ball* and *Aguilar*. . . . We therefore overrule *Ball* and *Aguilar* to the extent those decisions are inconsistent with our current understanding of the Establishment Clause. . . ."

3. Illustration: Factual Changes

In *Ladner v. Siegel*, 298 Pa. 487, 148 A. 699 (1930), Siegel wanted to build a 400 car garage on his property. The trial court enjoined construction of the garage on the basis that the area was almost exclusively residential, and that the proposed ventilation system (designed to remove gasses and odors and the other effects from the proposed garage) would not have given sufficient protection to the neighborhood. Over time, the surrounding area changed from residential to mostly commercial, and Siegel modified his plans in an effort to provide proper ventilation. The court agreed to lift the injunction.

4. The Limited Nature of School Desegregation Decrees

In a number of cases, the Court has recognized that desegregation decrees are not designed to last forever, and there is a presumption that they will eventually be terminated. For example, in *Board of Education v. Dowell*, 498 U.S. 237 (1991), the Court held that desegregation decrees must eventually terminate because of the preference for local control of schools. "Local control . . . allows citizens to participate in decisionmaking, and allows innovation so that school programs can fit local needs. The legal justification for displacement of local authority by an injunctive decree in a school desegregation case is a violation of the Constitution by the local authorities. Dissolving a desegregation decree after the local authorities have operated in compliance with it for a reasonable period of time properly recognizes that 'necessary concern for the important values of local control of public school systems dictates that a federal court's regulatory control of such systems not extend beyond the time required to remedy the effects of past intentional discrimination.' "

5. Partial Releases from Desegregation Decrees

In *Freeman v. Pitts*, 503 U.S. 467 (1992), the Court extended *Dowell*. In *Freeman*, the District Court concluded that a school district had not achieved unitary status in all respects but had done so in regard to student attendance and with regard to three other categories. The Court held that the district should be released from the decree in regard to "discrete categories in which the school district has achieved compliance with a court-ordered desegregation plan." "Upon a finding that a school system subject to a court-supervised desegregation plan is in compliance in some but not all areas, the court in appropriate cases may return control to the school system in those areas where compliance has been achieved, limiting further judicial supervision to operations that are not yet in full compliance with the court decree. In particular, the district court may determine that it will not order further remedies in the area of student assignments where racial imbalance is not traceable, in a proximate way, to constitutional violations."

H. Injunctions Against Criminal Activity

In general, courts have been reluctant to enjoin the commission of future crimes. As a result, if Jesse James were still alive and robbing banks, courts would be loath to enjoin him from committing future bank robberies.

1. Justifications for the Restriction

Various justifications have been offered for the reluctance to enjoin crime, including the fact that courts are reluctant to enter futile decrees, and the fact that the criminal laws are "sufficiently effective in deterring similar conduct of these parties, thereby affording plaintiff an adequate legal remedy" *City of Chicago v. Stern*, 96 Ill.App.3d 264, 51 Ill.Dec. 752, 421 N.E.2d 260 (1981). Moreover, if the criminal law doesn't deter James, with its substantial penalties for bank robberies, it's unlikely that a court order will do so.

2. Additional Justifications

There are other reasons as well. In *Amalgamated Clothing & Textile Workers Int'l Union v. Earle Industries, Inc.*, 318 Ark. 524, 886 S.W.2d 594 (1994), Justice Dudley, dissenting, offered the following explanation:

> "[Four] potential harms are always present when a case involves an injunction against criminal offenses. First, there is a potential harm in the possible conflict with the constitutional guarantee of the right to trial by jury. Equity does not afford a jury trial, and the absence of that protection is a substantial factor to be weighed against chancery assuming jurisdiction. Second, the proof necessary for a conviction in a criminal court is constitutionally designed to require a high standard of proof, proof beyond a reasonable doubt. The proof necessary to sustain a civil action for contempt is lesser, a preponderance of the evidence. Third, a court of equity can issue a show cause order, and the person cited must show why he should not be held in contempt. In a criminal proceeding the accused cannot be compelled to give evidence against himself. As a result, when a court of equity enjoins the commission of a crime, the person enjoined might

be cited for contempt in a court of equity and stands to lose these three constitutional guarantees. Fourth, the person enjoined will suffer some stigma or embarrassment comparable to that suffered by being labeled a habitual offender because, before a court of equity assumes jurisdiction, there must be proof that the person enjoined committed acts of violence with such systematic persistence as to warrant a finding that they would be continued unless restrained."

3. Exceptions to the Rule

Courts will frequently enjoin public nuisances even though the conduct at issue might also be regarded as criminal. For example, in *State v. H. Samuels Company, Inc.*, 60 Wis.2d 631, 211 N.W.2d 417 (1973), defendant's business generated a nuisance in the form of noise and ground vibrations. The trial court refused to issue an injunction until plaintiff at least tried to prosecute the crime. The Wisconsin Supreme Court disagreed with the trial court: "True, a court of equity will not enjoin a crime because it is a crime, *i.e.*, to enforce the criminal law, but the fact the acts complained of cause damage and also constitute a crime does not bar injunctive relief. The criminality of the act neither gives nor ousts the jurisdiction of equity. In such cases, equity grants relief, not because the acts are in violation of the statute, but because they constitute in fact a nuisance." Courts will also enjoin private nuisances even though the conduct may qualify as a crime.

I. Injunctions Against Litigation

In some instances, courts are asked to enjoin litigation pending in other courts. As we shall see, whether courts will grant injunctive relief against litigation is dependent on a variety of complex factors.

1. Early Equitable Injunctions Against Law Court Litigation

In the early common law, when separate courts of law and equity existed, courts of equity sometimes enjoined litigation in the law courts in order to protect their jurisdiction. For example, suppose that A agrees to buy 10 bushels of wheat from B at $10 per bushel, but the contract incorrectly states the price as $100 per bushel. In a law court, B sues A for $100 per bushel. If the law court refuses to rectify the mistake through reformation, as it would have refused to do at one time, then the legal action would have proceeded to judgment on the terms of the contract as written. In order to prevent this injustice, an equity court might reform the contract to the agreed-upon price. While the equity court was considering whether to do so, it might enjoin B from proceeding with the legal action. Since equity acts *in personam*, the equity court would have enjoined the parties to the law court proceeding rather than the law court itself. If reformation was granted, the legal action would have concluded based on the reformed contract. Following the merger of law and equity, a single court could hear B's contract claim and A's reformation claim at the same time, giving relief as appropriate. Thus, the need for injunctive relief was not needed in states where law and equity had been merged.

2. Modern Injunctive Contexts

Modern courts might also be asked to enjoin pending litigation, but in somewhat different contexts. Three separate and distinct contexts emerge: 1) state courts are asked to enjoin litigation in the courts of other states; 2) state courts are asked to enjoin litigation in federal courts; & 3) federal courts are asked to enjoin litigation in state courts. Because different rules apply in each context, we will examine them separately.

3. State Court Injunctions Against Foreign State Litigation

Assuming that a state court can obtain personal jurisdiction over the parties, a state court may have the power to enjoin litigation in other states. Of course, as at common law, the court does so by ordering the parties not to proceed with the foreign litigation rather than by issuing an injunction against the foreign court. Indeed, because it lacks personal and subject matter jurisdiction, the court might not have the power to directly enjoin the other court (the foreign court may be outside the court's jurisdiction and not subject to service of process within the enjoining state). Merely because a state has the power to enjoin litigation does not mean that it should exercise that power. There may be persuasive reasons why courts should refuse to enjoin foreign litigation.

a. The *James v. Grand Trunk Western Railroad Company* Deadlock

James v. Grand Trunk Western Railroad Company, 14 Ill.2d 356, 152 N.E.2d 858 (1958), provides the classic illustration of what can happen when state courts attempt to enjoin litigation in other states. In *James*, an administratrix sued the Grand Trunk Western Railroad Company in Illinois state court under the Michigan Wrongful Death Act. The defendant railroad, believing that the case should have been brought in Michigan where the accident occurred, obtained injunctive relief from a Michigan court prohibiting the administratrix from prosecuting the case in Michigan. The administratrix then moved the Illinois court for a temporary injunction enjoining enforcement of the Michigan injunction. Plaintiff was arrested and advised that she would be imprisoned for contempt unless she complied with the injunction. Although she wrote to her Illinois attorney discharging him and directing him to withdraw her case from the Illinois courts, she subsequently advised him that the letter did not express her true desires, but had been coerced by threat of imprisonment. A second injunction suit was instituted by defendant in Cass County, Michigan. Plaintiff did not appear, was defaulted, and an order was entered enjoining her from further prosecuting her Illinois action and directing her to withdraw it. The Illinois Supreme Court then denied defendant's motion to vacate the restraining order, and entered an injunction restraining defendant until it disposed of the case.

b. The *James* Holding

In *James*, the court noted that courts generally decline to issue injunctions against foreign litigation. Indeed, the "better view" is that "the exercise of such power by equity courts has been deemed a matter of great delicacy, invoked with great restraint to avoid distressing conflicts and reciprocal interference with jurisdiction." Indeed, the *James* case itself provides an example of such "distressing conflicts and reciprocal interference." Because of the conflicting and interlocking injunctions in that case, the case was deadlocked with injunction against both parties to the dispute. Nevertheless, the Illinois court concluded that it had the right to issue an injunction against the Michigan plaintiff: "[T]his court need not, and will not, countenance having its right to try cases, of which it has proper jurisdiction, determined by the courts of other States, through their injunctive process. We are not only free to disregard such out-of-State injunctions, and to adjudicate the merits of the pending action, but we can protect our jurisdiction from such usurpation by the issuance of a counter-injunction restraining the enforcement of the out-of-State injunction."

c. The Doctrine of *Forum Non Conveniens*

In general, cases like *James* are better resolved under the doctrine of *forum non conveniens* rather than through the issuance of an injunction. As the *James* court stated, "Where suits by nonresidents have no connection whatever with this jurisdiction, and the selection of this forum is purely vexatious, this court has held that the doctrine of *forum non conveniens* may be invoked to dismiss such cases. In the instant case, no such defense of *forum non conveniens* was interposed by defendant. Instead, it sought to remove the case from the Illinois court by enjoining plaintiff in the State of her residence from prosecuting the Illinois action."

d. Statutory Approaches to Conflicting Jurisdictional Claims

The Uniform Child Custody Jurisdiction Act (UCCJA) (L.1978, ch. 493, eff. Sept. 1, 1978), provides an alternate method for dealing with inter-jurisdictional conflicts. The UCCJA mandates that courts undertake a separate inquiry to determine where custody issues should be litigated. As the court explained in *Vanneck v. Vanneck*, 49 N.Y.2d 602, 404 N.E.2d 1278, 427 N.Y.S.2d 735 (1980):

> The UCCJA represents a considered effort to give stability to child custody decrees, minimize jurisdictional competition between sister States, promote co-operation and communication between the courts of different States, all to the end of resolving custody disputes in the best interests of the child. The act offers a standard for determining in the first instance whether the necessary predicate for jurisdiction exists. Custody may be determined in the child's "home state", defined as "the state in which the child at the time of the commencement of the custody proceeding, has resided with his parents, a parent, or a person acting as parent, for at least six consecutive months", or in the State that had been the child's home State within six months before commencement of the proceeding where the child is absent from the State through removal by a person claiming custody and a parent lives in the State. A jurisdictional predicate also exists in New York when "it is in the best interest of the child that a court of this state assume jurisdiction because (i) the child and his parents, or the child and at least one contestant, have a significant connection with this state, and (ii) there is within the jurisdiction of the court substantial evidence concerning the child's present or future care, protection, training, and personal relationships".
>
> The inquiry is not completed merely by a determination that a jurisdictional predicate exists in the forum State, for then the court must determine whether to exercise its jurisdiction. There, too, the act guides the determination, commanding the court to consider whether it is an inconvenient forum or whether the conduct of the parties militates against an exercise of jurisdiction. Notwithstanding that this State has jurisdiction, a court "shall not exercise its jurisdiction under

> this article if at the time of filing the petition a proceeding concerning the custody of the child was pending in a court of another state exercising jurisdiction substantially in conformity with this article". Once a court of this State learns of the pendency of another proceeding, the court "shall stay (its own) proceeding and communicate with the court in which the other proceeding is pending to the end that the issue may be litigated in the more appropriate forum and that information be exchanged in accordance with sections seventy-five-s through seventy-five-v of this article" (Domestic Relations Law, § 75–g, subd. 3).

4. State Court Injunctions Against Federal Litigation

In general, state courts lack the power to enjoin federal court proceedings. As the Court stated in *Donovan v. City of Dallas*, 377 U.S. 408 (1964), "state courts are completely without power to restrain federal-court proceedings in *in personam* actions like the one here. And it does not matter that the prohibition here was addressed to the parties rather than to the federal court itself." The only exception is for situations when a state court has custody of property (in other words, proceedings *in rem* or *quasi in rem*), and the state court enters an injunction to preserve its jurisdiction. As the Court recognized in *Donovan*, "[i]n such cases, the state or federal court having custody of such property has exclusive jurisdiction to proceed."

5. Federal Court Injunctions Against State Litigation

Although the federal courts have the power to enjoin state court proceedings, they generally abstain from doing so.

a. The *Younger* "Our Federalism" Doctrine

In its landmark decision in *Younger v. Harris*, 401 U.S. 37 (1971), the Court stated that "Since the beginning of this country's history, Congress has, subject to few exceptions, manifested a desire to permit state courts to try state cases free from interference by federal courts." *Younger's* so-called abstention doctrine, also known as "Our Federalism," stated a rule of policy rather than a rule of jurisdiction. The Court began by reiterating the "basic doctrine of equity jurisprudence that courts of equity should not act, and particularly should not act to restrain a criminal prosecution, when the moving party has an adequate remedy at law and will not suffer irreparable injury if denied equitable relief." An "adequate legal remedy" exists because plaintiffs can raise their claims in state courts. In addition to equitable principles, the Court found support for its approach in the Constitution noting that the "fundamental purpose of restraining equity jurisdiction within narrow limits is equally important under our Constitution, in order to prevent erosion of the role of the jury and avoid a duplication of legal proceedings and legal sanctions where a single suit would be adequate to protect the rights asserted." Finally, the abstention doctrine is reinforced by "the notion of 'comity,' that is, a proper respect for state functions, a recognition of the fact that the entire country is made up of a Union of separate state governments, and a continuance of the belief that the National Government will fare best if the States and their institutions are left free to perform their separate functions in their separate ways."

b. Application of the "Our Federalism" Doctrine

Younger itself provides the classic illustration of how the "Our Federalism" doctrine applies. In that case, Harris was charged with violating California's Criminal Syndicalism Act and filed suit in federal court to enjoin the District Attorney of Los Angeles County from prosecuting him. Younger alleged that the prosecution and even the presence of the Act inhibited him in the exercise of his free speech rights. In addition to requiring a showing of irreparable injury, the Court held that "in view of the fundamental policy against federal interference with state criminal prosecutions, even irreparable injury is insufficient unless it is both 'great and immediate.' Certain types of injury, in particular, the cost, anxiety, and inconvenience of having to defend against a single criminal prosecution, could not by themselves be considered 'irreparable' in the special legal sense of that term. Instead, the threat to the plaintiff's federally protected rights must be one that cannot be eliminated by his defense against a single criminal prosecution." As a result, if the defendant can defend the criminal proceeding, injunctive relief is inappropriate. In *Younger*, the "chilling effect" of an allegedly unconstitutional statute was deemed to be insufficient by itself to justify federal court intervention.

c. The *Dombrowski* Exception

Younger recognized that its prior holding in *Dombrowski v. Pfister*, 380 U.S. 479 (1965), established a limited exception to the Our Federalism doctrine. In that case, no valid criminal prosecution was pending. Instead, the prosecutor had threatened to enforce statutes, but had done so without any expectation of pursuing prosecution or any effort to secure convictions. On the contrary, there was a simple "plan to employ arrests, seizures, and threats of prosecution under color of the statutes to harass appellants and discourage them and their supporters from asserting and attempting to vindicate the constitutional rights of Negro citizens of Louisiana." The plaintiffs' offices were "raided and all their files and records seized pursuant to search and arrest warrants that were later summarily vacated by a state judge for lack of probable cause. Even though the state courts had quashed the warrants and suppressed the evidence that had been seized, the prosecutor continued to threaten to initiate new prosecutions of appellants under the same statutes, was holding public hearings at which photostatic copies of the illegally seized documents were being used, and was threatening to use other copies of the illegally seized documents to obtain grand jury indictments against the appellants on charges of violating the same statutes." The Court concluded that these circumstances revealed injury that could not be vindicated by the defense of a single prosecution. The facts "depict a situation in which defense of the State's criminal prosecution will not assure adequate vindication of constitutional rights."

d. Our Federalism and Threatened Prosecutions

In *Steffel v. Thompson*, 415 U.S. 452 (1974), a protestor was distributing handbills on a shopping center sidewalk when center employees asked him to stop and leave. When petitioner declined the request, the center called the police who told petitioner that he would be arrested unless he ceased and desisted. At that point, petitioner left to avoid arrest. Petitioner and a companion returned to the shopping center several days later and engaged in the same conduct again.

The police were called and once again demanded that petitioner stop or face arrest. Petitioner again left to avoid arrest. Although Petitioner desired to return to the shopping center to distribute handbills at a later time, he did not do so for fear that he would be arrested. The Court held that Our Federalism did not apply to a threatened prosecution. Since no state court prosecution was pending, plaintiff did not have an adequate legal remedy in the form of a pending proceeding in which plaintiff could assert his rights. In addition, since there was no pending state court proceeding, federal court intervention would not interfere.

e. Our Federalism and Requests for Declaratory (but Not Injunctive) Relief

In *Samuels v. Mackell*, 401 U.S. 66 (1971), appellants, who were indicted in a New York state court on charges of criminal anarchy, wanted to challenge the state's anarchy law in federal court on vagueness grounds. Fearing that *Younger* would bar a claim for injunctive relief, appellants sought only declaratory relief. The Court held that, even though only declaratory (and not injunctive) relief was sought, Our Federalism still precluded the federal court from hearing the case.

f. Subsequent Prosecutions and Pending Federal Proceedings

Our Federalism might also preclude a federal court from hearing a case in which there is no pending criminal proceeding, but there is a later criminal prosecution. In *Hicks v. Miranda*, 422 U.S. 332 (1975), plaintiff owned and operated an adult theater. The police seized four copies of one of plaintiff's films, and charged two of plaintiff's employees under a state obscenity statute. They did not file charges against plaintiff. Two weeks later, plaintiff filed a federal action seeking declaratory and injunctive relief regarding the seizure of the films. Shortly before a federal court hearing on the request for injunctive relief, local prosecutors (the defendants in the federal suit) amended the state criminal complaint to name plaintiff as a criminal defendant and moved to dismiss the federal suit under *Younger*. The Court held that the case should have been dismissed. Even though no charges had been filed against defendant when the federal court proceeding was filed, the subsequent charges provided him with a state venue for vindicating his objections.

g. The Anti-Injunction Statute

Younger's Our Federalism doctrine is reinforced by the federal anti-injunction statute. That statute provides that a federal court "may not grant an injunction to stay proceedings in a State court except as expressly authorized by Act of Congress, or where necessary in aid of its jurisdiction, or to protect or effectuate its judgments." The Act is subject to various exceptions including an *in rem* exception (that allows a federal court to enjoin a state court proceeding in order to protect its jurisdiction of a *res* over which it has acquired jurisdiction), and a "relitigation" exception (that permits a federal court to enjoin relitigation in a state court of issues already decided in federal litigation), and an exception that permits an injunction when the plaintiff in the federal court is the United States itself, or a federal agency asserting "superior federal interests."

h. The "Expressly Authorized" Exception

There is also an "expressly authorized" exception to the anti-injunction statute. In *Mitchum v. Foster*, 407 U.S. 225 (1972), the Court dealt with this exception that permits injunctive relief when "expressly authorized" by Congress. The question was whether 42 U.S.C. § 1983 expressly authorized a "suit in equity" to redress "the deprivation," under color of state law, "of any rights, privileges, or immunities secured by the [Constitution]" The Court held that it did, noting that the law need not specifically mention the anti-injunction statute, or explicitly authorize an injunction against state court proceedings. The Court held that the question is whether "an Act of Congress . . . created a specific and uniquely federal right or remedy, enforceable in a federal court of equity, that could be frustrated if the federal court were not empowered to enjoin a state court proceeding." The Court held that 1983 fit within this concept.

J. Structural Injunctions

Many injunction cases involve relatively discrete matters between private litigants (e.g., plaintiff seeks to enjoin defendant from trespassing on his property). Some cases involve broad challenges to the operation of a school district or prison system. In these latter cases, litigants sometimes ask a court to enter "structural injunctions" directed at governmental officials. These structural injunctions are designed to eliminate past violations and regulate the way a school, prison, or police department functions in the future.

1. Concerns Regarding Structural Injunctions

In general, courts are reluctant to enter structural injunctions for a variety of reasons. Such injunctions involve courts in continuously supervising governmental agencies, and courts are generally loath to engage in such supervision. Structural cases frequently present courts with separation of powers issues. Constitutionally, the power to operate schools or prisons is vested in the executive branch of government, rather than the judicial branch, and structural injunctions necessarily involve courts in the administration of prisons and other executive branch agencies. Moreover, administrators are usually more competent to administer entities like schools and prisons than judges.

2. The Justifications for Structural Injunctions

Despite these concerns, federal courts have entered structural relief in an extraordinary array of cases that have dramatically reshaped society, directly regulated state governments, and involved courts in issuing orders that involve continuing supervision problems. Indeed, courts have restructured school districts, and regulated the running of prisons, jails, institutions for the sick, the mentally insane and the mentally retarded. Courts have even mandated state apportionment schemes and reorganized city governments.

3. The Origins of Structural Relief

The development of structural remedies is generally traced to the U.S. Supreme Court's holding in *Brown v. Board of Education (Brown I)*, 347 U.S. 483 (1954). In that case, although the Court held that the Topeka, Kansas, school district was illegally segregated, the Court was unwilling to order immediate desegregation. Instead, the Court adopted a go slow approach and deferred a remedy until its decision in *Brown II*, 349 U.S. 294 (1955). Essentially, the Court did nothing to enforce *Brown II's* "all deliberate speed" mandate for many years. Even as late as the mid-1960s, many black children were still attending segregated schools. In *Swann v. Charlotte-Mecklenburg Bd. of Education*, 402 U.S. 1 (1971), the Court signaled an end to the Court's go slow approach. In *Swann*, although the trial court allowed school officials to submit three separate and distinct desegregation plans, the trial court rejected all three plans as constitutionally inadequate. In frustration, the trial court decided to desegregate the school system itself based on the advice of an outside consultant.

4. The Growth of Structural Injunctions Following *Brown II* and *Swann*

In the years that followed *Brown II* and *Swann*, the federal courts entered structural injunctions in a variety of cases. Some of these cases involved sweeping orders. *Missouri v. Jenkins*, 515 U.S. 70 (1995), represents the remedy's zenith. In *Jenkins*, the trial court found that the Kansas City, Missouri, school district was segregated. Since the school district was more than 68% black, it was difficult to reassign students in ways that would create meaningful integration. Unable to sweep suburban school districts into its decree, the court decided against additional intra-district reassignments because it feared that such transfers would drive non-minority students away and decrease stability. Instead, the court decided to improve the district's educational programs in the hope that the improvements would make the district attractive to non-minority students and thereby create "desegregative attractiveness." To that end, the Court allowed district officials to "dream" about how to improve their system, and the court then granted their dream by ordering the state to spend vast sums of money on the district. These sums included $220 million for quality education programs, $448 million for magnet schools, $260 million for capital improvements, and nearly $448 million for magnet schools. Although the U.S. Supreme Court initially upheld aspects of the trial court's order, the court ultimately held that the trial court had exceeded its authority by focusing on the principle of desegregative attractiveness, as well as by requiring the state to finance the program of attractiveness.

5. The Decline of Structural Remedies

In recent years, the use of structural remedies has declined. In many parts of the country, the courts have started terminating their control over local school districts and are returning control of those districts to local officials. For example, in *Oklahoma City Board of Education v. Dowell*, 498 U.S. 237 (1991), the Court held that the Oklahoma City school district should be released from a desegregation decree. Likewise, in *Freeman v. Pitts*, 503 U.S. 467 (1992), the Court released a Georgia school district from local control. In terminating the decree, the Court emphasized the importance of returning control over school districts to local officials, and the need for judicial intervention to be of limited duration. As the Court stated in *Jenkins*, "local autonomy of school districts is a vital national tradition" and "a district court must strive to restore state and local authorities to the control of a school system operating in compliance with the Constitution." The Court sounded similar themes in *Freeman v. Pitts* noting that, once a desegregation decree has been successfully implemented, the impetus and need for structural decrees diminishes.

6. *O'Shea* and Limits on Structuralism

The Court has also placed limits on the availability of structural remedies. For example, in *O'Shea v. Littleton,* 414 U.S. 488 (1974), respondents, black citizens who had been advocating for equality in employment, housing, education, and participation in governmental decisionmaking, began an economic boycott of local merchants opposed to equality. Respondents claimed that the county magistrate and judge had singled them out for harsh treatment because of their advocacy and boycott. Specifically, respondents alleged that the judge and magistrate discriminated against them by setting higher bond requirements and jury fees in criminal cases, and by imposing higher criminal sentences. The Court concluded that respondents were not entitled to injunctive relief, emphasising that none of the respondents could satisfy the Article III case or controversy requirement. The Court concluded that those who had been subjected to the alleged practices in the past could not show a case or controversy because "past exposure to illegal conduct does not in itself show a present case or controversy regarding injunctive relief, however, if unaccompanied by any continuing, present adverse effects." The Court found no "continuing effects" because none of the petitioners was then serving an allegedly illegal sentence or awaiting trial. Even if some had been unlawfully convicted, and were serving illegal sentences, the Court concluded that judicial intervention would have been inappropriate because "the complaint would inappropriately be seeking relief from or modification of current, existing custody." As for those that were subject to pending criminal proceedings, the Court held that federal intervention was inappropriate under Our Federalism principles. The Court did recognize that respondents might be arrested again, and therefore might be again subject to the illegal practices. However, the Court found this possibility insufficient to justify judicial intervention, noting that there was no allegation that any Illinois law was unconstitutional on its face. As a result, the Court found that the alleged injury was not "sufficiently real and immediate" since the Court was unwilling to "anticipate whether and when respondents will be charged with crime and will be made to appear before either petitioner." As a result, the allegations required the Court to engage in "speculation and conjecture." Moreover, the Court emphasized that federalism principles militated against judicial intervention, noting that respondents would have numerous judicial remedies available to them in the event that their rights were violated in the future.

7. *Rizzo v. Goode*

In *Rizzo v. Goode,* 423 U.S. 362 (1976), respondents sued a city and its mayor and other police officials claiming civil rights violations and seeking sweeping relief including the appointment of a receiver to supervise the police department and they also wanted to force civilian review of police activity. The trial court entered an extensive order, imposing procedures for the handling of complaints against the police (requiring ready availability of complaint forms, a screening procedure for eliminating frivolous complaints, prompt and adequate investigation of complaints, adjudication of nonfrivolous complaints by an impartial individual or body using fair procedures, prompt notification to the parties regarding the outcome of any proceedings), requiring the revision of police recruit manuals and rules of procedure, and requiring the maintenance of statistical records and summaries designed to allow the court to determine how the revised complaint process was working. In entering the order, the trial court recognized that respondents had "no constitutional right to improved police procedures for handling civilian complaints, but the court imposed the order nonetheless because violations of constitutional rights had occurred in 'unacceptably' high numbers and were likely to continue to occur absent judicial intervention. The trial court found that, in the absence of changed disciplinary procedures, even though unconstitutional incidents might not continue to affect the individual plaintiffs, they were likely to affect members of the classes that plaintiffs represented. In striking down the trial court's order, the U.S. Supreme Court invoked justiciability concepts and Our Federalism principles. Relying on *O'Shea*, the Court questioned whether respondents could show a 'real and immediate' injury because the claim depended 'not upon what the named petitioners might do to them in the future, but upon what one of a small, unnamed minority of policemen might do to them in the future because of that unknown policeman's perception of departmental disciplinary procedures.' " The Court found the connection too speculative.

K. Extra-Territorial Decrees

A number of cases have involved decisions regarding the permissibility of extra-territorial decrees. In doing so, courts have formulated special rules governing the permissibility of such decrees.

1. Decrees Affecting Land

In general, decrees affecting land are regarded as local in character, and it is generally inappropriate for a court in one state (e.g., California) or in a foreign country (e.g., Canada) to attempt to transfer property located in a U.S. state (e.g., New York). This principle—that a court cannot convey title to land located in a foreign jurisdiction—is well established. In *Fall v. Eastin*, 215 U.S. 1 (1909), a court in Washington state appointed a commissioner who purported to convey land located in Nebraska. The Court concluded that the conveyance was invalid, noting that "the court, not having jurisdiction of the *res*, cannot affect it by its decree, nor by a deed made by a master in accordance with the decree, is firmly established." But the Court went on to note that: "A court of equity, having authority to act upon the person, may indirectly act upon real estate in another state, through the instrumentality of this authority over the person."

a. *Deschenes* and Coerced Conveyances

In *Deschenes v. Tallman*, 248 N.Y. 33, 161 N.E. 321 (App.1928), although the court reaffirmed the general rule regarding foreign decrees, it created an exception. That case also involved a Canadian court that purported to transfer land located in N.Y. The N.Y. court held that the transfer was invalid. The Canadian court also coerced the company that owned the land into conveying it to the plaintiff. A New York court upheld the conveyance notwithstanding the coercion: "If the deed by the liquidators be assumed to be inoperative, there was none the less a conveyance of title upon delivery by the corporation of a confirmatory deed of grant. A judgment of a foreign court will not avail, of its own force, to transfer the title to land located in this state. But the rule is different where the conveyance is executed by the owner, though he acted under compulsion. The conveyance, and not the judgment, is then the source of title. His deed transmits the title irrespective of the pressure exerted on his will."

b. *Burnley v. Stevenson*

Although foreign courts are not required to accept out-of-state decrees affecting real property, they can choose to do so. For example, in *Burnley v. Stevenson*, 24 Ohio St. 474 (1873), a Kentucky court ordered a transfer of land located in Ohio, and appointed a master to make the transfer. Although the Ohio court noted that the Kentucky court did not have the power to make the transfer, the Ohio court chose to give it effect: "That this decree had the effect in Kentucky of determining the equities of the parties to the land in this state, we have already shown; hence the courts of this state must accord to it the same effect. True, the courts of this state cannot enforce the performance of that decree, by compelling the conveyance through its process of attachment; but when pleaded in our courts as a cause of action, or as a ground of defense, it must be regarded as conclusive of all the rights and equities which were adjudicated and settled therein, unless it be impeached for fraud."

c. *The Salton Sea Cases*: More on Potential Extra-Territorial Decrees

In *The Salton Sea Cases*, 172 Fed. 792 (9th Cir.1909), appellee diverted water from the Colorado River into irrigation canals for farming purposes. The water spilled over onto appellant's land which was used for mining, gathering, and refining salt. Since appellant's land was below sea level, the water created a lake more than 20 miles in length and several miles in width, and destroyed tons of appellant's salt and submerged its railroad. Eventually, the lake expanded and destroyed appellant's plant, sheds, mill and machinery. Appellant sought injunctive relief precluding appellee from diverting water "unless suitable headgates were provided to control the water, so that the flow would not be in excess of the amount used for irrigation purposes." Defendant admitted many of the complaint's allegations, but alleged that the waters were diverted from the Colorado river in Mexico by a corporation organized under the laws of the republic of Mexico (Sociedad Anonima), which owned all canals leading from the Colorado river in Mexico to the town of Calexico, California; and denied that it diverted any water from the Colorado river which flowed into either the Alamo or New river or upon any of complainant's land. The court held that defendant could nonetheless be required to remedy the problem because the most effective place to deal with the problem was in California.

2. Decrees Affecting Personal Property

Similar principles apply to personal property located in other states. In other words, a court in one state does not have the power to take control of property located in another state. Nevertheless, in *Madden v. Rosseter*, 114 Misc. 416, 187 N.Y.S. 462 (Sup.Ct.1921), a New York court appointed a receiver to take control of a racehorse located in California, and ordered the receiver to transport the horse to Kentucky. Although the New York court realized that it lacked the power to enter the decree, the court believed that the "courts of sister states may be relied upon to aid in serving the ends of justice whenever our own process falls short of effectiveness." In fact, the receiver was able to take control of the horse and transport it to Kentucky.

L. National Security

Courts are reluctant to sustain injunctions designed to prevent publication of information that may impact national security. In the landmark decision in *New York Times Company v. United States*, 403 U.S. 713 (1971), a Pentagon employee stole a classified study entitled "History of U.S. Decision-Making Process on Viet Nam Policy" (The Pentagon Papers), and turned it over to the *New York Times* and *Washington Post* newspapers who planned to publish the study. In a *per curiam* opinion, the U.S. Supreme Court rejected the government's attempt to enjoin the publication: "Any system of prior restraints of expression comes to this Court bearing a heavy presumption against its constitutional validity." The Court held that the government "thus carries a heavy burden of showing justification for the imposition of such a restraint." The Court concluded that the government could not satisfy that burden. Despite the holding, the case produced a plethora of concurring and dissenting opinions.

1. The *N.Y. Times Decision* and the Presumption Against Prior Restraints

In general, the U.S. Supreme Court has been reluctant to enter prior restraints prohibiting the publication of information. *See New York Times Company v. United States*, 403 U.S. 713 (1971). This presumption applies even when matters of national security are at stake. In the *N.Y. Times* case, the Court refused to prevent publication of the Pentagon Papers even though they had been stolen from the government.

2. Possible Exceptions

Although the *N.Y. Times* decision produced a variety of opinions, and divergent views regarding the circumstances under which an injunction might be appropriate, a majority of the justices seemed to suggest that an injunction could only be granted when exceptional circumstances existed that presented grave peril (*e.g.*, during war time, a newspaper planned to publish details regarding when a troop ship would sail).

3. *The Progressives Case* and Nuclear Weapons

In *United States v. Progressive, Inc.*, 467 F.Supp. 990 (W.D.Wis.1979), the U.S. government sought to enjoin the Progressive, Inc., from publishing an article entitled "The H-Bomb Secret: How We Got It, Why We're Telling It." The article provided information on how to build a hydrogen bomb. The government sought injunctive relief under 42 U.S.C. §§ 2274(b) and 2280 which authorized relief against anyone who sought to disclose restricted data "with reason to believe such data will be utilized to injure the United States or to secure an advantage to any foreign [nation]." The magazine responded that it wanted to publish the article to demonstrate laxness in the government's security system. The government argued that much of the article's information was not in the public domain, and that some of the information had in fact never been published. Even though the magazine sought to prove that the article was based entirely on publicly available information, the government responded that the information was not available in this form and that the article integrated information in way that would enable others to build thermonuclear weapons. In other words, the article exposed "concepts never heretofore disclosed in conjunction with one another" and would therefore help a medium sized nation build an H-bomb. Although the trial court judge initially entered an order enjoining publication, the court lifted the injunction when another magazine published a similar article.

4. The *Snepp* Case

In *Snepp v. United States*, 444 U.S. 507 (1980), while working for the Central Intelligence Agency (CIA), Snepp agreed not to disclose classified information without the agency's consent, and to submit all writings about the agency for prepublication review. After leaving the agency, Snepp violated the agreement when he wrote a book about CIA activities in South Vietnam and published it without submitting the book to the Agency for prepublication review. The court ordered that the government be awarded restitution of the proceeds from the book.

M. Injunctions for Breach of Contract

When a party breaches a contract, two types of injunctions may issue. The most common is an order of specific performance, compelling the defendant to perform as promised. In cases where specific performance is unavailable, plaintiffs facing irreparable injury might obtain a negative injunction, precluding the defendant from undertaking other duties inconsistent with performance of the contract. For instance, an opera singer who breaches a contract to perform at one theater might be enjoined from singing at a competing theater. Each type of order is discussed below.

1. Specific Performance

Specific Performance involves an injunction ordering a party to perform a contract as promised. That may involve delivery of goods or real estate, performance of services (such as completing construction) or any other performance—even, on rare occasions, payment of money.

a. Irreparable Injury Rule

Under the Uniform Commercial Code, specific performance is available when the goods are unique, "or in other proper circumstances." U.C.C. § 2–716. Outside the sale of goods, the irreparable injury rule—the requirement that the remedy at law is inadequate—applies directly. While courts often refer to uniqueness, this is simply one way to prove that the remedy at law is inadequate. Where goods are unique, money damages could not be used to replace them with a suitable substitute, making the remedy at law inadequate. In other circumstances, damages may be inadequate for other reasons. For instance, where goods are vital to a business, profits lost because of the breach may be extremely difficult to calculate. Rather than force the plaintiff to accept the jury's best estimate of profits (which would be limited by the certainty doctrine), courts may order specific performance. When goods are in short supply, damages measured by the cover price minus the contract price may suffice. But where the shortage is severe, locating substitute goods may be extremely costly, if possible at all. In these situations, the remedy at law is not as practical as specific performance, allowing courts to award specific performance. Under the UCC, these constitute "other proper circumstances."

(1) Real Estate Presumed Unique

No two parcels of real estate are completely identical. Thus, courts presume that the buyer of land is entitled specific performance of the contract. Modern tract homes may challenge this presumption. However, where a house is a little further from the freeway (or park) and facing north instead of south, these facts might be sufficiently different to justify specific enforcement of the contract. This eliminates the need to determine if the price of similar real estate reflects differences, however small, in the value or simply differences in the bargain. Plaintiff is not entitled to land that is more valuable, but is entitled to the benefit of a good bargain. Specific performance is a practical way to achieve that result.

(2) Goods Presumed Fungible

Goods often can be replaced with other, nearly identical goods. As such, courts generally presume that damages will protect plaintiff's interest adequately. A consumer buying a television can find another similar set at a different store—perhaps even the same manufacturer and model, with only the serial number different. A manufacturer buying leather to make boots can find goods from other tanneries if one breaches. To get specific performance, plaintiff must overcome this presumption.

Shortage—and uniqueness, the extreme case of shortage—offers the most obvious route to proving that damages will not put plaintiff in the position she would have occupied if the contract had been performed. Specially manufactured goods—goods made to the buyer's specifications, not generally available in the market—also may be harder to replace, making an injunction appropriate.

(3) Services

No presumption applies either direction to services. Services often will be unique. Even for menial tasks, where others might do the job as well, one hiring an individual might value other traits the person brings to the job, such as honesty, industriousness, initiative, cheerfulness, etc. Each individual is a unique combination of these attributes, making it plausible that damages would not be an adequate remedy. The reasons for avoiding injunctive relief of personal services contracts generally do not involve the irreparable injury rule, but other policy issues. Many service contracts do not permit the employer to choose who performs the work. A landowner who hires a contractor has no control over who actually performs the construction work, but must accept any workers (including supervisors) the contractor chooses to assign to the task. If one contractor breaches, damages may permit the owner to obtain a substitute on terms no different from those of the original contract.

b. Other Defenses

Even when the remedy at law is inadequate, difficulties may make specific performance unwise. Two problems that occur with some frequency are addressed here. All equitable defenses discussed earlier may be used in this context.

(1) Concerns for Practicality

In some cases, the court may be unable to frame an injunction in terms that permit it to supervise performance. This commonly occurs in construction contracts. Simply ordering the defendant to perform as promised may provide too little guidance on how to avoid contempt. It may also be impossible, as where a court orders a contractor to finish a building on the promised date. Courts do not order the impossible. On the other hand, more specific injunctions may be difficult to frame or to enforce. One problem concerns whether the contract actually requires defendant to perform in the way that the plaintiff now asks the court to order. If the contract does not specify the means, ordering defendant to adopt those means may give plaintiff something for which she did not bargain. In effect, the court becomes entangled in the details of defendant's business. Judges may not be able to find better ways to operate than defendant already is using.

A second problem involves the degree to which courts are willing to supervise performance. Some injunctions might generate constant litigation (usually in the form of contempt proceedings) over whether the defendant intentionally breached or made good faith efforts to perform as ordered, whether compliance with the order was possible, whether the conduct actually complied with the letter of the order but circumvented the goal, etc. If so, courts may be reluctant to issue the injunction in the first place—recognizing practical limits on their capacity to achieve a just result.

There are at least two settings where courts overcome these practical concerns. One involves contracts that include very specific plans and details of how their goals are to be achieved. The less the court must interpolate into the contract, the more willing it is to order specific performance. A second involves disputes of greater significance, such as civil rights disputes. Where the stakes are high, courts confront the practical difficulties head on as a matter of necessity. Private contracts rarely raise this second set of concerns.

(2) Concerns for Personal Freedom

Courts refuse to award specific performance of personal service contracts. Ordering an employee to return to work for an employer carries with it an implication of involuntary servitude. Even if not in violation of the XIII Amendment to the United States Constitution, courts prefer not to approach the boundaries of this rule too closely. The rule also may involve concerns for practical difficulties. An employee ordered back to work may not perform with enthusiasm. Rather than decide whether half-hearted efforts constitute contempt of a court order, courts refuse to order specific performance in the first place.

(a) Mutuality

In some cases, courts deny specific performance no matter which party seeks it. Thus, employees may be denied specific performance of employment contracts on the basis that a personal service contract cannot be specifically enforced. The justification often reflects a misplaced concern for mutuality: since the employer could not receive specific performance, neither can the employee. That argument is unsound: it would suggest that courts should deny specific performance to buyers of land simply because sellers could not get specific performance for the payment of money. A serious concern for mutuality is more likely to allow courts to order specific performance to a buyer or seller in the real estate context. While some employers may have legitimate reasons for resisting specific performance—concerns for employee misconduct or sabotage following the deterioration of the relationship—mutuality has little to recommend it as an explanation.

(b) Statutory Changes

Modern statutes, especially civil rights laws, often embody an employee's right to reinstatement or other specific performance of an employment contract. As courts become more comfortable with orders of this type, concerns for mutuality seem likely to recede. Instead, concerns for compelling people—whether employees or employers—to maintain a relationship at least one of them no longer wants, are likely to govern these disputes.

2. Negative Injunctions

When specific performance is not available, courts may offer lesser injunctive relief. Specifically, a party may be ordered to refrain from any conduct inconsistent with performance. For example, even though an employee might not be ordered to return to work for an employer, the employee can be ordered to refrain from working for any other employer during the period covered by the employment contract.

a. Contractual Source of Injunction

Negative injunctions usually have a contractual source. Sometimes contracts explicitly preclude certain conduct, such as working for a competitor for a period of time after leaving an employer. Noncompetition clauses of this type may appear in technology licenses, joint ventures, and other types of contracts, not just employment contracts. In other cases, courts infer the obligation from the contract. For instance, an agreement to work full time for one employer and devote all one's professional energies to that employer's benefit implicitly precludes outside employment during the duration of the contract. Courts may enforce this implied term by a negative injunction.

b. Rationale as a Limit on Injunctive Relief

Courts divide on the advisability of negative injunctions. To some, the negative injunction seems like an attempt to coerce the employee to return to the original employer. A court that would not order the employee to return may balk at making it impossible for the employee not to return.

More realistically, negative injunctions protect employers against part, but not all, of the harm caused by the breach. An employer who loses an employee's service (especially a unique employee) inevitably suffers some loss, even if the employee does not begin to work for competitors. Allowing the employee to work for competitors may increase the loss the first employer would suffer. For example, when an opera singer who draws crowds refuses to perform for one theater, some people who would have come to see the opera may not come, causing some loss of profit. The loss might be even greater, however, if the opera singer performs for a competitor. People who might have attended the plaintiff's opera house if the star performed at neither one might decide to visit the competitor if the star performs there instead. A negative injunction prevents the second harm, even though it cannot prevent the first.

This rational suggests a limit to negative injunctions. Where no competitive losses seem likely, a negative injunction is unnecessary. Thus, if the opera singer performs on another continent instead of across town, the competitive loss might be nil, requiring no injunction. Similarly, if the job does not involve competitive losses—as where the employee served in a menial capacity—a negative injunction might not prevent any loss to the first employer.

c. Public Policy Concerns

Injunctions that prevent employees from earning a living raise public policy concerns. Thus, courts prefer not to grant negative injunctions where the harm might outweigh the gain. This can be handled in three ways. First, a noncompetition clause might be declared void as against public policy. Courts often consider whether a clause is too broad, in that it covers either too large a geographic area, too many alternative jobs, or extends for too long a period of time. A clause reasonably limited to the area, jobs, and time when the employee's competition might injure the employer is more likely to be enforced. (Some states, however, simply refuse to enforce noncompetition clauses.) Note that declaring the clause unenforceable precludes damages for breach, not just injunctive relief. Second, a court might apply the undue hardship defense. Where the harm to the defendant (from being denied suitable employment) significantly outweighs the benefit to the plaintiff (the competitive harm suffered), a court might deny the injunction. This is a standard application of the equitable defense. Third, a court may balance public policy concerns favoring employment in using its discretion over whether to issue the injunction.

N. Injunction-Like Special Remedies

Three bodies of law have the feel of injunctions, but do not quite fit into the standard mold described above: ejectment, replevin, and conversion. This section examines each in turn.

1. Ejectment

Ejectment, a remedy available in an action for trespass, enables a possessor of land to regain sole possession of her property. Because an order of ejectment is directed to the sheriff, rather than to the trespasser, it is a legal rather than an equitable remedy—a rare example of specific legal relief. An ejectment order might direct the sheriff to remove a trespassing person or object (or even, in a few cases, a trespassing building) from the plaintiff's property. In addition to the specific remedy, an ejectment order may also include a judgment of mesne profits—the fair rental value of the land during the time it was wrongly occupied by the defendant. Although ejectment is also sometimes used to resolve title disputes, courts often hold that an action for quiet title is the more appropriate remedy in such situations.

2. Replevin

Replevin is a remedy to a cause of action for trespass to chattels, which returns to the plaintiff property wrongfully in the possession of the defendant. Replevin is available in two forms—legal and equitable.

a. Legal Replevin

The procedure for obtaining legal replevin is statutory and varies considerably from state to state. The enforcement mechanism is homogenous, however—the court orders the sheriff to seize the property in possession of the defendant and return the property to the plaintiff. Thus, legal replevin (like ejectment) is one of the few types of specific relief that may be awarded by a court sitting at law.

Legal replevin is available as pre-trial relief (analogous to a temporary restraining order and preliminary injunction) and permanent relief. In most states, the plaintiff is required to post a bond of twice the value of the property—the rationale for this burden is that pre-trial replevin hearings can often be heard *ex parte* and because plaintiff might attempt to use replevin strategically to deflate the value of the property by casting a cloud over its title. Once the sheriff seizes the property pursuant to a pre-trial replevin order, the defendant then has the chance to post a counter-bond, regaining the property pending resolution of the case. In most states, a defendant has no right to appeal pre-trial legal replevin.

The primary advantage of legal versus equitable replevin is that the enforcement mechanism of legal replevin is, in some circumstances, faster. As mentioned before, enforcement of legal replevin operates via seizure of the property by the sheriff. By contrast, equitable replevin is enforced like any other injunction—the sheriff delivers the injunction decree to the defendant ordering her to return the property to the plaintiff, then the court waits to see if the defendant complies. If the defendant does not comply, then contempt proceedings may begin. Thus, where property is able to be located, legal replevin is often the quicker route to recovery.

b. Equitable Replevin

Equitable replevin is merely a form of injunction, with all the same attendant rules. The primary wrinkle is that due to the availability of legal replevin, the equitable requirement of "inadequate legal remedy" is more difficult to prove.

Pretrial equitable replevin may be either mandatory in form or prohibitory: if mandatory, it involves an order to the defendant to return the property to the plaintiff; if prohibitory, it involves an order prohibiting the defendant from damaging, selling, or hiding the property pending trial. Such pre-trial equitable replevin can arise in the context of a request for a temporary restraining order or a preliminary injunction. Proving that legal damages or legal replevin would be inadequate is a requirement for the remedy of equitable replevin.

With pre-trial equitable replevin, the plaintiff must of course post a bond, although there is no requirement that it be twice the value of the property—simply a bond sufficient to compensate the defendant for any harm that might be caused by the wrongful issuance of the replevin order. A defendant cannot regain the property pre-trial by counter-bonding. In some states, courts have ameliorated this problem by allowing for pre-trial court impoundment of the property, so that neither party has possession of it until the dispute is resolved.

The appealability of pre-trial equitable replevin is governed by the rules applicable to other types of injunctions—TROs are not typically appealable; preliminary injunctions are, subject to requests for stay pending their appeal.

Whereas speed is the advantage of legal replevin, equitable replevin also has its usefulness. Because equitable replevin is an *in personam* order, enforceable by contempt, a defendant is incentivized not to secrete, damage, use, sell, or otherwise dispose of the property. By contrast, a sheriff cannot seize—via legal replevin—what no longer exists or what the sheriff cannot find. The other side of this point is that a plaintiff will typically only be able to show that legal replevin is inadequate where there is a danger that the defendant might secrete or damage the property before the sheriff has the chance to seize it.

3. Conversion

Conversion, also traditionally referred to as "trover," is either a tort in its own right or a remedy to an action for trespass to chattels—many jurisdictions are nebulous on this point. Regardless, the conversion remedy is a "forced sale" of personal property to which the plaintiff has title to the defendant, in exchange for payment of the property's market value at the time of the conversion (or at resolution of the case, if the property has risen in value). The court's order creates a legal fiction that title in the plaintiff's property passed to the defendant at the time of conversion, creating a duty on the part of the defendant to pay for it. Conversion is limited to cases that require payment for the full value of the chattel. Although conversion has elements similar in some respects to an injunction, it is in fact a legal remedy. The conversion order issued by the court is not an *in personam* order, but an order that "P is entitled to the value" and "D is entitled to ownership."

There is some disagreement among courts as to whether conversion is available as against a bona fide purchaser. Most jurisdictions hold that because a bona fide purchaser (BFP) fails to obtain legal title, a plaintiff may obtain conversion against a BFP. In a minority of jurisdictions, plaintiffs cannot succeed against a BFP.

TRUE-FALSE QUESTIONS

Please answer the following questions "true" or "false":

1. Whether an injunction is denominated "mandatory" or "prohibitory" depends on how the injunction is worded (e.g., an injunction that prohibits an act is necessarily regarded as prohibitory).
2. Various types of injunctions exist including, inter alia, temporary restraining orders, temporary injunctions, and permanent injunctions.
3. Temporary injunctions, and temporary restraining orders, are used to preserve the status quo during the pendency of a lawsuit.
4. Since equity demands that no wrong be without a remedy, courts automatically grant injunctive relief to aggrieved parties.
5. Since temporary restraining orders are only designed to last for a limited period of time, they are ordinarily issued *ex parte*.
6. Since equity delights in doing justice, and not by halves, it is common for injunctions to be worded broadly enough to bind the entire world.
7. When a court order purports to apply to an individual, the individual is bound regardless of whether he has received notice of its existence and content.
8. In order for notice of an injunction to be valid, two things must be shown: First, the notice must come from a source that is entitled to credit. Second, it must adequately inform defendant of the act or acts sought to be prohibited.
9. Ordinarily, in order to obtain preliminary injunctive relief, plaintiff must post security.
10. For a wrongfully issued injunction, all states limit recovery to the amount of the bond.
11. By definition, an injunction that limits a protestor's free speech rights is content-based and viewpoint-based.

MULTIPLE CHOICE QUESTIONS

1. Under the Federal Rules of Civil Procedure, injunctions can bind which of the following:

   A. The parties to a lawsuit;

   B. The parties' officers, agents, servants and employees;

   C. Those in active concert or participation with the parties in a suit.

   D. All of the above.

2. Plaintiff believes that a nearby factory causes a private and public nuisance, and plaintiff seeks injunctive relief against the factory. Plaintiff can demonstrate that the factory emits a significant amount of dirt and causes loud noises. Defendant can show that the factory is extremely important to the community employing, as it does, 350 people. In the ordinary case, which of the following injunctions is the court *least likely* to grant:

   A. An order requiring the factory to take steps to ameliorate the noise and pollution.

   B. An order precluding the factory from operating in the middle of the night.

   C. An order requiring the factory to shut down while the court decides what to do.

   D. None of the above.

3. In some instances, when a federal court enters injunctive relief (e.g., in a school desegregation case), it needs to bring in third parties (e.g., outlying school districts) in order to grant the plaintiff complete relief. Under existing rules, it is safe to say:

   A. To the extent necessary to provide complete relief to the parties before the court, a trial court has discretion to extend its order to third parties.

   B. A trial court is not permitted to enjoin third parties unless they are implicated in the segregative conduct.

   C. Under existing precedent, a trial court judge is required to bring third parties into its decree.

   D. None of the above.

ESSAY QUESTIONS

1. An injunction is entered against abortion protestors that restricts their ability to protest outside an abortion clinic. In particular, the judge prohibits the protestors from chanting outside the clinic, and from approaching those entering or leaving the clinic. The protestors believe that the injunction was not framed with sufficient specificity and therefore is invalid. They have come to you (a local attorney) for advice about whether they should obey the injunction or whether they are free to violate it. How would you advise them?

2. Defendant runs a pawn shop in Kansas City, Missouri, but lives in Kansas City, Kansas. Plaintiff, who also lives in Kansas, suffered a burglary at his house that deprived him of an heirloom watch. Two months later, after faithfully scouring local pawn shops, he believes that he has found the watch in defendant's Missouri shop. Since defendant lives in Kansas, plaintiff sues him there for conversion (alleging that defendant converted the watch when he purchased it from the burglar). Since the purchase occurred in Missouri, defendant files suit in Missouri seeking injunctive

relief to prevent plaintiff from prosecuting the case in Kansas and requiring him to prosecute the case in Missouri. If you are the judge in the Missouri case, how should you rule on the request for injunctive relief?

3. A wife, fearful that her husband is running around with another woman, seeks injunctive relief precluding the other woman from doing any of the following things: 1) Approaching the husband; 2) Speaking to the husband; 3) phoning him; 4) sending him letters. The wife seeks to present evidence showing that she is legally married to her husband, that the husband is having an affair with the other woman, and that the affair is having a detrimental impact on her marriage. If you are the judge in this case, would you grant the wife's request for injunctive relief? Why? Why not?

ANSWERS TO TRUE-FALSE QUESTIONS

1.	False	Whether an injunction is denominated "mandatory" or "prohibitory" is determined by substance rather than form. As a result, even though an injunction is worded in prohibitory terms, it can be a mandatory injunction if it requires performance of an affirmative act.
2.	True	While there are different ways of categorizing injunctions (e.g., mandatory versus prohibitory), one method of categorization involves a division into temporary restraining orders, temporary injunctions, and permanent injunctions.
3.	True	Temporary injunctions, and temporary restraining orders, are in fact used to preserve the status quo during the pendency of a lawsuit.
4.	False	Equitable relief, including injunctive relief, is inherently discretionary. As a result, it is simply incorrect to state that, because equity demands that no wrong be without a remedy, courts automatically grant injunctive relief to aggrieved parties.
5.	False	Under the Federal Rules of Civil Procedure, *ex parte* injunctions are explicitly disfavored and can only be issued in limited situations.
6.	False	The Federal Rules of Civil Procedure provide that injunctions can only bind the parties to an action, their agents, servants and employees, and those in active concert or participation with them. For a variety of reasons, courts should not draft injunctions broadly enough to bind the entire world.
7.	False	Even when an injunction purports to bind an individual, courts generally require that the bound individual receive notice of its existence and content.
8.	True	As a general rule, there are two predicates to effective notice: First, the notice must come from a source that is entitled to credit. Second, it must adequately inform defendant of the act or acts sought to be prohibited.
9.	True	Under the Federal Rules of Civil Procedure, in order to obtain preliminary injunctive relief, plaintiff must post security.
10.	False	Although many states limit recovery to the amount of the bond, some do not.

11. False One can make a strong argument that an injunction that limits a protestor's free speech rights is necessarily content-based and viewpoint-based. However, in *Madsen*, the Court concluded otherwise.

ANSWERS TO MULTIPLE CHOICE QUESTIONS

1. Answer (D), "all of the above," is correct. Under the Federal Rules of Civil Procedure, injunctions can bind all of those listed in Answer (A)—Answer (C) including the parties to a lawsuit; the parties' officers, agents, servants and employees; and those in active concert or participation with them.
2. Answer (C) is correct. Because of the importance of the factory to the community, the court is least likely to enter an order requiring the factory to shut down. Since Answer (C) is correct, Answer (D) is necessarily incorrect because it provides that "none of the above" is correct. Answer (A) is a realistic option because, even though the court is unlikely to order the factory to shut down, it might enter an order requiring the factory to take steps to ameliorate the noise and pollution. Likewise, the court might limit the factory's operation, as in Answer (B), by precluding the factory from operating in the middle of the night.
3. Answer (B) is correct. In general, a court may not join third parties unless they are implicated in the segregative conduct. Because of this fact, Answer (A) is necessarily incorrect because it provides that "to the extent necessary to provide complete relief to the parties before the court, a trial court has discretion to extend its order to third parties." Answer (C) is likewise incorrect because it provides that existing precedent "requires" a trial court judge to bring third parties into its decree. Answer (D), which provides that "none of the above" is correct, is necessarily incorrect since Answer (B) is correct.

ANSWERS TO ESSAY QUESTIONS

1. In general, a lawyer should be reluctant to advise clients to simply disobey or ignore an injunction. There is a significant likelihood that the protestors will be held in contempt of court. The proper approach is to obey the injunction while seeking to have it overturned at either the trial court or appellate level.
2. The request for injunctive relief should be denied. In general, it is inadvisable and potentially counterproductive for courts to try to enjoin litigation in other states. Once a court does so, there is a significant possibility of interlocking injunctions and stalemate. It is far preferable to deny the request for injunctive relief thereby forcing the pawn shop owner to seek relief from the Kansas court. Relief is potentially available under the doctrine of *forum non conveniens.*
3. The request for injunctive relief should be denied for a variety of reasons. For one thing, courts are reluctant to grant injunctions that involve them in continuing supervision problems. Because of the nature of the case, this request for injunctive relief is likely to present continuing problems. In addition, it is noteworthy that the wife is seeking the injunction rather than the husband. The court might be more inclined to grant the requested relief if the husband sought it on the basis that he was being harassed by the other woman. As it is, the husband may be receptive to the other woman's attention and disinclined to break it off with her. It may be preferable for the court to allow the parties to work this problem out between themselves.

Chapter Four

Restitution

A. General Principles

The doctrinal core of restitution is misleadingly simple: "A person who has been unjustly enriched at the expense of another is required to make restitution to the other." The RESTATEMENT OF RESTITUTION § 1 (1937). The purpose of restitution is to prevent a defendant from retaining benefits unjustly derived from plaintiff. Despite the simplicity, restitutionary remedies can be extremely powerful and flexible.

1. Quasi-Contract Distinguished

Quasi-contract is perhaps the best-known aspect of restitution. The foundational decision was rendered in *Moses v. MacFerlan*, 2 Burr. 1005, 97 Eng.Rep. 676 (King's Bench 1760), in which Jacob issued four promissory notes to Moses. Moses endorsed the notes to MacFerlan in order to allow MacFerlan to proceed directly against Jacobs. MacFerlan expressly agreed that he would not hold Moses liable on the endorsements. In breach of his agreement, MacFerlan sued Moses on the notes and obtained a judgment in what might be called the modern analogue to small claims court. Because of the limited "subject matter" jurisdiction of the court, Moses was not allowed to interpose his agreement with MacFerlan as a defense. Moses then sued MacFerlan for a refund, and the King's Bench held in Moses favor. Lord Mansfield writing for a unanimous Court stated that "[t]he ground of this action is not, 'that the judgment was wrong:' but, 'that, (for a reason which the now plaintiff could not avail himself of against that judgment,) the defendant ought not in justice to keep the money.' " Lord Mansfield concluded that "the defendant [MacFerlan], upon the circumstances of the case, is obliged by the ties of natural justice and equity to refund the money."

2. Quasi-Contract Today

Today, quasi-contract extends to many different types of situations. For example, when a motorist is rendered unconscious and receives emergency medical assistance at a hospital, the motorist can be held liable to the hospital for the value of the services rendered. Even though there was no express contract between the hospital and the motorist (because the motorist was unconscious and unable to enter into a contract), the principle of restitution-is designed to prevent unjust enrichment, and therefore-can form the basis of an obligation to pay the hospital for the value of the emergency services.

3. Other Forms of Restitution

As we shall see, restitution extends far beyond quasi-contract. It also includes special restitutionary devices such as constructive trusts, equitable liens and subrogation.

a. The Mistaken Home Builder

For example, in *Beacon Homes, Inc. v. Holt*, 266 N.C. 467, 146 S.E.2d 434 (1966), defendant's mother contracted with plaintiff to build a house on defendant's land. Once the house was built, the mother refused to pay for it. Defendant also refused to pay for it but claimed ownership of the house and began renting it out. Defendant kept the rental proceeds and rejected plaintiff's offer to remove the house and restore the land to its original condition. The court concluded that defendant had been unjustly enriched: "The question is, can the owner of a lot upon which a house has been built by another, who acted in good faith under a mistake of fact, believing he had a right to build it there, keep the house, refuse to permit the builder to remove it so as to restore the property to its former condition, enjoy the enhancement of the value of the property and pay nothing for the house? For the owner to do so is as contrary to equity and good conscience as it would be if the builder had believed itself to be the owner of the land."

b. Legal Versus Equitable Restitution

Restitution has roots in both law and equity. The earliest suits were brought in equity: "[They] were bills for restitution, such as bills for the recovery of property obtained by fraud, for the return of consideration paid for an unperformed promise, for the recovery of a chattel from the bailee after the death of a bailor, and, of most importance, for the recovery of land which had been granted with a promise of its return." RESTATEMENT OF RESTITUTION, Introductory Note to Part I, Topic 1. Over time, the law courts developed a restitution action of their own called assumpsit. This action, which initially involved "an action of trespass on the case brought for a failure to perform an undertaking or for performing negligently the duties of a public calling," eventually expanded in scope and use and came to be referred to as an action in "quasi-contract." However, even after the law courts developed the quasi-contract action, equity courts still heard restitution cases when the plaintiff sought a special restitutionary remedy such as a constructive trust, equitable lien or subrogation. *Id.*

c. The Cheating Bettor

Stewart v. Wright, 147 Fed. 321 (8th Cir.1906), presents an interesting example of restitution. In that case, a group of swindlers specialized in arranging rigged foot races. They lured wealthy "pigeons" to bet on those races by claiming that the races were rigged in the pigeon's favor. In fact, the races were rigged against the pigeon. When a defrauded pigeon sued to recover his losses, the swindlers defended, relying on the clean hands doctrine. Under that doctrine, when two individuals enter into an illegal betting arrangement, a court might be inclined to deny the loser recovery for any losses because the loser might be regarded as having come to court with unclean hands. However, if there is a relative discrepancy between the culpability of the parties (*e.g.*, the defendant is a swindler who routinely takes advantage of folks like plaintiff), and the court wants to discourage defendant's conduct, the court might order that the defendant pay restitution to the plaintiff. In *Stewart*, the court balanced the relative equities and concluded that the swindlers should be required to disgorge their profits. Given the relative culpability of the parties, the court overlooked plaintiff's misconduct.

d. "Volunteers" and "Officious Intermeddlers"

Even though defendant receives an enrichment at plaintiff's expense, it may be "just" for defendant to retain that benefit. As a rule, courts are reluctant to permit "volunteers" and "officious intermeddlers" to recover sums expended on behalf of others. As the Restatement of Restitution states, "A person who without mistake, coercion or request has unconditionally conferred a benefit upon another is not entitled to restitution, except where the benefit was conferred under circumstances making such action necessary for the protection of the interests of the other or of third persons." RESTATEMENT OF RESTITUTION § 112. For example, suppose that defendant adequately provides for his children, but the children's aunt decides that they deserve to go to a fancy restaurant. After taking them, she sues the father for "restitution" on the theory that the father is responsible for the children's health and welfare and should be required to reimburse her for the meal. The aunt will be denied relief as a "volunteer" or an "officious intermeddler."

e. Limits of the Officious Intermeddler Doctrine

Just because plaintiff has voluntarily conferred a benefit on defendant does not necessarily make him a volunteer or an officious intermeddler. For example, in *Western Coach Corporation v. Roscoe*, 133 Ariz. 147, 650 P.2d 449 (En Banc., 1982), plaintiff, who held a lien against a mobile home, repossessed it and spent money to refurbish it (the mobile home had been vandalized). When plaintiff sued to recover the refurbishment costs from defendant (who was obligated on a purchase note on the mobile home), defendant responded that plaintiff was an officious intermeddler. The court disagreed: "Western was not an 'officious intermeddler.' At the time Western took possession of the mobile home and made the alleged repairs, the payments were in default. Western had an interest in seeing that the security for the debt was preserved and was therefore not an 'officious intermeddler.' "

B. Measuring the Enrichment

Even when a court finds that defendant has been unjustly enriched, it must decide how to measure the enrichment. In fact, as we shall see, the measurement can vary depending on circumstances.

1. General Principles

The RESTATEMENT OF RESTITUTION, Comment to § 1, at 13, provides for the following measure of recovery in restitution cases: "*d.* Ordinarily the benefit to the one and the loss to the other are coextensive, and the result of the remedies given under the rules stated in the Restatement of this subject is to compel the one to surrender the benefit which he has received and thereby to make restitution to the other for the loss which he has suffered."

2. Alternative Measures

In contrast to damages, which are usually measured by plaintiff's loss, restitution can also be measured by defendant's gain. The issue that frequently arises, however, is how to measure or value the benefit to the defendant. There are many alternatives. The appropriate choice will depend in large part upon the facts of the case, and on the nature of the benefit conferred (*i.e.*, money, property, profits, services, etc.), the nature or degree of defendant's wrongdoing, and the substantive policies underlying the claim or defense.

3. Example #1: The Tree Thief

George Johnson stole 3 mahogany trees from James Mail's property. The trees were worth $15,000. Johnson milled the trees into lumber and used the lumber as studs in a new house that he was building. Since the studs could not be seen, Johnson could have used much cheaper lumber (that would have been equally sturdy and effective) in place of the mahogany. This other wood could have been purchased for $4,000. Nevertheless, Mail would be entitled to recover $15,000. Given Johnson's status as a thief, the higher measure of recovery is preferable because Johnson should bear the loss of value rather than Mail.

4. The Tree Thief: Redux

Suppose that, instead of stealing the trees, Johnson had taken them mistakenly (he cut them down thinking that the trees were on his own property, and later found out that they were on Mail's property). In this situation, the trees would still be valued at $15,000. Even though Johnson was only negligent, rather than a thief, he should bear the loss vis-a-vis Mail since he made the mistake and Mail was entirely blameless.

5. The Tree Thief: Third Variant

Jacob Weber owned a lumber yard, and Jane Shoemaker ordered lumber for use as studs in the building of a house. Ordinarily, such wood would cost $4,000. Weber mistakenly shipped Shoemaker mahogany wood (worth $15,000). Shoemaker did not notice the mistake and used the mahogany for studs. Weber demanded payment of $15,000. Shoemaker refused to pay, claiming that Weber is only entitled to $4,000. In this situation, since Weber was at fault, he would be forced to bear the loss.

6. The Defaulting Publisher

Professor Younger agrees to write a property casebook for South Publishing Co. Professor Younger dutifully prepares a wonderful book, but South refuses to accept it. South agrees that Professor Younger produced an excellent book. However, the casebook market has changed (publishers are now producing electronic casebooks rather than hard copy books), and South no longer wishes to publish the book. Professor Younger is entitled to restitution based on an hourly rate for the time he spent in preparing the manuscript.

C. Special Restitutionary Remedies

The equitable side of restitution includes a number of special restitutionary devices, including the constructive trust, the equitable lien, tracing and subrogation. Because each of these devices is powerful and flexible, each can provide a plaintiff with unique litigation advantages.

1. The Constructive Trust

A constructive trust is created and imposed by operation of law, without any reference to the trustee's actual or supposed intent to create a trust, and sometimes in contravention of the "trustee's" intent. It is imposed simply to prevent unjust enrichment.

a. Distinguished from Express Trusts

Comment a to the RESTATEMENT OF RESTITUTION § 160 explains how a "constructive trust" differs from an "express trust." An "express trust" if created by an active and consensual decision of the creator. By contrast, as the Restatement notes, a "constructive trust" is "in fact something quite different from an express trust: An express trust and a constructive trust are not divisions of the same fundamental concept. They are not species of the same genus. They are distinct concepts. A constructive trust does not, like an express trust, arise because of a manifestation of an intention to create it, but it is imposed as a remedy to prevent unjust enrichment. A constructive trust, unlike an express trust, is not a fiduciary relation, although the circumstances which give rise to a constructive trust may or may not involve a fiduciary relation."

b. Illustration: The Defaulting Wife

Special restitutionary devices might be applied in an array of contexts. For example, in *Sieger v. Sieger*, 162 Minn. 322, 202 N.W. 742 (1925), a husband, who was unable to read or to write, entrusted his wife with the power to purchase real estate. Of the $3,400 purchase price, $2,000 came from plaintiff's separate funds and the remaining $1,400 came from defendant's separate funds. The remainder of the purchase price came from community property. Although both parties subsequently lived on the real estate, the wife arranged to have the property titled solely in her own name. When plaintiff learned what his wife had done, he demanded a conveyance to him. The court held that plaintiff was entitled to an undivided share of the property and ordered defendant to hold the property in trust for plaintiff. In imposing the trust, the court found that: "[The] conduct of defendant as found by the court shows that she obtained the title to this property in bad faith, and in taking advantage of a fiduciary relation. She did this in such an unconscientious manner that she should not in equity and good conscience be permitted to keep it."

c. Second Illustration: The Defaulting Niece

Plaintiff was the maternal aunt of the defendant, Constance Sawicki. Plaintiff, who was 86 years old, had no children and her only living relatives were the defendant and the defendant's mother, the plaintiff's sister. In 1975, she prepared a will leaving all her estate to the defendant. Subsequently, defendant told plaintiff that, should she enter a nursing home, social services and creditors would attach the plaintiff's house for the payment of debts. Defendant asked plaintiff to convey the house to her to ensure that the house passed to her. Defendant promised to help plaintiff with the bills pertaining to the house and to reconvey the house to the plaintiff should she so desire at a future date. In 1991, the plaintiff sought to obtain a home equity loan to enable her to make repairs to the house and pay several debts she owed. The bank required that she obtain legal title to the house before she could get the loan. Defendant refused to reconvey the house to the plaintiff. Defendant admitted that, during the 15 years the deed was in her name, she did not help plaintiff with the payment of taxes on the property or with any other bills pertaining to the property, with the exception of $200 to assist the plaintiff in repairing the roof. The court imposed a constructive trust on the property.

2. Equitable Lien

An equitable lien is similar to a constructive trust, but instead of requiring defendant to hold the property in trust, the court imposes a lien against property as security for plaintiff's interest.

3. Special Advantages of Constructive Trusts and Equitable Liens

Both constructive trusts and equitable liens offer plaintiffs special advantages over other remedies. The two most important advantages are that both devices allow plaintiffs to "trace" their property into other forms and can be used to give plaintiffs priority over other creditors.

a. Tracing

"Tracing" is the idea that plaintiffs can trace their property into different forms and impose a constructive trust or equitable lien on the property in those other forms.

(1) Illustration: The Embezzling Employee

In *G & M Motor Company v. Thompson*, 567 P.2d 80 (Okla.1977), an accountant embezzled money from his employer, combined it with some of his own money, and invested it in life insurance for his wife and child. In imposing a constructive trust on the proceeds, the court relied on the RESTATEMENT OF RESTITUTION § 160, Comment c (1937), "Where a person wrongfully disposes of property of another knowing that the disposition is wrongful and acquires in exchange other property, the other is entitled [to] enforce a constructive trust of the property so acquired."

(2) Second Illustration: The Bank and the Ex-Wife

In *In re Allen*, 724 P.2d 651 (Colo., En Banc, 1986), after a husband and wife dissolved their marriage and divided their assets, the employer learned that the husband had embezzled funds from the employer. Following the dissolution, the wife had transferred her share of the marital assets (which included a portion of the embezzled funds) into a bank account and eventually into a piece of real estate in Florida. The bank was allowed to trace the embezzled proceeds from the marital home (in which they were originally invested) into the bank account and eventually into the Florida real estate. The court held that the bank could impose either a constructive trust or an equitable lien on the now ex-wife's property.

(3) Third Illustration: The Defrauded Purchasers

Diana and Donald Coppinger sold their home to Diane McKay for $152,000. The Coppingers, due to prior inspections, were on notice that the foundations of the home were infested with termites. After the sale, McKay discovered termites in the interior walls in the living room. Meanwhile, the Coppingers had used the proceeds from the sale to purchase another residence. In *Coppinger v. Superior Court of Orange County*, 134 Cal.App.3d

883, 185 Cal.Rptr. 24 (1982), the court held McKay could trace her money into the Coppingers' new home and impose a special restitutionary remedy on the new home.

b. Priority over Other Creditors

A second advantage of the special restitutionary remedies (e.g., constructive trusts, equitable liens and tracing) is that they can be used to gain priority over other creditors. In other words, rather than standing in line with other creditors and receiving pennies on the dollar, plaintiff can assert a constructive trust or equitable lien against the property and receive priority over other creditors.

(1) Illustration: The Defrauded Real Estate Purchaser

In *In re Radke*, 5 Kan.App.2d 407, 619 P.2d 520 (1980), plaintiff claimed that he was defrauded in the purchase of real estate, and that the money was invested in other real estate. Plaintiff sought to trace his money into the other real estate and impose an equitable lien on it (rather than stand in line as a general creditor). The Court allowed him to do so, stating that: "Equity permits the tracing of assets and the impression of a trust or equitable lien on them without the showing that a money judgment against the party who precipitated the fraud would be uncollectible. PALMER, LAW OF RESTITUTION § 3.14(a)(1978)."

(2) The Rule in *Knatchbull v. Hallett*

In *Knatchbull v. Hallett*, L.R. 13 Ch. D. 696, the court held that "where a fund was composed partly of a defrauded claimant's money and partly of that of the wrongdoer, it would be presumed that in the fluctuations of the fund it was the wrongdoer's purpose to draw out the money he could legally and honestly use rather than that of the claimant, and that the claimant might identify what remained as his *res*, and assert his right to it by way of an equitable lien on the whole fund, or a proper pro rata share of it."

(3) Lowest Intermediate Balance Theory

The "lowest intermediate balance theory" is articulated in the RESTATEMENT OF RESTITUTION § 212 as a way of determining a plaintiff's portion of co-mingled funds: "Where a person wrongfully mingles money of another with money of his own and makes withdrawals from the mingled fund and dissipates the money so withdrawn, and subsequently adds money of his own to the fund, the other can enforce an equitable lien upon the fund only for the amount of the lowest intermediate balance, unless: (a) the fund or a part of it earns a profit; or (b) the subsequent additions were made by way of restitution."

(4) The Limits of Tracing: Ponzi Schemes and Defrauded Investors

In *Cunningham v. Brown*, 265 U.S. 1 (1924), Charles Ponzi ran the original "Ponzi Scheme" in which he encouraged individuals to invest in his operation in exchange for exorbitant rates of return. Ponzi was not investing the money, but instead was paying prior investors out of money given to him by later investors. When the scheme went belly-up, as it inevitably would have done since Ponzi was paying out more money than he was taking in, plaintiffs sued trying to rescind their contracts and "trace" their funds into the monies remaining in the bank account. The Court refused to permit the tracing, noting that "to succeed they must trace the money, and therein they have failed." In *Cunningham*, the Court refused to apply "the fiction of *Knatchbull v. Hallett* [noting that the] rule is useful to work out equity between a wrongdoer and a victim; but, when the fund with which the wrongdoer is dealing is wholly made up of the fruits of the frauds perpetrated against a myriad of victims, the case is different. To say that, as between equally innocent victims, the wrongdoer, having defeasible title to the whole fund, must be presumed to have distinguished in advance between the money of those who were about to rescind and those who were not, would be carrying the fiction to a fantastic conclusion." In essence, the court held that all of the defrauded investors must stand in line together as defrauded creditors.

c. Circumvention of Debtor Exemptions

An additional advantage of special restitutionary remedies is that they can be used to circumvent debtor exemptions. Each state provides debtors with certain "exemptions" that allow them to protect assets against creditors. The "homestead exemption" is one such exemption. Special restitutionary remedies allow creditors to circumvent the exemptions and assert a claim against the property that is the subject of the exemptions.

d. Subrogation

Subrogation is yet another special restitutionary remedy. The RESTATEMENT OF RESTITUTION § 162 (1937), provides that: "Where property of one person is used in discharging an obligation owed by another or a lien upon the property of another, under such circumstances that the other would be unjustly enriched by the retention of the benefit thus conferred, the former is entitled to be subrogated to the position of the obligee or lien-holder."

(1) Subrogation and Tracing

Tracing can be used in subrogation cases to give plaintiff the benefit of a secured interest and/or a preferred position. However, one who tries to subrogate is subject to all defenses the defendant might have raised against the discharged creditor.

(2) The Defrauder

In *Wilson v. Todd*, 217 Ind. 183, 26 N.E.2d 1003 (1940), Todd defrauded Wilson and used the proceeds to pay off a mortgage on real estate. After Wilson obtained a judgment against Todd, and was unable to satisfy it, he asked to be subrogated to the original mortgage holder's rights against the real estate. The court allowed the subrogation, noting that: "Subrogation is the substitution of another person in the place of a creditor, so that the person in whose favor it is exercised succeeds to the right of the creditor in relation to the debt."

TRUE-FALSE QUESTIONS

Please answer the following questions either "true" or "false":

1. The operative goal of restitution is to prevent "unjust enrichment".
2. By its nature, the focus in restitution cases is solely on the benefit received by the defendant.
3. In measuring the amount of restitution, a court may consider both parties' conduct.
4. Special restitutionary devices can be used to provide plaintiffs with priority over other creditors.
5. Special restitutionary devices can provide plaintiffs with the ability to "trace" their property into other forms.

MULTIPLE CHOICE QUESTION

Which of the following statements about "special restitutionary devices" is correct:

A. Quasi-contract is the quintessential special restitutionary device.

B. While the special restitutionary devices are powerful, they cannot be used to do certain things (e.g., circumvent debtor exemptions).

C. Special restitutionary devices include the constructive trust, the equitable lien and subrogation.

D. None of the above.

ESSAY QUESTION

Defendant burglarizes plaintiff's home and steals a diamond ring worth $15,000. Defendant sells the ring through a flea market vendor to an unknown purchaser for $2,000. Defendant spends the entire proceeds on lottery tickets. Against all odds, defendant wins the lottery and nets $100 million. Is plaintiff entitled to restitution? If so, in what amount?

ANSWERS TO TRUE-FALSE QUESTIONS

1. True — In fact, the operative goal of restitution is to prevent "unjust enrichment."

2. False — Because restitution tends to focus on the amount by which defendant was unjustly enriched, there is a tendency to assume that the measurement is the amount received by the defendant. In fact, when courts determine the amount of an enrichment, they focus on a variety of factors including the nature of what plaintiff lost and defendant received, as well as on each party's conduct. The net effect is that the ultimate determination of the amount of an enrichment is really a policy judgment.

3. True — As the prior answer indicates, in measuring the amount of restitution, a court may consider both parties' conduct.

4. True — In fact, one of the major advantages of special restitutionary devices is that they can be used to provide plaintiffs with priority over other creditors.

5. True Another major advantage of special restitutionary devices is that they can be used to provide plaintiffs with the ability to "trace" their property into other forms.

ANSWER TO MULTIPLE CHOICE QUESTION

Answer (C) is correct because special restitutionary devices include the constructive trust, the equitable lien and subrogation. Answer (A) is incorrect because quasi-contract is *not* the quintessential special restitutionary device. Answer (B) is incorrect because special restitutionary devices can be used to circumvent debtor exemptions.

ANSWER TO ESSAY QUESTION

Plaintiff is clearly entitled to restitution. Defendant was unjustly enriched by the amount of the ring and therefore should be required to disgorge the benefit. However, this result can be obtained through a conversion action which allows plaintiff to recover the value of the ring at the time of the theft. Restitution would produce the same result. In theory, although the amount of the enrichment could be determined either at the time of the theft or the time of the sale, the former measurement would be used since defendant was a thief and plaintiff was blameless. Perhaps the more interesting question is whether plaintiff can recover the lottery proceeds. The simple answer is probably "yes." It is possible for plaintiff to "trace" his property into lottery tickets and ultimately into the proceeds of those tickets. Since defendant probably didn't exercise any skill or judgment in obtaining the lottery proceeds, he may have no entitlement to any of the proceeds.

Chapter Five

Declaratory Judgments

A. Generally

A declaratory judgment decides disputed rights, obligations or status of parties without providing for further enforcement of the judgment. Thus, although the declaratory remedy can be combined with other remedies (e.g., injunctive relief), it can function independently as a mere declaration of the parties' respective legal rights.

1. Development of the Declaratory Remedy

The declaratory remedy was developed in various states early in the last century. The remedy was adopted by many states in the form of the Uniform Declaratory Judgments Act (UDJA) and by the federal government as the Federal Declaratory Judgment Act (FDJA).

2. The Function of Declaratory Relief

A declaratory judgment may either adjudicate the validity of proposed conduct, interpret a legal writing—for instance, a statute or deed, or decide copyright and trademark rights. The remedy is especially valuable to individuals who may be unsure about what they may or may not legally do. For example, an individual may want to engage in a protest demonstration outside city hall, but fear prosecution under an ordinance that proscribes protesting at that location. Similarly, a businesswoman may believe that her contract with another business is not valid and need not be obeyed. Rather than risk prosecution in the protest case, or breach of contract in the business case, the individuals might prefer to seek a declaration of their rights before acting.

3. The Uniform Declaratory Judgment Act

The Uniform Declaratory Judgment Act (UDJA) has been adopted, in whole or in an amended form, by approximately 43 states.

a. Scope

Section 1 of the UDJA provides that "Courts of record within their respective jurisdictions shall have power to declare rights, status, and other legal relations whether or not further relief is or could be claimed. No action or proceeding shall be open to objection on the ground that a declaratory judgment or decree is prayed for. The declaration may be either affirmative or negative in form and effect; and such declarations shall have the force and effect of a final judgment or decree."

b. Power to Invoke

Section 2 of the UDJA provides that "[a]ny person interested under a deed, will, written contract or other writings constituting a contract, or whose rights, status or other legal relations are affected by a statute, municipal ordinance, contract or franchise, may have determined any question of construction or validity arising under the instrument, statute, ordinance, contract, or franchise and obtain a declaration of rights, status or other legal relations thereunder."

c. Discretionary

The issuance of a declaratory judgment is not mandatory, even when the claimant has established the required elements under the statute. The discretionary nature of the remedy is captured by Section 6 of the UDJA, which states that a "court may refuse to render or enter a declaratory judgment or decree where such judgment or decree, if rendered or entered, would not terminate the uncertainty or controversy giving rise to the proceeding."

d. Jury Trial

The declaratory judgment remedy is neither legal nor equitable. Thus the availability of equitable defenses, for example, or the right to a trial by jury is determined according to how a court would have resolved the case had the plaintiff sought substantive relief. Accordingly, Section 9 of the UDJA states that the right to jury trial is as applicable as it would be "in other civil actions in the court in which the proceeding is pending."

e. Harmony Between States

The UDJA provides that it should be interpreted to promote harmony between the states, as well as with "federal laws and regulations on the subject of declaratory judgments and decrees." UDJA, Sec. 15.

4. Federal Declaratory Judgment Act

The Federal Declaratory Judgment Act (FDJA) is similar to the UDJA. *See* Federal Declaratory Judgment Act, 28 U.S.C. §§ 2201–02.

a. Authority to Declare

Under the FDJA, § 2201, federal courts have the authority to "declare the rights and other legal relations of any interested party seeking such declaration, whether or not further relief is or could be sought." However, such declarations can only be made when a case or controversy exists.

b. Jury Trial

The right to jury trial under the FDJA is similar to that provided under the UDJA, although defined by the Seventh Amendment rather than state jury trial law. Under Rule 57 of the Federal Rules of Civil Procedure, the "procedure for obtaining a declaratory judgment" is governed generally by the federal rules.

Notwithstanding any similarities to equitable proceedings, "the right to trial by jury may be demanded" in accordance with Rules 38 and 39. As with the right to jury trial in other contexts, the right to obtain a jury determination depends on whether, at the time the Seventh Amendment was ratified, the relevant issue would have been resolved by a court of law or equity.

c. Adequacy of Legal Remedy

A declaratory judgment is neither legal nor equitable. Thus, under Rule 57, the existence of an adequate remedy does not "necessarily" preclude a declaratory judgment.

d. Statute of Limitations and Laches

As with the other procedural aspects discussed above, the applicable statute of limitations (or laches) in a declaratory judgment action depends on the underlying substantive claim. *See, e.g.*, Stone v. Williams, 873 F.2d 620 (2d Cir. 1989) (holding that because the underlying relief sought was in the nature of an accounting, an equitable remedy, laches was an appropriate limitation).

e. Speedy Resolution

As appropriate, courts "may order a speedy hearing of an action for a declaratory judgment and may advance it on their calendar."

B. Case or Controversy Requirement

A declaratory judgment looks rather like an unconstitutional advisory opinion, but for one important requirement. Under the FDJA, and consistent with Article III of the Constitution, declaratory relief is only available when "a case of actual controversy" exists between the parties. 28 U.S.C. § 2201.

1. The Principles of Justiciability

The case or controversy requirement incorporates other principles of justiciability—namely, standing, ripeness, and mootness. Each of these justiciability principles apply in declaratory judgment cases. Indeed, the seminal opinion declaring a prohibition against advisory opinions was *Muskrat v. United States*, 219 U.S. 346 (1911), and involved a request for declaratory relief.

2. The *Haworth* Principle

In *Aetna Life Insurance Co. v. Haworth*, 300 U.S. 227 (1937), the Court was confronted by a dispute regarding the meaning of insurance policies. The Court concluded that the case was justiciable, noting that determinations of justiciability are to be made based on the distinction that a " 'controversy' in this sense must be one that is appropriate for judicial determination. A justiciable controversy is thus distinguished from a difference or dispute of a hypothetical or abstract character; from one that is academic or moot. The controversy must be definite and concrete, touching the legal relations of parties having adverse legal interests. It must be a real and substantial controversy admitting of specific relief through a decree of a conclusive character, as distinguished from an opinion advising what the law would be upon a hypothetical state of facts." *Haworth* concluded that the dispute between the parties was sufficiently definite because the defendant had begun to claim benefits under the plaintiff's insurance policy, and the plaintiff had denied coverage.

3. The *Mitchell* Decision

In *United Public Workers of America v. Mitchell*, 330 U.S. 75 (1947), employees of the federal government sought declaratory relief regarding the validity of the Hatch Act (which prohibited officers and employees in the executive branch of the Federal Government, with exceptions, from taking "any active part in political management or in political campaigns. . . . ") Employees who wished to engage in political management and political campaigns sought to challenge the Act. Except for a single employee who had been charged under the Act, the Court concluded that the case was not justiciable: "Appellants want to engage in 'political management and political campaigns,' to persuade others to follow appellants' views by discussion, speeches, articles and other acts reasonably designed to secure the selection of appellants' political choices. Such generality of objection is really an attack on the political expediency of the Hatch Act, not the presentation of legal issues. It is beyond the competence of courts to render such a decision." This holding captured three points: (1) the proposed conduct was not sufficiently definite that the Court might determine its validity under the statute; (2) the political nature of the plaintiff's claims led the Court to require even greater definiteness than would otherwise be required; and (3) the government had not yet threatened prosecution for the defendants' proposed actions. This final point should be narrowly interpreted, however, for in *Steffel v. Thompson*, 415 U.S. 452 (1974), the Court held that where two friends were distributing leaflets protesting the Vietnam War, the threat of prosecution, even implied by the arrest of one friend, was sufficient to create a definite case or controversy in a suit brought by the other.

4. The Case or Controversy Requirement in State Courts

The UDJA does not specifically require a case or controversy. Nor are state courts bound to require it by Article III of the federal Constitution. Many state courts nonetheless require an analysis parallel to that found in the federal cases.

C. Jurisdiction

The FDJA cannot be invoked by a court that lacks personal or subject matter jurisdiction over the matter in question. In other words, the FDJA is "procedural" and does not create an independent cause of action. As a result, in order to invoke federal jurisdiction, individuals must be able to demonstrate that diversity or a federal question exists. Similarly, by itself the FDJA does not provide an independent basis for removal of actions from state to federal court or for bringing state claims into federal fora.

D. Standard of Review

1. Adequacy of Remedy

As previously noted, declaratory judgments generally are not conditioned upon the inadequacy of remedial alternatives. F.R.Civ.P. 57 specifically provides that "another adequate remedy does not preclude a judgment for declaratory relief in cases where it is appropriate."

2. Judicial Discretion

Courts are free to exercise discretion in deciding whether to grant declaratory relief. Section 6 of the UDJA provides that courts may refuse "a declaratory judgment or decree when such judgment or decree would not terminate the uncertainty or controversy giving rise to the proceeding." Courts may also refuse to issue declaratory relief on a variety of other grounds, including that the action was for the purpose of harassment or was merely a tactical maneuver, or that that there is a pending proceeding in which the rights of the parties may be adjudicated adequately. For example, in *Wilton v. Seven Falls Co.*, 515 U.S. 277 (1995), the Supreme Court declined to issue a declaratory judgment in light of a pending state court action in which the plaintiff sought interpretation of an insurance provision under state law. Courts also sometimes decline to issue a declaratory judgment due to concerns regarding the separation of powers or due to a desire to avoid weighing in on a constitutional question. *See, e.g., National Wildlife Federation v. US,* 626 F.2d 917 (D.C. Cir. 1980) (declining to intervene in a political dispute by issuing a declaratory judgment stating that the President had violated statutory reporting requirements with respect to forming a budget for the National Forest Service). Courts are mixed regarding whether the same discretion is allowed regarding interpretation of a federal statute.

E. Declaratory Judgments in Context

1. Written Instruments

Declaratory relief is frequently sought (and granted) in cases involving wills, trust agreements, commercial contracts, and other written instruments. In this context, declaratory relief allows the parties to ascertain their rights in advance, and avoid the possibility of breach or repudiation. For example, Section 2 of the UDJA provides that declaratory relief is available for persons "interested under a deed, will, written contract, or other writing constituting a contract, or whose rights, status, or other legal relations are affected by a constitutional provision, statute, [or] rule."

2. Intellectual Property

Declaratory relief is also sometimes sought in disputes relating to patents, copyrights and trademarks. Such declarations are frequently necessary to allow the parties adequate information regarding their obligations and enables them to assure purchasers that they are not infringing others' patents or copyrights.

3. Constitutional Claims

Declaratory relief is also available in cases involving constitutional claims. In some instances, those requests for declaratory relief will be denied on the basis that the claim involves injury that is too remote or speculative to present a justiciable controversy.

F. The Effect of Declaratory Judgments

Declaratory judgments bind the parties so that principles of *res judicata* and collateral estoppel apply. A frequent litigation pattern is for a plaintiff to seek a declaratory judgment (which is often more expedient and cost-effective than litigation seeking a substantive remedy) then wait to see if the relevant parties comply. If not, the plaintiff files a subsequent action seeking damages or an injunction, using the declaratory judgment as binding precedent. A plaintiff need not wait to seek a substantive remedy, of course. Both the UDJA and FDJA provide for "further" relief when "necessary and proper," including coercive remedies. UDJA, Sec. 8; FDJA, 28 U.S.C. § 2202.

TRUE-FALSE QUESTIONS

Please answer the following questions "true" or "false":

1. Declaratory relief is generally disfavored today.
2. Declaratory relief is never available except when coupled with a request for injunctive relief.
3. Declaratory relief will be denied when plaintiff has an adequate remedy at law.
4. Declaratory relief is frequently sought and granted in cases involving disputes relating to patents.
5. At both the federal level and the state level, special statutes provide for declaratory relief.
6. Once a plaintiff establishes the requisite *prima facie* elements (justiciability and the underlying substance of the claim), the plaintiff has a right to a declaratory judgment.

MULTIPLE CHOICE QUESTION

Federal courts were reluctant to grant declaratory relief prior to 1900 for which of the following reasons:

A. Because plaintiffs almost invariably had an adequate remedy at law available to them.

B. Because federal statutes disfavored the granting of such relief.

C. Because of justiciability concerns.

D. None of the above.

ESSAY QUESTION

Can you explain why declaratory relief is sometimes refused as non-justiciable in constitutional cases?

ANSWERS TO TRUE-FALSE QUESTIONS

1.	False	At one point, prior to 1900, it was accurate to state that declaratory relief was generally disfavored. Today, with the passage of the Federal Declaratory Judgment Act and the Uniform Declaratory Judgment Act, declaratory relief is more accepted and available.
2.	False	Declaratory relief can be granted with or without a corresponding request for injunctive relief.
3.	False	By statute, declaratory relief is available whether or not plaintiff has an adequate remedy at law.
4.	True	Declaratory relief is frequently sought and granted in cases involving disputes relating to patents. In such cases, a patent dispute can make it difficult or impossible to license the patent and there is a need for quick resolution of any disputes (rather than after the fact resolution).
5.	True	At both the federal level and the state level, special statutes provide for declaratory relief.
6.	False	Declaratory judgments are broadly discretionary, even if the plaintiff establishes the requisite *prima facie* elements.

ANSWER TO MULTIPLE CHOICE QUESTION

Answer (C) is correct. Prior to 1900, federal courts were reluctant to grant declaratory relief because of justiciability concerns. As you know from your civil procedure and constitutional law classes, federal courts do not have general jurisdiction and in fact are limited by the "case and controversy" requirement. At one point, courts were concerned about their power to issue declaratory judgments. They feared that such judgments would amount to nothing more than advisory opinions which were non-justiciable under the case and controversy requirement. Today, while courts will render declaratory judgments, they are careful to make sure that a concrete case or controversy actually exists. Answer (A) is incorrect because, prior to 1900, courts would sometimes deny relief even when plaintiffs did not have an adequate remedy at law available to them. Answer (B) is incorrect because, prior to 1900, there were no federal or state statutes that disfavored the granting of such relief. Finally, Answer (D) is incorrect because it provides that "none of the above" are correct, and Answer (C) is correct.

ANSWER TO ESSAY QUESTION

A number of constitutional cases are non-justiciable because they involve abstract rather than concrete disputes. In other words, they are brought by so-called "ideological plaintiffs" whose injury is more abstract and theoretical and does not constitute a definite case or controversy. The classic example is *Frothingham v. Mellon* in which plaintiff disliked a regulatory program and sought declaratory relief holding that the program was invalid. The only alleged injury was that the program might result in higher taxes. The Court rejected the claim, noting that plaintiff's injury was remote and speculative. Plaintiff was unable to show that the existence or non-existence of the program would have any impact on her taxes.

Chapter Six

Damages

A. General Approach to Compensatory Damages

Compensatory damages seek to place the plaintiff (the victim of a legal wrong) in the position that she would have occupied if the defendant had not committed the wrong. Most of this chapter explores the ways courts evaluate as closely as possible the amount of money needed to advance plaintiff from the position she now occupies to the position she should occupy, a position unaffected by the wrong—as one casebook author puts it, her "rightful position." *See* DOUGLAS LAYCOCK, MODERN AMERICAN REMEDIES 16 (3d ed. 2002). While exceptions may reduce or increase the ultimate award, this principle alone (properly applied) will typically approximate the appropriate compensatory award. Courts sometimes apply detailed formulae to remind juries of factors that affect the calculation. Most formulae, however, are just longer versions of this basic rule.

1. Clarifying Common Misinterpretations of the Rule

a. Position Today, Not Position Before the Wrong

Courts sometimes refer to the position a plaintiff occupied before the wrong. More accurately, the rule seeks to recreate the position the plaintiff would have occupied today (at the time of judgment) if the wrong had not occurred. This includes the benefits a plaintiff would have enjoyed after the date of injury but before the date of judgment as well as future losses caused by the defendant's wrong.

b. Would Have Occupied, Not Could Have Occupied or Hoped to Occupy

The test is objective, not subjective. Plaintiffs may anticipate significant gains that fail to materialize after the wrong. In some cases, these gains would not have materialized even if defendant had not committed the wrong. The rule here turns on the position the plaintiff *would have occupied* if the wrong had not occurred. Put differently, the plaintiff must prove, more likely than not, that the defendant's wrong caused the alleged losses. As will be discussed later with regard to "foreseeability" and "certainty," the plaintiff need not show that *the amount* of damages is certain (e.g., damages for pain and suffering cannot be determined with certainty), but the plaintiff must show by a preponderance of the evidence *the fact* that the loss occurred and was caused by the defendant's wrong.

c. Double Recovery

Courts remain vigilant, if not always perfect, in seeking to avoid double counting any element of recovery. The danger arises in multiple count complaints, where the losses in each count address the same injury. It can also happen in a single count complaint, where similar components of a damage award overlap. For instance, damages for lost enjoyment of life may address the same loss as pain and suffering damages. Similarly, subjective value may overlap with emotional distress.

2. Generality of the Rule

The basic compensatory damages principle applies throughout the law. The temptation to differentiate remedies for torts from remedies for breach of contract—or remedies for sales of goods from remedies for employment contracts or construction contracts—should not obscure the fundamental unity of compensatory awards. Some details differ with context—sometimes because the law differs, but usually because the facts differ. Those details may have significant effects on how to plead a case. For instance, the availability of emotional distress and punitive damages in tort leads many attorneys to cast wrongs in a tort mold, where a contract action would be more straightforward and intuitive. The basic rule, however, applies across all settings. Even statutory provisions, which may specify remedial rules for a particular cause of action, usually adhere fairly closely to the general principles identified here—or to principles of equity and unjust enrichment discussed in other chapters.

3. Where the Plaintiff's Rightful Position Is Unclear: Expectation, Reliance, and Restitution Damages in Contract

In some cases, discerning the plaintiff's rightful position is intuitive. In the tort context, for example, the court and jury's job is to imagine what the plaintiff's body, psyche, and finances would have looked like without the defendant's tortious act. The process of determining the loss sometimes might be fraught, but the concept is not. In other scenarios, the plaintiff's rightful position is susceptible to different conceptual approaches—for instance, the choice in contract cases between expectation, reliance, and sometimes restitution damages. Expectation seeks to place the plaintiff in the position she would have occupied if the contract had been performed (that is, had no breach occurred). Reliance seeks to put the plaintiff in the position she would have occupied if the contract had never been made (that is, no duty to perform had arisen). Restitution—not really a measure of damages at all, but the subject of a different chapter—seeks to put the *defendant* in the position she would have occupied if the contract had never been made. (A fourth choice—seeking to put the defendant in the position if the contract had been performed—receives less attention and has no settled name. Courts rarely choose this measure intentionally.)

a. Communication as the Wrong

Sometimes the wrong consists of a deceptive communication. This may be a false statement of fact or a promise that one never intended to perform. In either case, the wrong involves making the statement. The plaintiff's position but for the wrong focuses on where she would have been if the communication had never been made. Usually, this means plaintiff would not have entered a transaction that the misleading communication induced. This leads some courts to award out-of-pocket costs incurred in relation to that transaction. For instance, where a false statement led a plaintiff to buy property (land, stock, goods) that she otherwise would not have purchased, she can recover the price paid (out of pocket) minus the value of the property received. (This assumes that plaintiff does not elect to rescind the transaction and return the property in exchange for a full refund. *See* Chapter 4 Restitution A.3.b., *supra.*)

Many states allow more than out-of-pocket losses, despite the logic of the preceding paragraph. They follow the benefit-of-the-bargain rule, which treats the misleading communication as true. Thus, plaintiff recovers the value the property would have had if the statement had been true minus the value of the property received. This measure of damages is slightly more generous than the general rule would justify. The explanations are pragmatic. The more generous recovery offers a disincentive to misrepresentation. (If the only cost to defendant were a refund of the excess price, there would be no risk in trying to deceive. If not caught, she keeps the unjust profit; if caught, she keeps the just profit, but loses nothing more than attorneys' fees.) It also eliminates the difference between fraud and warranty. Plaintiffs can elect to treat some misrepresentations as promises to deliver goods of certain quality. *See, e.g.,* U.C.C. § 2–313 (allowing express warranties to arise from "affirmation[s] of fact"). Thus, a plaintiff could sue for breach of warranty, collecting expectation damages: the position she would occupy if the goods had been as promised. That is indistinguishable from the position if the statement had been true. Moreover, misrepresentation often is a greater wrong than breach of contract. It seems anomalous to offer a more generous remedy for breach contract than for the tort of deception.

b. Problems Proving Expectation Losses

The general rule favors expectation—the position if the wrong did not occur, where the wrong is the breach. In some cases, however, it may be difficult to prove expectation damages, particularly when the law requires reasonable certainty in the calculation. *See* E.5, *infra.* In these situations, it may be possible to calculate the reliance interest and, thus, to allow some recovery rather than deny all recovery. This approach, though called reliance, often reflects an effort to come as close as possible to the expectation interest. For example, in a contract action a plaintiff may recover unavoidable expenses (usually those incurred before breach) plus lost profits. (The same measure may apply where a tort destroys a business venture.) If plaintiff cannot prove the amount of its lost profits, she nonetheless should recover expenses to date. This result may assume the promise would not have been made (and thus no expenses incurred—reliance) or that profits would have been zero (and thus sales would cover expenses, but not exceed them—expectation).

c. Special Contexts

In some contexts, expectation recoveries may seem excessive. In those settings, recourse to the reliance interest or a similar measure based on plaintiff's expenditures has some appeal.

(1) Problems with Title to Real Estate

When a defendant promises to sell real estate, but cannot deliver good title, courts often limit recovery to expenditures plaintiff made in preparation for the transaction (such as title searches or surveys). This limitation, sometimes called the English rule or the *Flureau* rule (after *Flureau v. Thornhill,* 2 W. Bl. 1078, 96 Eng.Rep. 635 (C.P.1776)), denies plaintiff the full profit on the transaction. It contrasts with the American rule, which allows plaintiff to recover the market value of the land minus the contract price of the land (in addition to a refund of any portion of the price already paid)—the expectation interest. The English rule assumes that mistakes about title are understandable and forgivable, so that only the harm generated by wasted preparations should be recovered. The English Rule does not apply to defendants who know their title is bad at the time they enter the contract, who cause the problem of title (such as by selling to someone else after entering the contract with the plaintiff), or who could deliver good title but choose to breach instead. (Specific performance usually is available in the last situation, but not the first two.) The American rule assumes that recording statutes make mistakes of title less understandable or forgivable. It also adheres to the general premise that plaintiff should be left in as good a position as she would have occupied but for the wrong. Defendant, not plaintiff, should bear the risk of failure to deliver good title. While more states adhere to the American rule, some of the largest states (CA, MI, NY, PA, TX, VA) follow the English rule, with the limitations noted here.

(2) Fantastic Promises

Sellers sometimes make warranties that are impossible to fulfill. In effect, they promise to deliver a product that does not exist, a fantasy. Because the product as warranted does not exist, assessing the value of the product if it did exist poses serious difficulties. Awarding the plaintiff the benefit of the bargain—the value of a fantasy—often seems excessive. One could rein in the excesses by limiting recovery to reliance damages. Because the U.C.C. does not include provisions for reliance damages, courts often award the benefit of the fantastic bargain. *See, e.g., Chatlos Systems, Inc. v. National Cash Register Corp.*, 670 F.2d 1304 (3d Cir. 1982) (purchaser of a $46,000 computer awarded over $200,000 because only computers costing more than that could possibly perform as warranted).

(3) Disproportionate Recoveries

When the gain plaintiff expected from a transaction grossly exceeds the cost of the transaction, it may seem harsh to ask the defendant who had so little to gain to pay the full cost of its default. Disproportionate recovery may help explain why full recovery in both of the preceding sections seems unjust to some. It also helps explain other limitations on damages, such as foreseeability. *E.g., Hadley v. Baxendale,* 9 Ex. 341, 156 Eng.Rep. 145 (1854) (plaintiff paid 2*l.* 4*s.* to ship mill shaft; when negligent delivery delayed reopening of mill, plaintiff sought £300 in lost profits; jury award of £25—over 10 times price of shipping—reversed); *see* E.4, *infra.* Some secondary sources invite courts to limit disproportionately large awards to the reliance interest. *See* RESTATEMENT (SECOND) OF CONTRACTS § 351(3). Given the prevalence of contract clauses disclaiming liability for consequential damages, *see* U.C.C. § 2–718, relatively few courts today find it necessary to invoke this invitation.

4. Terminology

Although each of the following terms is described at greater length in later sections (and some in the Glossary), an initial view of basic terminology helps provide structure to damages law. Damages remedies might be understood to fall into four general categories: compensatory, punitive, nominal, and statutory.

Compensatory damages are for the purpose of compensating the plaintiff for losses she suffered as a result of the defendant's wrong and also (many would argue) to deter the defendant and other potential future wrongdoers from engaging in similar behavior.

Punitive damages are awarded as an addition to compensatory or nominal damages for the purpose of punishing a defendant for particularly bad behavior or to deter a defendant (and other potential wrongdoers) that might not be deterred by compensatory damages alone.

Nominal damages are a representative sum (e.g., $1 or $100) awarded in cases in which compensatory damages are difficult to prove or where policy reasons counsel against allowing a jury to award compensatory damages. Nominal damages represent society's judgment that the defendant committed a wrong. They also serve the practical purpose of acting as a hook to which a jury might attach punitive damages, where compensatory damages are not available.

Statutory damages are damages provided by statute rather than the common law. Legislatures pass statutory damages provisions for various reasons, perhaps most often (1) to cabin jury discretion in issuing damages for wrongs for which a plaintiff's actual harm is particularly inscrutable (e.g., for copyright violations), (2) to provide predictability for both plaintiffs and defendants, and (3) to deter particularly odious behavior (e.g., the treble damages available for antitrust violations).

Within the category of compensatory damages, courts often break down damages awards into subcategories, each with its own particular rules and guidelines. These subcategories include: general damages, special damages, incidental damages, pre- and post-judgment interest, costs and fees, and attorneys' fees.

General damages are the fundamental damages on which an action is based. In a breach of contract action, general damages are those that are the natural consequence of the breach, often measured by the expectation interest. In the tort context, general damages are nonpecuniary damages—for example, pain and suffering, loss of consortium, emotional distress, or loss of enjoyment of life.

Special damages might also be thought of as "ensuing damages," or damages that are one step removed from the immediate harm of a defendant's wrong. In a breach of contract action, special damages, also known as "consequential damages," are damages that do not flow directly from the breach—for example, a loss of downstream business that occurred as a result of a defendant's failure to promptly repair the plaintiff's broken mill. *See supra Hadley v. Baxendale*. In an action for tort, special damages are out of pocket pecuniary expenses stemming from the plaintiff's injury—for example, medical expenses, lost wages, or harm to property.

Incidental damages are costs incurred in mitigation. In a contract action, incidental damages might be, for example, the cost to replace undelivered goods or of finding a replacement buyer. In a tort action, incidental damages might be the cost of renting a car while a car damaged by the defendant is repaired. The concept of incidental damages is a slippery one, as certain types of damages might be considered either special or incidental. For example, the cost of physical therapy in a tort action might be a medical expense or an attempt to mitigate long-term damages.

Prejudgment interest is interest on compensatory damages from the time of the defendant's wrong to the final resolution of the case. *Post-judgment interest* is interest from the time of final resolution to the actual payment of the judgment.

Costs and fees are expenses required by the court in the course of litigation. They might, for example, consist of filing fees and the cost of making required copies of documents.

Attorneys' fees are exactly what they sound like—the fees charged by the attorneys in representing their client in the litigation.

5. Organization of the Chapter

Because "general" and "specific" damages mean different things depending on the cause of action, this chapter is first divided into sections on direct losses (damages that are a direct consequence of the wrong) and ensuing losses (more remote effects of the wrong). Because losses that have a market value are scrutinized differently from losses that do not have a market value (nonpecuniary losses such as pain, suffering, joy, indignity, distress, consortium and grief), the chapter covers intangible losses (even those that are "direct" losses) as a third section. The chapter next covers doctrinal and contractual limitations on damages before turning to punitive damages and attorneys' fees.

REVIEW QUESTIONS

1. To calculate the expectation interest, determine the amount necessary to:
   a. Put the defendant in the position the defendant would have occupied if the contract had been performed
   b. Put the plaintiff in the position the plaintiff would have occupied if the contract had never been made.
   c. Put the plaintiff in the position the plaintiff would have occupied if the contract had been performed.
   d. Put the defendant in the position the defendant would have occupied if the contract had never been made.
2. Which of the answers to question 1 is so rarely used that commentators cannot agree on what to call it?
3. The benefit of the bargain rule for deception closely resembles which remedial interest?
   a. Expectation
   b. Reliance
   c. Restitution
   d. None of the above
4. In cases of deception, should states employ the benefit of the bargain rule or the out-of-pocket loss rule to determine plaintiff's recovery?

ANSWERS

1. C.
2. A.
3. A.
4. The out-of-pocket rule gives plaintiff (P) the difference between the amount she gave up because of the deception (usually the price paid) and the amount she received, the value of whatever defendant (D) provided in exchange. This returns P to the same net position she occupied before the transaction, no better and no worse. This is the position she would have occupied but for the wrong, since if told the truth she probably would not have entered the transaction and, thus, would have retained the money. As compensation, this measure is complete.

   The benefit of the bargain rule would award P the difference between what she was promised—as if the deceptive statement had been true—and what she received. Presumably, she was promised more than the price she paid, so the benefit of the bargain would give a larger recovery. It would leave plaintiff in a better position than she occupied before the breach, in much the way that contract suits leave parties better than they were before the breach by giving P more than she had before—the benefit of the bargain. This is not necessary to put plaintiff in the position she would have occupied but for the wrong. Benefit of the bargain overcompensates her.

   Nonetheless, some state courts pursue benefit of the bargain, with good reason. P could plead breach of warranty, alleging the deceptive statement was a promise relating to quality. If so, she could recover expectation. It seems odd to limit her recovery for tort to out-of-pocket loss while allowing a more generous recovery if she pleads the action a little differently. Doubly odd, deception seems a worse wrong than breach of contract. Allowing a more generous recovery for breach of contract than for deception seems backwards. (Perhaps an award of punitive damages would correct the imbalance without altering the basic recovery rule.) Finally, out-of-pocket loss seems too little to deter future deception. If the only sanction D faces is to refund the overcharge, D has little reason not to continue deceiving others. If not caught, D keeps the entire price. If caught, D still keeps the fair price of the thing sold. There is no downside to deception—again, unless punitive damages apply. The benefit of the bargain rule builds a disincentive to lie into the basic recovery rule. This may be the better choice.

B. Direct Loss

Direct loss refers to the thing injured by the wrong. It may be physical property (a car, a building), a legal right (a patent, a contract right), or a person's body. Harm to the thing itself is called direct loss. The inability to use the thing in other projects (to drive the car to work, to resell the contract performance to another, to use the body in gainful employment) will be discussed later as ensuing loss.

Discussion of direct loss is broken down into specific contexts. In each section, the ultimate goal remains the same: to identify how much money it will take to restore plaintiff to his rightful position. Different contexts generate different terminology and different components—and in some cases involve different economic concerns. In many ways, however, each section is an example of the general rule. You may be able to master the rule without every single example.

1. Reduced Value

When property is damaged, direct loss may be measured by **its value immediately before the injury minus its value immediately after the injury**. *But see* B.1.c, *infra*. (The measure works even when property is totally destroyed rather than damaged; its value immediately after the injury is $0, or perhaps some salvage value.) This measure applies to real property, as where a building is damaged or destroyed, and to personal property, as when a car is damaged or destroyed. A similar approach can apply to contract cases, where the plaintiff receives and keeps property not in compliance with the requirements of the contract. **The value of performance as promised (on the date for delivery) minus the value of the performance as received** has been applied to construction contracts. *See, e.g., Jacob & Youngs v. Kent,* 230 N.Y. 239, 129 N.E. 889 (1921) (contract required Reading pipe, but contractor substituted another manufacturer's pipe). That formula is codified in the U.C.C. for goods that do not live up to a warranty, if buyer keeps the goods instead of rejecting them. *See* U.C.C. § 2–714. In each case, reduced value may not measure the entire loss; additional recovery for ensuing losses may be needed to make the plaintiff whole.

a. Definition of Value

When addressing pecuniary losses, value usually means fair market value: the amount that a willing buyer would give and a willing seller would accept in exchange for the property in an arm's-length transaction, each being reasonably informed and neither being under any compulsion to enter the transaction. Actual transactions are good evidence of market value. Mere offers may not be, since at least one party had not yet agreed and might insist upon better terms. Forced sales, where one party cannot await a better offer, are not good evidence of value. If a relationship between buyer and seller might induce them to deal on terms more advantageous to one of them, the transaction is not at arm's length and, thus, not good evidence of what the property would be worth on the market. Similarly, the price agreed to by a deceived party may not reflect fair market value.

b. Calculating Value

Four different techniques may be used to calculate value (both for purposes of calculating value before wrong and value after wrong): market value, replacement cost less depreciation, capitalization of earnings, and value of repaired property minus the repair costs. Each should produce about the same result. (Note: Book value, a concept useful in tax law, has no use in calculating remedies. Full replacement cost, while occasionally promised in insurance contracts, also is not a remedial concept.)

(1) Market Value

Market value seeks the amount it would cost a person to buy similar property in the market. Similar includes similar age, similar condition, similar features, etc. Evidence of similar property available in the market is the best evidence. Appraisers may offer estimates of current market value based on recent market transactions.

(2) Replacement Cost Less Depreciation

This measure starts with the cost to buy new property (or services) similar to those lost, then adjusting the cost to reflect differences in age and condition. Full replacement cost (with new property) would overcompensate a plaintiff who held used property before the transaction. Adjustments often subtract a percentage of the price based on the amount of useful life the original property had left at the time of injury compared to the amount of useful life in the new property.

(3) Capitalization of Earnings

Where property produces income, its value often depends on how much income it will produce over time. The amount a person will pay today depends directly on the amount of income the property will produce, how long it will take to generate that income, and the risk that the property might produce less income than projected. For example, property (a machine, a shopping mall) that might produce $50,000 in profit in each of the next five years might be worth about $190,000 today (to a purchaser who wants a 10% return on investment). (The calculation is the same as for present value of future income. *See* C.5.c, *infra*.) The rental value of real property is sometimes referred to as *mesne profits*. Capitalization of earnings does not always capture the full value of the plaintiff's loss, however. For example, where a defendant inflicts fire damage on a plaintiff's apartment building, plaintiff's lost value might be both in lost mesne profits as well as cost of repairing the structure.

(4) Repairs as Evidence of Value

The cost to repair the property is some evidence of the amount of value lost. Subtracting repair costs from the value the property will have once repaired is a reasonable estimate of the value of the property in its injured condition. For example, if spending $5,000 on repairs would produce property worth $20,000, it seems likely that the damaged property is worth about $15,000. Anyone offering much more than $15,000 is likely to lose money on the deal (unless the $20,000 value after repairs is wrong). Anyone offering much less than $15,000 is likely to be outbid by someone willing to take a slightly smaller profit on the repairs. If the property remains useful or valuable without repairs, the value might exceed $15,000. And in some cases, the value of repaired property may be greater than the property before the injury—e.g., if a damaged car is repaired with new, rather than used parts. Nonetheless, in many cases, cost of repair will approximate the decreased value caused by the injury.

c. Problems of Timing

Statements of the rule relying on "before" and "after" assume a relatively sudden accident, as where a car is in good condition one moment, but damaged by impact a moment later. Where property damage occurs over time, the value before the accident and the value after may reflect more than just the injury caused by the defendant. Property (such as cars) may depreciate over the time even if not subjected to the injury. Defendant should not pay for depreciation he didn't cause. Similarly, property (such as art or land) may appreciate over time, despite being subject to the injury. Defendant should not pay less because of appreciation she didn't cause. Damages must reflect the value the property would have had if not injured minus the value of the property does have in its injured condition, measured on the same day. Measuring loss on the date the injury is complete should correct for depreciation defendant did not cause.

A second problem involves appreciation after the injury. Prejudgment interest on the loss, measured from the date of the injury, plus any appreciation to the damaged property, may compensate plaintiff for lost appreciation in the value of the property. In some cases, however, this may be inadequate. For instance, an artwork that cannot be repaired might have appreciated more than the interest rate if it had not been damaged. (If repaired, appreciation might not be affected by the wrong.) Damages might be measured by the value the undamaged property would have had on the date of judgment minus the value the damaged property has on the date of judgment. This would eliminate the effects of intervening appreciation or depreciation that differed from the market interest rate. The approach presents problems in other settings, making it uncommon for courts to express the rule this way. For instance, where future appreciation depends on additional investment or effort by the plaintiff (as when a business or a crop is damaged), assessing the value the property would have had after additional investment poses difficulties. The problem is exacerbated when the tort obviates the investment (as by destroying the business or crop).

2. Alternative Measure: Cost of Repair

In many cases, plaintiff will not leave damaged property in its damaged condition, but will repair it. Allowing plaintiff to recover **the cost of repair** (plus any ensuing losses during the time required for repairs) often puts her in the position she would have occupied if the wrong had not occurred: she has the property in its original condition), at no cost to her (once compensated by defendant). Some courts allow plaintiff to elect the cost of repair as an alternative measure of damages, instead of the reduced value of the property. As will be seen below, repair costs are not always the same as diminution in a property's value, and courts have adopted rules to delimit their recovery.

a. Market Value of Repairs

The amount the plaintiff actually spent on repairs may not be recoverable if plaintiff spent more than the repairs were worth. A plaintiff who expects defendant ultimately to pay for the repairs has less incentive to keep the cost down than a plaintiff who expects to bear the cost himself. Thus, courts often limit recovery to the fair market value of repairs. Alternatively, courts may award actual repairs unless unreasonable. The latter approach resembles the avoidable consequences doctrine: plaintiff cannot recover for losses she reasonably could have avoided, such as by shopping for a more reasonable price for the repairs. *See* E.3, *infra.*

b. Excessive Repair Costs

In some cases, it may make no sense to repair the damaged property. Rules that allow plaintiff to choose cost of repair generally include some restriction on plaintiff's ability to choose this measure when repairs are excessive relative to the benefit of repairs. Several rules have been stated by various jurisdictions for when plaintiff may not recover the cost of repairs:

i. When the cost of repairs exceeds the increase in value resulting from the repairs;

ii. When the cost of repairs exceeds the value before the injury;

iii. When the cost of repairs exceeds the value after the repairs are completed;

iv. When the cost of repairs is disproportionate to the diminution in value of the property.

The first approach makes economic sense: where repairs increase value by more than the cost of the repairs, a reasonable person would undertake the repairs, but not where the opposite is true. The last three also avoid repair costs where the repairs are not economically justified. The second and third disallow high repair costs on expensive goods where the repairs would restore very little value to the goods. The fourth shares this feature, but allows the judge to determine whether costs would be "disproportionate" to the property's diminution in value. The fourth guideline has appeal for two reasons. First, it allows some room for plaintiff to err when arranging for repairs. A plaintiff will not always be able to predict the amount of diminution a court eventually will find. As long as repairs are not disproportionate to the loss in value, some leeway for miscalculation may be justified. Second, it leaves some room for subjective value. Plaintiff may value the property more than the market does. (If the market valued it more, it might have bought plaintiff out before the injury.) Even if repairs exceed the value of the property to others, they may not exceed the value of the property to the plaintiff. Thus, when repairs are not disproportionate to the reduced value, it may make sense to allow plaintiff to make repairs. Thus, secondary sources often favor the last approach. *See* RESTATEMENT (SECOND) OF TORTS § 929; RESTATEMENT (SECOND) OF CONTRACTS § 348(2).

On the other hand, the last approach leaves room for strategic behavior. A plaintiff might assert subjective value in an effort to collect repair costs not justified by the market (that is, costs that exceed the increase in value that repair will achieve). Once awarded, plaintiff might sell the property without repairing it, ending up in a better position than she would have occupied but for the wrong. For example, suppose plaintiff owns a farm worth $500,000. Defendant floods part of the land, reducing the value of the farm to $400,000. By spending $130,000, plaintiff could recover the land and return the value of the farm to $500,000. As the ancestral homeland of plaintiff's family, plaintiff might persuade a court that it is worthwhile to him to repair the land, even though an objective party would not spend $130,000 to increase the land's value by $100,000. If plaintiff can recover $130,000, then sell the land for $400,000 without repairing it, plaintiff ends up with $530,000—more than the value of the land before the injury. For this reason, courts scrutinize claims of subjective value with some skepticism—and some reject the disproportionality test altogether, preferring one of the other approaches. Note that the second approach—where repairs exceed the value before the wrong—would still allow plaintiff to recover repair costs: $130,000 is less than $500,000, even though it exceeds the value repairs will add to the land.

Exception: Environmental Harm to Real Property

For reasons of public policy, in cases in which a defendant's wrong causes environmental damage to a plaintiff's real property, courts frequently award repair costs even where such an award might violate the rules outlined above. *See, e.g., Terra-Products v. Kraft Gen. Foods, Inc.*, 653 N.E.2d 89 (Ind. App. 1995).

c. Incomplete Repairs

Most rules assume that repairs will restore the property to its original value. That is not always true. Where repairs do not restore property to its full value, courts must award cost of repairs plus any residual lost value. That is, the difference between the value the property would have had if never injured and the value the property has as repaired must be added to the award. For example, a car worth $30,000 before an accident may require significant repairs, costing $10,000. While repairs may make the car fully functional, the car may be worth only $22,000 after repairs—even though cars of similar make, model, age, mileage, features, etc., would be worth $30,000. Buyers generally pay less for cars that have undergone significant repairs than for cars that have never been damaged in the first place. Thus, even after receiving the cost of repairs, plaintiff will not be in the position she would have occupied but for the wrong unless she receives an additional $8,000 to cover the residual loss in value.

3. Undelivered Value

Sometimes the wrong does not damage property already possessed by the plaintiff, but prevents plaintiff from obtaining additional property. This can happen in tort (such as destroying or diverting property en route to plaintiff or interfering with another's performance of a contract), but more commonly involves a breach of contract. The goal is to allow the plaintiff to obtain the things promised (or their monetary equivalent) at no greater cost than if the wrong had not been committed. The value of the property itself is direct loss. Value plaintiff hoped to create by using the property involves ensuing losses.

Most contract remedies can be reduced to a simple approach: the value the plaintiff would have received if the contract had been performed minus costs the plaintiff avoided because of the breach. Costs avoided because of the breach typically involve any performance plaintiff would have needed to provide under the contract, but has not yet provided (and, because of the breach, no longer needs to provide.) Ensuing losses can be added to this formula, if the value plaintiff would have received is limited to direct losses. Sometimes ensuing losses may be included in the value plaintiff would have received. Care must be taken not to double count ensuing losses.

One can approach this from the other direction and achieve a functionally identical approach: the costs plaintiff cannot avoid incurring plus any profit plaintiff would have earned had the contract been performed. Recovery of unavoidable costs brings the plaintiff back to the break-even point. Awarding profits on top of that gives the plaintiff the gain it expected on the transaction. (Profit equals total gains minus total costs. Thus, unavoidable costs plus profit always should equal total gains minus avoided costs.) Again, profit may be limited to direct gains or may include ensuing losses. Care must be taken to avoid double counting ensuing losses or overlooking them entirely.

The issues below focus on nonperformance rather than partial performance. When a party's performance is incomplete or not up to the promised quality, the issue generally involves the reduced value of that performance. The preceding sections apply to those situations. When a party fails to perform, the rules below apply. At the edges, nonperformance and inadequate performance may overlap. Delivery of half the promised goods could be treated as a performance of reduced value or as nonperformance as to half the goods (and full performance as to the other half). Because both approaches aim at the same general rule—the plaintiff's position if the wrong had not occurred—the result should be the same no matter which approach the court takes. Where the approaches produce different results, usually some component has been omitted from the calculation on one of the approaches.

a. Sales of Goods

Article 2 of the Uniform Commercial Code codifies contract remedies for sales of goods. These provisions are a useful illustration of how contract remedies work. Once we review these provisions, it will be easy to see how the same principles apply in other contract contexts, such as employment and construction.

(1) Nondelivery by Seller

Buyer is entitled to receive a refund of any amount paid to seller. U.C.C. § 2–711(1). In addition buyer may recover the cover price (the cost to obtain substitute goods in good faith, without unreasonable delay, in a reasonable transaction) minus the contract price promised to the original seller. U.C.C. § 2–712. Alternatively, buyer may decide not to make a substitute deal and recover the market price of the goods (the amount it would have cost if he had made a reasonable substitute purchase) minus the contract price promised to the original seller. U.C.C. § 2–713. (One could frame the rule as the cover price or market price minus unpaid portion of the contract price. If the goods cost less than the contract price, that rule might allow defendant to keep a portion of any down payment. Allowing a full refund, then subtracting the entire contract price, codifies a restitution component of these remedies.) Of course, a plaintiff could seek specific performance if "the goods are unique or in other proper circumstances." U.C.C. § 2–716. Specific Performance is discussed elsewhere. *See* Chapter 3 Injunctions M, *infra.* Damages when buyer keeps goods that do not conform to the contract are measured by the reduced value of the goods (value as warranted minus value as received). *See* B.1, *supra.* In each case, plaintiff receives the goods or their money equivalent, minus any amounts saved (the contract price). Additional losses—such as the time required to make substitute arrangements, any losses if substitute goods arrive later than those promised by the seller, and any losses to the venture of which the goods were a part (such a lost profits on resale) will be discussed under ensuing losses.

(2) Nonpayment by Buyer

When a buyer refuses to pay for goods, seller may refuse to deliver the goods—including recovering the goods from a third party, such as a transportation company or warehouse. U.C.C. § 2–703. In addition, seller may recover the contract price minus the resale price (the amount seller realized in a good faith and commercially reasonable sale of the goods to another buyer). U.C.C. § 2–706. Alternatively, seller may decide not to make a substitute deal. If so, she recovers the contract price minus the market price (the amount she would have received if she had made a reasonable substitute sale). U.C.C. § 2–708(1). In some cases, there will be nothing to subtract from the contract price; the market value the seller could receive will be zero. For instance, buyer may already have the goods, so seller cannot resell them. The goods may have been destroyed after the risk of loss shifted to buyer. In some cases, seller may have the goods but may be unable to resell them at any reasonable price. In these cases, seller may recover the entire contract price but must hold the goods (if she has them) available for buyer. U.C.C. § 2–709. In each case, any savings to the seller would be subtracted from the recovery—perhaps the cost of shipping the goods or insuring them during transit. In addition, plaintiff may recover ensuing losses, such as the cost incurred trying to resell the goods and of storing and insuring them pending resale.

Seller's remedies do include one unusual provision: lost volume sellers. The rules stated above assume that a resale by the seller was a substitute for the sale to the buyer. In some cases, however, seller could have made both sales. For instance, a manufacturer of potato chips might have been able to fill both the order of the new buyer and the order of the original buyer. (Hence the slogan "Munch all you want; we'll make more.") By breaching, the original buyer reduced the seller's total profit. Instead of making a profit on two sales, seller only made the profit on one—the substitute transaction. Where seller could have earned profits on both sales, the breaching buyer must pay the profit (plus reasonable overhead) on the contract breached, plus ensuing costs, but minus any savings (such as shipping costs or warranty service) in relation to the contract. U.C.C. § 2–708(2). Thus, seller ends up where she belongs. She collects the profit on two sales: one via the resale, the other via the damage award.

(3) Comparing the Remedies

The remedies for buyers and sellers are almost exactly parallel, as can be seen in the chart below. Each can make a reasonable substitute transaction and collect the difference between the substitute transaction and the transaction to which they were originally entitled. Each can eschew substitute transactions and recover based on market price—the price at which a substitute transaction would have been made if plaintiff had so elected. And each can recover exactly what they bargained for—the goods (via specific performance) or the price (as damages) in an appropriate case. The only difference involves the seller's inability to recover for the reduced value of nonconforming delivery. This set of cases probably is empty: where buyer pays in something other than money, seller would be treated as a buyer of that something, able to invoke buyer's remedies; where buyer was to pay money, the nonconformity must relate to the amount, leaving an unpaid balance that seller may claim under these provisions.

SUMMARY OF U.C.C. DAMAGE REMEDIES

SELLER	BUYER
Contract Price - Resale Price + Incidental – Savings (2–706) [+ Consequential]	Refund + Cover Price - Contract Price + Incidental + Consequential (2–712)
Unpaid Contract Price - Market Price + Incidental - Savings (2–708) [+ Consequential]	Refund + Market Price - K Price + Incidental + Consequential (2–713)
	Value Warranted - Value Received + Incidental + Consequential (2–714)
Contract Price (2–709) + Incidental – Savings [+ Consequential]	Specific Performance + Damages Not Avoided by SP (2–716)

b. Employment Contracts

In employment contracts, employees sell services and employers buy them. Most of the remedies will be identical to sales of goods.

Where an employee breaches, the employer may need to hire a substitute (in good faith and reasonably). If the substitute costs more than the contract with the employee, the employee should be liable for the difference—cover price minus contract price. Price here should reflect both wages and fringe benefits. Ensuing losses—the cost to find the new employee and any damages caused in the interim—remain a part of the picture.

Where an employer breaches, the employee may need to find substitute employment (similar to reselling the goods). If the new job pays less (considering both wages and fringe benefits), the employer should be liable for the difference—contract price minus resale price.

In either case, if no substitute transaction occurs, the market price may be substituted for cover price or resale price: the employer may be limited to the excess amount it would have cost to replace the employee; the employee may not recover the amount she could have earned if she had found new employment. (This rule is usually discussed under the avoidable consequences doctrine. *See* E.3, *infra.*) If the new employment does not substitute for the old—if the employee would have worked both jobs, not just one—she is a lost volume seller, so the new wages are not subtracted from the amount owed under the employment contract. If substitute employment is unavailable—the resale value of the services is zero—the employer may be liable for the entire contract price. In either event, ensuing losses—profits lost because of employee's nonperformance, foreclosures because of employer's nonpayment—might be needed to round out the remedy, if they can survive the doctrines limiting recovery of ensuing losses.

The remedies discussed here assume complete nondelivery of services. Lesser breaches will be more analogous to the reduced value situation. Where an employee doesn't work as long or as hard as promised, the value of the services might be adjusted. That is relatively common when the employee is late or absent; pay for time not worked can be subtracted from a paycheck. Suing a lazy employee for damages caused by inactivity, while theoretically possible, is relatively rare. Employers probably replace poor quality employees instead of suing them for damages. Other breaches, such as trade secret violations or breach of a noncompetition agreement, involve the same principles: putting the plaintiff where she would have been if the breach had not occurred. Almost all of the loss in these cases falls within ensuing losses.

c. Construction Contracts

As with employment, construction contracts involve services—in this case, services related to creating or repairing buildings, usually on real estate owned by the buyer of the services. As with goods and employment, when the seller (contractor) breaches, the buyer (landowner) may need to make substitute arrangements. These may involve the entire contract or the unfinished work. The owner recovers the cost to complete the project minus the unpaid portion of the contract price (the savings from not paying the original contractor the rest of what she would have collected had she finished the job). As usual, the substitute transaction must be a reasonable one made in good faith. Ensuing losses may be recoverable, though many construction contracts exclude damages for delay.

When the landowner breaches—dismissing the contractor without cause—the contractor is in the position of a discharged employee. She may recover the amount promised for the full job, minus any expenses saved by not needing to complete the job. (Savings may include salvage value of materials already purchased for the job.) The amount the contractor earns or could have earned on other jobs usually is not subtracted from the award. Most contractors are treated as lost volume sellers. Contractors often can handle many projects at one time, simply hiring more laborers as they work more sites. Instead of treating other jobs as substitutes for the job the owner breached, the courts award profits lost on this job and assume that the builder could have performed the other jobs, too.

d. Real Estate Contracts

The same principles apply to real estate, but with some differences.

(1) Seller Breaches

When seller fails to deliver real estate, buyer normally is entitled to specific performance. Where damages are awarded instead, buyer may recover a refund of any payments, plus the market value of the land minus the contract price of the land. This is the American rule discussed earlier—along with the tendency of some courts to award reliance damages under the English rule. *See* A.3.c.(1), *supra*. Courts almost never award cover price minus contract price, even if plaintiff enters a substitute transaction. Each parcel of real estate is unique. Courts have difficulty discerning whether a higher cover price is attributable to the good deal the plaintiff made on the promised parcel or to better quality of the substitute parcel. If the latter, a remedy based on cover price might make plaintiff better off than if the contract had been performed by providing him with a better parcel than promised for the price of the promised parcel. The basic rule—putting plaintiff in the position she would have occupied if the wrong had not occurred—does not encompass allowing plaintiff to buy a better parcel at defendant's expense. Thus, even a good faith and reasonable substitute purchase will not be used as the measure of recovery in most jurisdictions. The second parcel, if sufficiently similar, might be evidence of the market value of the promised parcel. (Market value for real estate often depends on the price of similar land in the vicinity.) But the substitute transaction has no direct effect on the measure of damages.

(2) Buyer Breaches

When buyer refuses to take delivery and pay for a parcel, seller can resell the parcel and collect the original contract price minus resale price, minus any savings (*e.g.,* brokerage commissions, if lower because of the resale—and perhaps the value of retaining possession of the land, as where it produces a crop before it is resold). As always, ensuing losses (such as cost of resale, insurance while resale was pending, etc.) may be necessary to fill out the remedy. Here, the parcel is exactly the same, so any difference in the resale price must reflect the deal itself. (If an uninsured loss damaged the property in the interim, that might be an ensuing loss; the parcel is different, so the lower resale price may not reflect how good a deal the first contract was. But defendant would have suffered the uninsured loss but for the breach, making it appropriate to use this measure anyway.) If buyer does not resell, the contract price minus the market value (on the date of the breach) remains a viable remedy—again, taking account of any savings and any ensuing losses.

(3) Leases

When the estate being sold is less than a fee simple, the same principles apply. The values become the values of the estate actually being sold. Thus, the fair rental value might substitute for the fair market value in the formulations offered above. The same concerns arise if a tenant enters a substitute transaction for a different property. The actual transaction will not be used to measure the loss, though it might be evidence of the fair rental value of the original premises. If the fair rental value of the original exceeds the contract price, the tenant might recover the difference from the breaching landlord.

Where the tenant breaches, a more difficult issue arises. To what extent are the premises retained by the landlord and to what extent are they retained by the tenant? If the landlord retains the premises, then their value is a savings to him that results from the breach and should offset the rent due (especially if the landlord succeeds in reselling part of the lease to another tenant). If the premises are retained by the tenant—who is entitled to use them for the full period, though she now wishes to renounce that right—then the landlord saves nothing, the tenant retains the benefit. The latter represents the traditional view: the landlord collects the full rent, without any offset; that the tenant doesn't use the premises is the tenant's business, and not the landlord's. At least for residential real estate, many states now hold that the repudiation of the lease by the tenant constitutes an immediate breach of contract, returning any unused portion of the leasehold to the landlord. The approach tends to be partial: the landlord's recovery decreases by the amount that it realizes by a substitute lease; but recovery is not reduced by the value of the leasehold unless the landlord did (or could have with reasonable efforts) enter a substitute lease. As with discharged employees, the landlord's potential resale of the premises tends to be treated under the avoidable consequences doctrine. *See* E.3. *infra.* Note that the traditional view continues to prevail for commercial leases in many jurisdictions.

4. Loss of Intangible Property

Some losses involve intangible property, such as contract rights, patent rights, insurance, or stock certificates. Where these rights have a market value, the techniques described above can apply with full force. Failure to deliver a stock certificate can be compensated by cover price minus contract price or, if buyer does not cover, market price minus contract price. Failure to pay for the stock can be compensated by contract price minus resale price or, if seller does not resell, contract price minus market value. Thus, direct loss for many intangibles presents no new issue. In some cases, however, intangibles raise new wrinkles.

a. Insurance Policies

When defendant breaches a promise to obtain insurance for plaintiff, cover price minus contract price will suffice only if plaintiff discovers the problem with enough time to obtain insurance coverage elsewhere before an insured loss occurs. After an insured loss, no one will issue a policy covering the risk of that loss. Thus, to put plaintiff in the position she would have occupied if the breach had not occurred, the law must award the full amount of insurance plaintiff would have received under the policy promised by defendant. Defendant promised to deliver intangible property (an insurance policy) but failed to deliver it. The value of the policy might have been very small (if no insured loss occurred) but turns out to be large (compensation for the insured loss). If the thing itself is not delivered, its value should be provided.

b. Contract Rights, Intellectual Property Rights

The failure to pay for intangible rights poses no theoretical difficulties: the promised payments, less any savings, should be awarded. (Where price depends on volume, but no volume is produced or sold, price might be difficult to calculate. *See* E.5, *infra.*) Failure to deliver promised rights pose a different story. In many cases, all losses will be ensuing losses: the profits plaintiff would have made by using the rights. But in some cases, rights may have a market value. This is particularly true where they can be resold (for example, the movie rights to a book). While resale sounds like just another use (and thus another ensuing loss), plaintiff is deprived of a piece of property, however intangible, that has measurable value. This is direct loss, as much as the destruction, damage, or nondelivery of tangible property is a direct loss. Of course, intellectual property rights and other contract rights may be unique, allowing for injunctive relief.

5. Personal Injury

Personal injury—both physical and emotional—tends to be seen as sui generis. The general approaches detailed above can apply with equal force, but some of the questions raised simply don't arise in the context of personal injuries.

a. Physical Injury to a Person

In some ways, physical injury to a person is much like physical injury to property. Courts could theoretically award the value immediately before the injury minus the value immediately after the injury—for example, the value of a plaintiff's body with two working legs minus the value of the plaintiff's body with only one working leg. Measuring the value of the human body in the abstract, however, is difficult, if not impossible. How much money might one accept to give up a leg, or pay to avoid losing a leg? There is no legitimate market to aid us in answering such questions. Instead, courts award reasonable medical costs plus pain and suffering plus any ensuing losses (such as lost earnings). Medical costs are the costs of repair. In some ways, medical costs are not direct losses, but costs incurred in an effort to minimize the loss caused by injury to the person—thus, medical costs are typically referred to by courts as "special damages." Pain and suffering and ensuing losses are the best available proxies for measuring the value of plaintiff's physical injury itself. Together, these various damages mirror a court's measure of recovery for property damage which, once repaired, yet retains some decreased market value—in the case of personal injury, the recovery is repair costs, plus the lost value that repair costs do not compensate, in the form of pain and suffering and ensuing losses.

(1) Future Medical Costs and Medical Monitoring

In addition to medical costs necessary to repair a plaintiff's immediate injury, the plaintiff may also recover reasonably certain future medical expenses, such as foreseeably necessary surgeries, physical therapy, nursing care, prostheses, etc. The difficult issue whether to award the costs of continued testing—referred to as "medical monitoring"—in cases where the defendant's wrong has put the plaintiff at risk for currently undetectable future harm. This is most common in toxic tort cases in which the plaintiff has been exposed to a potentially disease-causing agent, although the issue can also arise in normal injury scenarios. Where the plaintiff has not suffered any initial injury or symptoms, courts are often reluctant to award medical monitoring costs—some courts are willing, some are not. (*See* E.1.c, *infra.*) Where the plaintiff has suffered initial injury, however, courts are more willing to award medical monitoring costs. For example, where a plaintiff currently suffers from asbestosis, courts often award the costs of testing for asbestos-related cancer.

b. Anguish Accompanying Physical Injury

The pain caused by an injury—including the pain suffered as of the time of recovery in the lawsuit as well as any unavoidable future pain—is a second component of the value of the body itself and is a direct loss that requires compensation. Indeed, pain and suffering has long been considered the central basis for recovery in torts cases involving personal injury and is thus referred to as "general damages." Although pain and suffering is a direct loss, because it is subject to extensive special rules, the topic is considered at greater length in the section on Intangible Loss below. (*See* D.3, *infra.*)

(1) Emotional Injuries Without Physical Injury

As noted above, the pain and suffering that accompanies physical injury is typically recoverable, subject to the limitations described in Sections D and E, *infra*. Tort law has imposed stringent limits, however, on plaintiffs' recovery in claims for pure emotional distress—that is, in cases in which the plaintiff suffered no physical injury, but only emotional harm. The general rule is that plaintiffs cannot recover purely emotional distress. Courts have allowed exceptions, however, in a variety of fact-specific categories—for example, where the defendant's wrong negligently put the plaintiff in a zone of physical danger, where the defendant's wrong involved the corpse of a relative of the plaintiff, or where the defendant negligently caused serious injury to a close relative of the plaintiff in the plaintiff's presence. Courts have typically couched such rules in the language of negligence duty, rather than describing the rules as damages limitations—although one might argue that the opposite might make more conceptual sense. Courts have adopted similar limitations on claims for purely economic injuries, as described in Section E.6, *infra*.

(2) Awards for Physical Injuries Without General Damages

Juries occasionally return personal injury damages awards for medical costs and/or lost wages (special damages) without a corresponding award for pain and suffering (general damages). Depending on the particular case, such a result might be explained by the jury's disbelief in the plaintiff's testimony on pain and suffering, by difficulty in sorting out the causal determinant of the plaintiff's pain (for example, where the plaintiff already suffered from pain before the tort, the jury might find it difficult to determine whether the plaintiff's pain was exacerbated by the tortious injury), or by the jury's determination that any pain associated with the plaintiff's injury was incidental. In many jurisdictions, as a matter of law a jury may not award special damages without accompanying general damages. The rationale behind this rule is that if a conscious, feeling plaintiff (*see* D.3.b, *infra*) suffered tortious physical injury, pain and suffering must necessarily have accompanied it and ought to be compensated. In other jurisdictions, personal injury awards of special damages alone are not per se invalid, but are merely suspect and subject to the applicable standard of review by the court (*see* E.8, *infra*).

REVIEW QUESTIONS

1. Define fair market value.
2. Which method for computing value lacks validity when calculating damages?
   a. Capitalization of Earnings
   b. Book Value
   c. Replacement Cost Less Depreciation
   d. Market Value
3. When seller delivers goods of lower quality than buyer ordered, but buyer decides to keep them, how much damage can buyer collect for the direct loss caused by seller's breach?

a. Cover Price minus Contract Price

b. Market Price minus Contract Price

c. Contract Price minus Market Price

d. Value as Warranted minus the Value as Received

4. P owned an airplane worth $2 million. P hired D to perform some routine maintenance on the plane. While performing the maintenance, D negligently drove a truck into the plane's landing gear, severely damaging that part of the plane. It will take $100,000 to repair the plane. Until it is repaired, it is useless as a plane, though as spare parts it might be sold for $200,000. Once repaired, it will have the same value it had before the injury, minus about $75,000 due to depreciation caused by the age of the plane. How much should P recover for direct loss caused by P?

5. On the facts of question 4, how would your answer differ if the value before the injury was only $200,000, the value of spare parts was $50,000, and the value after repairs and depreciation were only $140,000? (Repairs still cost $100,000.)

6. D foreclosed on land owned by T and sold it at auction to P for $30,000. P had invested about $5,000 in studying the feasibility of building a shopping center on the land. The shopping center might produce profits over the coming years with a present value of $130,000 (after all expenses, including building expenses). Unknown to D, T redeemed the land just before the sale, depriving D of any right to sell it. D, therefore, cannot deliver title to P. Similar parcels of land nearby sell for about $45,000 in the market. How much can P recover from D for direct loss?

7. Which of the following would be compensable in the typical personal injury case?

   a. Emotional distress without accompanying physical injury

   b. Damages for medical monitoring, where plaintiff has no current injury or symptoms

   c. Pain and suffering that accompanies physical injury

   d. Medical costs of $500,000 where plaintiff consciously suffered permanently disfiguring injuries, with no accompanying award for pain and suffering

ANSWERS

1. Fair market value the amount that a willing buyer would give and a willing seller would accept in exchange for the property in an arm's-length transaction, each being reasonably informed and neither being under any compulsion to enter the transaction. [This definition is fairly important; you may want to memorize it.]

2. B.

3. D.

4. P should recover the $100,000 cost of repairs. The plane is nearly worthless now, except to someone who wanted to repair it. Repairs, therefore, will add almost $2 million in value to the plane ($1,925,000). Even assuming the plane's current value is the value after repairs minus the cost of repairs ($1,825,000), repairs still restore $100,000 in value to the plane. This case does not meet any of the criteria for rejecting cost of repairs as a measure of loss in value.

5. The case here becomes much closer. On the traditional test, the cost of repair is less than the value before the injury, suggesting that repairs are recoverable. But investing $100,000 to increase the value of the plane by only $90,000 seems wasteful.

On the other hand, value before minus value after would require defendant to pay $150,000 ($200,000–$50,000 value as spare parts). Defendant is unlikely to oppose an award of $100,000 for repairs unless she can persuade the court to evaluate plaintiff's position but for the wrong on the date of judgment (or the date repairs would be completed). But for the wrong, P would have owned a plane worth $140,000 (because it would have depreciated even if uninjured). Instead, P has a plane worth at least $50,000 as spare parts. (No one seems likely to buy the plane for purposes of repairing it.) The true loss is only $90,000. However, P might not have suffered the depreciation if P had sold the plane for $200,000 shortly after the injury—a realistic possibility, if D hadn't damaged the plane making it unsalable at that time. Focus on the date of the injury may be justified.

If you noted that P may also recover for ensuing loss, since it could not use the plane pending repairs, you are correct, though the question asked you to focus on direct loss. If you noted that these numbers don't make sense, you again are correct. How does damage to the landing gear require repairs worth half the price of the plane? And how long would the repairs have to take for the plane to depreciate 30% in the interim? The numbers don't make a lot of sense.

6. If D had title, P could claim specific performance, eliminating the need to calculate damages. The damage issue begins with finding out whether this state follows the English or American rule. If the English rule, P may collect only $5,000 spent on the study—and that only if it was spent in reliance on the sale. If P spent the money before buying the land, D's promise to sell the land did not cause the investment. (D's breach turned an investment that seemed about to pay off into one that was worthless, but that may not fit the English rule.)

   Under the American rule, P recovers market value minus contract price (because P need not pay the contract price and can recover any amount already paid). Market value appears to be $45,000, based on similar plots. Thus, at least $15,000 should be recoverable. But P believes this land would return $130,000. Viewed as P's lost profit on the land, the damages are ensuing loss, not direct loss, and probably would be denied because they were unforeseeable to D—both points covered in other sections of this chapter. But the prospective income flow also represents a stream of earnings, allowing the value to be calculated under the capitalization of earnings technique. If the court will accept the survey as evidence of the fair market value based on capitalization of earnings, P might recover as much as $100,000. (Capitalization of earnings may be harder to justify here, since it does not involve earnings from the land as purchased, but from improvements on the land that P intends to build. Thus, the earnings are not really of the asset D refused to provide, but of the way P intended to use the asset D refused to provide. This probably crosses the line into ensuing loss.)

7. C.

C. Ensuing Loss (Consequential Damages, Loss of Use)

Often, awarding the plaintiff the direct loss will not place him in the position he would have occupied if the wrong had not occurred. Repairing a damaged car or house does not compensate for the inability to use the property while repairs are performed. Buying substitute goods may not compensate for the inability to use (or resell) the promised goods between the promised delivery date and the time plaintiff manages to cover. In short, replacing the thing lost does not always cover the inability to use the thing for a period of time. And where replacement is impossible—as with many physical injuries—loss of use may be the primary element of damage.

1. Terminology

Different words describe ensuing losses depending on the context. In contract, the inability to use the goods is called consequential damages or the more specific lost profits. In tort, especially property torts, the ensuing loss is called loss of use; again, lost profits are a common example, though the cost to rent replacement property (and thus avoid losing profits) often suffices. In personal injury actions, courts usually refer to loss of earning potential or loss of income, specific examples of ensuing losses, rather than use a general name for ensuing losses.

2. Failure to Pay Money: Interest as Damages

When defendant's breach deprives plaintiff of money, a judgment that only includes the amount owed would fall short of plaintiff's rightful position. Receiving money after trial is not nearly the same as receiving the same amount of money when it originally should have been received. Without damages for ensuing loss, defendant in effect receives an interest-free loan of whatever amount it owes plaintiff. On the other hand, allowing plaintiff to prove exactly how much she would have gained if the money had been paid on time—such as by identifying an investment that, with 20-20 hindsight, would have been exceptionally profitable—puts defendants at risk for large and sometimes imaginary losses plaintiffs claim to have suffered. The law balances these concerns with rules that limit plaintiffs to interest on the amount due.

Traditionally, courts apply two different rules to late payments. One states that consequential damages are not available for failure to pay money. The other states that prejudgment interest is available for damages if the amount is liquidated—that is, either a sum certain or an amount capable of calculation once the inputs are known (such as price and quantity), even if disputes about the inputs require resolution by the finder of fact. These two rules combine into a single general rule: consequential damages for failure to pay money are limited to interest on the sum that should have been paid.

a. Rationale and Critique

Failure to pay money arguably does not prevent a plaintiff from using the money as planned. Rather, nonpayment forces plaintiff to find a substitute source of money—that is, a loan. Plaintiff then can invest the borrowed money as planned and earn the same profit (or loss) that she would have earned if the wrong had not occurred. The loss caused by defendant is measured by the interest on the loan, not by the return on the investment.

In effect, this is an application of the avoidable consequences doctrine. *See* E.3, *infra*. Plaintiff could minimize the loss by borrowing money and using it as planned. Failure to do so caused the losses to be larger than necessary, thus limiting plaintiff to the interest she would have had to pay on the loan. (In cases where defendant breached a promise to loan money, the difference between the cost of the original loan and the cost of the substitute loan would be the loss.) Note how this turns the ensuing loss into direct loss. The loss of use of the money no longer measures the loss; the loss of the money itself is the measure.

The rationale suffers from two problems. First, it assumes that plaintiff could have arranged a substitute source of funds in time to pursue the original venture. Some plaintiffs cannot borrow at all, others may be unable to replace the money in time to pursue the lost investment. The rule here eliminates the inquiry into the reasonableness of plaintiff's failure to replace the money and to avoid the investment losses. Under the avoidable consequences doctrine, defendant would bear the burden of proof on that matter. Second, it assumes that interest rates awarded in court will reflect the rates plaintiffs would need to pay—or, in some cases, actually did pay—in order to borrow money. Prejudgment interest rates typically are fixed by statutes, without regard to the amount plaintiff actually paid. Some statutes point to a market rate (such as 90-day Treasury Bills), some of which may approximate the cost to borrow funds. If interest rates reflect the amount plaintiff could have earned on the money (if it had been paid on time), the interest awarded may be much lower than the interest the rationale justifies.

b. Prejudgment and Post-Judgment Interest

All judgments earn post-judgment interest—that is, interest from the date of judgment to the date of payment. This rule operates as an incentive for defendant to pay on the judgment as soon as possible. Prejudgment interest covers the period from the date of the injury to the date of judgment. The rationale for prejudgment interest is to create an incentive for a wrongdoer to pay the wronged party without resort to litigation.

Many courts order recovery of prejudgment interest only if the claim is liquidated, meaning where the amount of plaintiff's loss could be ascertained, either as a sum certain or by application of a simple formula. This approach allows prejudgment interest on claims involving property and in contract cases involving a definite sum of money or good that have a fixed or easily ascertainable value. In tort claims, this approach allows recovery of prejudgment interest on pecuniary damages, but denies interest on pain and suffering, emotional distress, or injury to reputation.

The rule may relate to the rationale above. *See* C.2.a, *supra*. Borrowing an ascertainable amount makes sense, but borrowing a completely indeterminate amount may not. In any event, the limitation to liquidated claims precludes prejudgment interest in many cases. Plaintiff bears the cost immediately, but recovers the cost later without compensation for the time value of the money (or other loss). The defendant benefits from an interest free loan for as long as judgment can be deferred.

Throughout the Twentieth Century, courts began to abandon the rule limiting prejudgment interest to liquidated claims and pecuniary damages. The RESTATEMENT THIRD OF TORTS: REMEDIES § 14 thus provides for prejudgment interest in all tort cases "at a reasonable market rate . . . from the date or dates the damage was incurred (or a reasonable approximation thereof) to the date of judgment," explaining in a comment that: "Awarding interest on all or most tort damages is the clear trend of decisions and the better rule, and it has become the majority rule."

c. Exceptions

In jurisdictions that retain the traditional rule, its shortcomings have produced a number of exceptions. While some cases fit general patterns, others are more ad hoc.

(1) Bad Faith

When a party who owes money lacks a good faith justification for not paying, courts may award damages that exceed interest. Insurers are particularly prone to judgments of this sort. Courts often allow consequential damages for a bad faith refusal to pay claims. (Bad faith also may justify emotional distress and punitive damages, despite the rule that these recoveries do not apply to contract actions. Calling bad faith breach of insurance contracts a tort circumvents these restrictions.) The same result applies when liability insurers use bad faith in refusing to settle litigation against the insured. Consequential damages typically include the entire judgment against the insured, even if it exceeds the policy limits specified in the insurance contract. No limitation to interest on the amount not paid remains. Other cases of bad faith, especially bad faith by banks that refuse to let depositors withdraw their money, extend the principle. Bad faith refusal to settle a lawsuit occasionally produces a judgment in excess of the amount owed. These other examples have not achieved the widespread acceptance of insurance cases.

(2) Lenders

Some states have recognized liability for lenders who refuse to fund specific projects. Here, the investment opportunity is contemplated by both parties. Plaintiff must prove losses to that project; she cannot identify some other investment that might have proven profitable. For example, where defendant breaches a promise to provide plaintiff a mortgage for purchase of specific land, consequential damages may include appreciation on the land. This principle could be extended to other investors, such as partnerships. In most cases, however, the lost investment has been relatively easy to measure. Real estate investments, where appraisal is fairly standard and reliable, produce judgments for ensuing losses more readily than business investments, where the profit on the business might be difficult to prove.

(3) Actual Interest Losses

Where the evidence establishes the amount of interest plaintiff actually lost, courts sometimes substitute that amount for interest at the legal rate. In effect, this recognizes the original project: to put plaintiff in the position she would have occupied if the wrong had not occurred. The interest plaintiff actually paid to replace the money hews closer to the general rule of damages, occasionally supplanting the simplifying assumptions noted above. *See* C.2.a, *supra.*

3. Loss of Use

When anything has been damaged or destroyed, the inability to use the thing pending repair or replacement is an ensuing loss. Loss of use usually is measured one of three ways. First, where a temporary substitute can be obtained, the cost of that substitute (typically, rental cost) will be awarded. Second, where a temporary substitute cannot be obtained, the loss of profits plaintiff would have earned with the original may be awarded. Where lost profits are unavailable (usually because uncertain), the lost rental value—the amount plaintiff might have received for renting out the thing, not the amount it would have cost plaintiff to rent a substitute—may be awarded. All three measures share a focus: how much is it worth to have the property for a period of time? Repair or replacement eventually restores the property itself to the plaintiff; but the value of losing the property for these few days requires additional recovery.

a. Cost of a Temporary Substitute

If plaintiff can obtain a temporary substitute for the property, to cover the time between injury and repair or replacement, courts usually award the cost of a reasonable substitute transaction. Rental cars or even cabs may substitute for a damaged car pending repair or replacement. A hotel or apartment may substitute for a house pending repair or replacement. A temporary employee may substitute for a regular employee pending his return or replacement. In each case, any amount saved in the interim (say, the wages the regular employee would have made, the gas needed to run the original car) would offset the losses. The net loss (the difference in salary, the difference in fuel costs) would be recoverable, not the gross temporary costs.

This rule tends to be the preferred measure. A substitute often avoids any lost profits or other consequences of the loss, which may be required by the avoidable consequences doctrine. *See* E.3, *infra.* The cost of a substitute usually can be ascertained relatively easily by looking at the market or, better still, at the actual substitute transaction plaintiff made. Lost profits, on the other hand, can be difficult to measure. Similarly, if no substitutes are available in the market, estimating the amount plaintiff could have obtained in the market by renting the one she had poses difficult issues.

(1) Reasonable and in Good Faith

As with cover transactions discussed earlier, *See* B.3.a.(1), *supra*, the amount recoverable for a substitute must be reasonable and in good faith. When plaintiff does not make substitute arrangements, the market price of a reasonable substitute should prevent excessive damages. But if plaintiff makes an actual substitute transaction, courts will award the actual cost only if it is reasonable and in good faith. If the substitute either gives the plaintiff more than she had before or costs the defendant more than necessary, the court may not allow the full cost of the substitute.

For example, a substitute of vastly superior quality may be unreasonable. But even a vastly superior substitute may be reasonable if it is the least expensive substitute that is at least as good as the original. For instance, few rental companies carry 20-year-old cars. To obtain a substitute, plaintiff may be forced to rent a better (at least newer) vehicle.

Similarly, paying more than the market price for a substitute may be unreasonable—though plaintiff need not find the least expensive substitute, only a reasonable substitute, one within the range of prices acceptable in the market. (More time looking for a better substitute price may increase both the cost of seeking a substitute and the losses pending the arrival of the substitute. A deal may be good enough to make it unnecessary to keep looking for a better price.)

b. Lost Profits

For any period during which a plaintiff reasonably cannot obtain a temporary substitute, any losses caused by being deprived of the thing are recoverable. Where the thing generated income, lost profit provides a measure of the damage to plaintiff during the interim. For example, manufacturing equipment sometimes is so specialized it cannot be rented. If defendant injures plaintiff's equipment, forcing a plant to shut down for three weeks pending repairs, production for the year may be lower than it would have been but for the wrong. Assuming plaintiff would have sold all that it produced, the inability to produce during those three weeks reduced sales and profits.

In some cases, profits may be delayed rather than lost. That is, additional effort after the substitute is obtained may provide as much profit as plaintiff would have received if no deprivation ever occurred. For example, once a machine is back in service, a manufacturer may be able to increase production for a few days, eventually selling as much product as it would have but for the injury. If no sales were lost and no costs increased (e.g., no overtime to increase output), the profit may have been delayed rather than lost. (Unlike the previous example, this one assumes demand is limited: plaintiff could not sell all it produced, but only a certain amount per year. If plaintiff could have sold both the production from the lost days and the increased output later, it is a lost volume seller; the later production did not substitute for the earlier production, since plaintiff could have done both and earned even more profit.)

c. Rental Value

Where no substitute was available and no profits lost—or lost profits cannot be proven—courts still need to assess loss of use. Some suggest recourse to the amount that plaintiff could have gained by renting the property to another. This may be hard to ascertain. If a rental market were available, the first measure (cost for plaintiff to rent) would apply. Thus, courts may need to use the capitalization of earnings technique to appraise the rental value. This technique estimates how much a reasonable person would pay to rent property by evaluating how much profit the person could earn with the property. In effect, this is the lost profits technique, but focused on some other (hypothetical lessee's) profit instead of the actual profit lost by the individual plaintiff. To the extent that plaintiff claims an unusual profit, moving to a hypothetical lessee may limit damages. More commonly, the technique allows courts to estimate profits that plaintiff cannot prove with reasonable certainty.

d. Archaic Limitations

Traditionally, loss of use was available when property was damaged, but not when it was destroyed. The implication was that it takes time to repair property, but no time to replace it. Recently, courts have recognized the error of this assumption and have begun awarding loss of use for damaged or destroyed property. To the extent that replacement takes less time than repair, loss of use will be smaller in these cases, but not denied.

Similarly, courts traditionally capped recovery for loss of use at the value of the damaged property. The rule has some basis. If the cost to replace the property is less than the cost of a substitute pending repairs, a reasonable person probably would replace rather than repair the property—at least if they were spending their own money instead of another's. Thus, ensuing loss might affect the decision regarding the reasonableness of undertaking repairs in the first place. *See* B.2.b, *supra*. In some cases, however, repairs may be a reasonable choice, but delays drive up the damages for loss of use. To limit recovery for loss of use would leave plaintiff in a worse position than if defendant had never damaged the property in the first place. The remedial goal does not support this limitation in all cases. Courts are beginning to recognize this problem and treat cases individually, rather than mechanically apply the traditional cap to all cases.

4. Lost Profits

A wrong may deprive the plaintiff of something that is more valuable to the plaintiff than it is to the market. Sometimes that surplus will be measurable in the value of the thing itself, particularly when plaintiff simply values having the thing (as a collector might). Often, however, the value to the plaintiff reflects the way the plaintiff intended to use the thing. The use would have generated additional benefits to plaintiff. Where the additional benefits take the form of money, plaintiff suffers lost profits.

Courts historically exhibited some reluctance to award lost profits. The further removed from the value of the thing itself, the more other factors intervene to limit the loss. Courts found rationalizations for this reluctance: causation, remoteness, uncertainty, foreseeability, avoidability, etc. Most of the surviving doctrines are addressed below. *See* E, *infra*. Today, as long as the evidence sufficiently establishes that, but for the wrong, plaintiff would have benefited from the project, ensuing losses are permissible.

a. Losses to a Project

Lost profits can be directly related to the asset defendant injured. Thus, destroying (or failing to deliver) items that plaintiff intended to resell directly deprives plaintiff of the resale profits. In other cases, the use may be less direct. The item may be one input into a larger project. For instance, a plaintiff may buy or rent land as part of a business (whether farming, ranching, retail, or manufacturing). If defendant deprives plaintiff of the land, the entire project may suffer. Simply awarding the value of the land may not restore the plaintiff to the position she would have occupied if the wrong had not occurred. Similarly, when plaintiff intends to use defendant's services as part of a larger project, depriving plaintiff of those services may threaten an entire project (whether a movie, a concert, a lecture, or some other service). In some cases, direct loss will permit plaintiff to replace the key element in time to prevent loss to the venture. When that is not possible, loss to the project, not just loss of the services, is necessary to put plaintiff in the rightful position.

b. Limitations Significant

The legitimacy of awarding lost profits has been recognized in almost every context. The most important issues surround concerns that profits might be exaggerated. Thus, the limitations on remedies, discussed below at E, take on great significance in this context. Thus, where a plaintiff could avoid losing profits by reasonable use of substitutes, profits may be limited. Where the profits claimed were unforeseeably large, recovery may be limited. Where the evidence of lost profits leaves uncertainty, profits may be limited. Where the link between the wrong and the lost profits becomes too remote, profits may be limited. Naturally, any loss that would have been suffered despite the breach will not be included in recovery.

(1) Measurement

Aside from the limitations, the only issue of lost profits involves accurately measuring them. The issues tend to involve accounting rather than law. The goal is accurate calculation. The arguments center on the accuracy of revenue projections, the inclusion of all appropriate costs, allowance for any costs saved as a result of the wrong, proper calculation of overhead, and similar issues. Watch carefully for ways in which plaintiffs seek double compensation, including in lost profits elements already compensated in other components of the remedy.

(2) Present Value and Inflation

Any profit that would have been earned in the years following judgment must be reduced to present value. Plaintiff will be able to invest the award and earn returns on it. Present value estimates how much the plaintiff must receive today in order to have the right amount, after investment income, in the year the profit would have been earned. For example, suppose that plaintiff would have earned $100,000 in profit in the third year after judgment and can invest the money safely at a 4% return. If awarded the full $100,000 in the judgment, after two years she would have $108,160—more than the profit she would have earned in the third year. Instead, the court should award $92,455.62. After two years at 4%, this will produce $100,000, the amount plaintiff deserves in the third year. On the other hand, any money paid now will be worth less over the course of time due to the likelihood of inflation. This requires an upward adjustment to the verdict. For additional discussion of the methods by which courts deal with these factors, *see* C.5.c *infra.*

5. Lost Earning Potential

The primary ensuing loss physical injuries produce is lost earning potential. This can include the temporary lost earnings when a wrong prevents work, whether while the body heals or simply because the wrong delayed the plaintiff. Those costs are relatively easy to calculate and uncontroversial. More significant are the lost earnings from a long-term disability that prevents plaintiff from pursuing her career. The same calculation issues can arise from breach of an employment contract, wrongful discharge torts, or discrimination suits.

a. Future Increases

Earnings are not limited to the plaintiff's current income or even the plaintiff's current job. In some cases, especially children, earning potential may have been destroyed before plaintiff's career path was set. While certainty issues arise, some effort to project future income is required. Even when plaintiff's career choices seem fixed, variations such as promotions, transfers, and raises require attention.

b. Ending Liability

The period for which defendant is liable will vary with the wrong and the injury.

(1) Permanent Disability

Where plaintiff is permanently disabled from any work, the issue focuses on determining when the plaintiff would have retired. Some experts rely on actuarial tables showing work-life expectancy, which projects how many months a plaintiff would have worked during the rest of her life. The projections include not only retirement, but also the likelihood that layoffs or other events that might interrupt the plaintiff's work life, reducing the number of months during which she earned income.

(2) Temporary Disability

Some injuries leave plaintiff able to resume work—either after rehabilitation or by changing careers to one he can still perform. This raises two issues: when will plaintiff return to work?; and how much will he earn after returning? The first involves estimates of the time required to recover from the injury or to retrain for a more suitable position. For the period before return, plaintiff should recover full lost wages (subject to avoided or avoidable consequences).

Income after return to work poses fewer difficulties when plaintiff returns to the same career path. Income may follow the same pattern it would have followed but for the wrong, in effect eliminating losses following return. In some cases, however, a period of absence will set plaintiff behind on the career path, so that earnings after return will not equal the earnings he would have had if service had not been interrupted. (Seniority may be lower, promotion may be slower, etc.) As a result, some residual losses may exist even if plaintiff returns to the same job. These should be included in the damage calculation: but for the wrong, plaintiff would have received more income in those years.

Where plaintiff changes careers, projecting earnings in the new career may be more difficult. That is particularly true if the new career has large variations in income potential. (Consider the differences between starting salaries in big law firms, small law firms, government offices, and public interest law groups.) If the projected new income stream is lower than the projected original income stream, then residual losses should be included in the damage calculation. When the new income stream is greater than the old, differences arise in the treatment. The benefit rule would permit the increased income to offset some of the other harms caused by the wrong. *See* E.2.d, *infra*. Alternatively, courts may decide that liability ends at the time plaintiff recovers from the injury, as indicated by resuming work at a higher income. No further losses or gains require calculation thereafter. The latter approach is a double-edged sword, cutting off both subsequent harms and subsequent gains. Where medical expenses or pain would continue past reemployment, seeking to cut off liability at that date may be disadvantageous for plaintiff.

(3) Discharge from Employment

Discharge does not disable the plaintiff but merely deprives her of income from one employer. The period during which defendant remains liable for the loss varies with context. In contract claims, the contract duration term will set the end of liability. Having not promised income to the plaintiff past a certain date, losses after that date are not attributable to the wrong. (Where the contract does not specify an end date, it is terminable at will by either party, so discharge usually is not a breach at all.) In tort claims and discrimination claims, the duration is not so easily fixed. With no date upon which employment would have ended but for the wrong, defendant's liability could continue indefinitely. This probably is unrealistic; assuming that defendant never would have fired plaintiff for a legitimate reason is a bit harsh. Effectively it turns defendant into a guarantor of plaintiff's future employment—something plaintiff never could claim but for the breach.

One technique is to allow the avoidable consequences doctrine to fix the end. Once plaintiff obtains substitute employment of similar nature, defendant's liability ends. *See Ford Motor Co. v. EEOC*, 458 U.S. 219, 102 S.Ct. 3057, 73 L.Ed.2d 721 (1982). The approach poses problems. First, it may not include recovery if substitute work pays less than the position with defendant. Second, it may extend recovery for long periods of time, where plaintiff does not find substitute work despite reasonable efforts.

c. Present Value and Inflation

As with lost profits, future wages (and future medical expenses, although in most jurisdictions *not* future nonpecuniary damages—the Third Torts RESTATEMENT § 15 defines the relevant damages as those "that can be valued by prices in a market") require discounting to present value. Awarding full future wages today would overcompensate plaintiff, once he earned investment income on the award. Simultaneously, the likelihood of inflation means that plaintiff will be undercompensated by a present recovery of future earnings. Several techniques have been devised for adjusting for these factors, usually in an effort to simplify calculations and increase accuracy. Each technique will be discussed here. But first, a simple example of the procedure appears.

(1) The Procedure

The calculation below assumes that plaintiff earned $50,000 a year at the time judgment and that plaintiff's income would have increased by 5% per year until retirement five years after the judgment. (Note: this calculation covers only the years after the judgment. For income lost before judgment, prejudgment interest should be added to reflect plaintiff's inability to invest—or need to borrow—this money up to the date of judgment.) It also assumes that plaintiff can invest the award at a rate of 2%. These assumptions would need to be supported by facts and expert testimony, such as evidence that income had risen by an average of 5% for the last several years and that interest rates were likely to average 2% for the coming years. On these assumptions:

Year	Salary	Discount	Award
Judgment + 1	$ 52,500.00	0.98039216	$ 51,470.59
Judgment + 2	$ 55,125.00	0.96116878	$ 52,984.43
Judgment + 3	$ 57,881.25	0.94232233	$ 54,542.79
Judgment + 4	$ 60,775.31	0.92384543	$ 56,146.99
Judgment + 5	$ 63,814.08	0.90573081	$ 57,798.38
Total	$290,095.64		$272,943.18

The Salary column shows the amount plaintiff actually would have earned. The Discount column is a number pulled from a table of discount rates. Multiplying Salary times Discount gives an amount that, if invested at 2% for the number of years available (one for Judgment + 1, five for Judgment +5, etc.), will produce a total equal to the Salary column. In other words, if awarded $272,942.95. Plaintiff can invest it at 2% and, after one year, withdraw $52.500, after two years withdraw $55,125, etc. After the fifth year, when she withdraws $63,814.08, nothing will be left. Plaintiff will have withdrawn $290,095.64 over the years, exactly what she would have earned if the wrong had not occurred.

(2) Traditional Method

The example above uses the traditional method. It projects actual increases in future wages and discounts by an actual interest rate at which the plaintiff might invest. Thus, increases in wages include increases for inflation and the interest rate includes an amount believed necessary to account for inflation. This introduces two problems. First, inflation is not constant. Projections based on the current inflation rate may underestimate or overestimate actual increases in income. Second, projections of investment income may be too high or too low, as changes in inflation produce interest rates that are higher or lower than those used in calculating present value. If plaintiff's investments perform better or worse than the rate assumed in the present value calculation, then the compensation may be excessive or inadequate. Because inflation is very hard to project, especially over long periods, the likelihood of accurately assessing damages may be quite small. Despite these concerns, the traditional method has been accepted by many courts.

(3) Partial Offset Method

The partial offset method seeks to remove inflation from the calculation of present value. In projecting future income and interest rates, it projects real increases—that is, the extent to which increases in income and long-term interest rates exceed the inflation rate. Income increases in excess of inflation are sometimes referred to as productivity increases, reflecting the tendency of wages to increase as productivity (in a particular industry or the economy as a whole) increases. Thus, rather than increasing income by 5%, it would project income increases at 5% minus the rate of inflation. For example, if inflation had been about 2%, it would project income increases at 3%, the rate at which real income increased. Similarly, in discounting income, the method would project the long-term real interest rate—the difference between interest rates and inflation rates, over the long term. While plaintiff might earn 2% on an investment, some of that would offset inflation. The real interest rate might be 1% or so. (If inflation has been at 2%, the implication is that, in the short term, no interest has been charged on money. That rate is unstable; people will demand more than a break-even interest rate on their investments over time, even if temporarily the interest rate equals the inflation rate. This kind of anomaly illustrates why the long-term real interest rate is used.) Thus, our calculation above might look something like this:

Year	Salary	Discount	Award
Judgment + 1	$ 51,500.00	0.99009901	$ 50,990.10
Judgment + 2	$ 53,045.00	0.98029605	$ 51,999.80
Judgment + 3	$ 54,636.35	0.97059015	$ 53,029.50
Judgment + 4	$ 56,275.44	0.96098034	$ 54,079.59
Judgment + 5	$ 57,963.70	0.95146569	$ 55,150.48
Total	$273,420.49		$265,249.47

The calculation produces a slightly smaller award on these assumptions. In part, that reflects the use of a long-term interest (1%) rather than the short-term real interest rate (0%, where inflation of 2% eats up the entire 2% investment income). On different assumptions, the result could be larger rather than smaller. Both the traditional and partial offset methods have been approved, but not compelled, by the U.S. Supreme Court. *See Jones & Laughlin Steel Corp. v. Pfeifer*, 462 U.S. 523, 103 S.Ct. 2541, 76 L.Ed.2d 768 (1983).

Note: Plaintiff will invest $265,249.47 at a market rate, higher than the 1% used to calculate present value. Thus, she can withdraw more than $273,420.49 over the years. The additional amounts reflect inflation, both of wages and interest rates. If inflation affects wages and interest rates equally, the excess amount of investment income will roughly equal the amount inflation would have increased her wages.

(4) Total Offset Method

The total offset method assumes that real increases in wages will exactly match real interest rates. If so, it becomes unnecessary to project increases and discount to present value. Instead, just multiplying current wages by the number of years of remaining work will produce a reasonable estimate of future wages. In this example, the award would be $250,000—current income times five years. The method is acceptable, if the parties stipulate to it. But it cannot typically be forced on either party over its objection.

(5) Selecting an Interest Rate

The interest rate selected has a significant effect on present value calculations. The larger the interest rate, the lower the damage award; a large interest rate assumes plaintiff will earn more money by investing the award, requiring less initial money from defendant to make plaintiff whole. As a result, plaintiffs seek to keep the interest rate small while defendants seek to use a larger interest rate. Because the interest rate reflects investments, that means defendants urge investments that produce large returns on capital, while plaintiffs urge the use of interest rates that reflect smaller returns. Using a smaller return overcompensates plaintiff if she then invests the money at a higher rate of return. But using a larger interest rate undercompensates plaintiff unless she invests the money at a higher rate of return. Because higher rates of return often involve higher risk, a plaintiff who invests at these rates may lose money, facing undercompensation. As a result, courts normally instruct the jury to employ an interest rate that allows plaintiff to invest safely—that is, at a lower interest rate. The factfinder typically hears testimony on the relevant rates by expert economists and chooses rates that it deems most accurate.

d. Issues of Race and Gender

Disparities in income and longevity based on gender and race continue to exist in America. Should such disparities be reflected in jury awards in personal injury cases? For example, in estimating lost wages of an African-American decedent, should the jury be allowed to consider evidence that the average African-American lives four fewer years than the average Caucasian and earns 59 percent of what the average Caucasian is paid? How about evidence that the average woman earns 77 percent of what the average man is paid, a gap that grows with age and also exists for women without children? In calculating future lost wages, courts often provide juries with charts reflecting average wages in specific fields throughout an average worker's career. Some charts are broken down by gender and race; others are not. As a matter of public policy, many courts have refused race or gender-specific wage and life-expectancy information, instead requiring an average or upper-end range. Nonetheless, it has been clearly documented that juries award lower damages, on average, to women and people of color. *See* Martha Chamallas & Jennifer B. Wriggins, THE MEASURE OF INJURY: RACE, GENDER AND TORT LAW (New York University Press, 2010). For these reasons, the RESTATEMENT THIRD OF TORTS: REMEDIES § 19, cmt. h provides that average wages and life expectancy should be determined on the basis of data for all Americans, not predicated on a plaintiff's race or sex.

REVIEW QUESTIONS

1. When a buyer of goods takes delivery of them but fails to pay for them, seller may recover the price plus ensuing losses measured by:

   a. The amount of interest seller paid or would have paid to borrow the money at market rates.

   b. The gains on the investment seller would have made with the money, provided the project can be identified with sufficient certainty.

   c. Nothing, because ensuing losses are not allowed for nonpayment of money.

   d. The statutory rate for prejudgment interest.

2. P parked his car—an older car, worth about $2,000—in D's garage. P returned for the car before the posted closing time, but D had already locked the garage for the night. P paid $30 to take a cab home and returned for the car the next day, but D insisted on charging P for a second day of parking. P refused to pay beyond the time he tried to remove his car the night before. D refused to allow the car out of the garage until P paid. P parked the car, paid $10 to take a cab to a lawyer's office, and

thereafter rented a car as similar to the one P owned as the rental agency offered—about 9 years newer than P's car, but the same size and quality. P paid $25 a day for the car. Meanwhile, the lawyer demanded release of P's car and, after D refused, filed suit seeking an injunction ordering D to release P's car. After 100 days (of rental car payments), the court finally ordered D to release P's car, but retained jurisdiction to determine whether either party could collect damages from the other. How much, if anything, can P recover from D if the court determines D's retention of P's car was wrongful.

a. $2,540, because P acted reasonably to minimize the loss

b. $2,000, because loss of use cannot exceed the value of P's car

c. The cost of a car similar to P's on the day P consulted a lawyer, minus the amount P could have sold a substitute car for on the day P's car was returned.

d. Nothing, because P's car was not destroyed

e. Nothing, because P's expenses exceed the value of P's car

ANSWERS

1. D.

2. A. C is a reasonable answer, if P had known from the outset that it would take 100 days (or even 80) to get his car back. It certainly would have been cheaper to buy a $2000 car and resell it when P got his own back. But if P reasonably believed that the preliminary injunction would be issued before 80 days of rentals (the $2000 mark), renting a car might have kept damages lower. Other issues under the avoidable consequences doctrine could arise. Was it reasonable to rent a much newer car? Maybe, if older cars were not available for rent or if the older cars available were less reliable than P's car. Should P have paid D and sued to recover the overcharge? Maybe, especially since P needed to sue D either way. But getting the car back might have been quicker, since preliminary injunctions don't usually take as long as a final judgment on damages. And perhaps P preferred not to bring the action in small claims court, where a small overcharge would be handled, but wanted a more experienced judge, as the injunction would require. Like retreat rules in self-defense, perhaps giving in to bullies is not required, even by the avoidable consequences doctrine.

D. Intangible Loss

Pain, distress, and indignity are real. Most people would prefer to live without them rather than suffer through them. But few people have the chance to bargain their way out of these harms. Thus, no market sets the price for pain, distress, and indignity. The resulting difficulty of calculation can produce awards that are wildly excessive or wildly inadequate. With no benchmark against which to compare the award, no one can say whether an award is too high, too low, or just right. This section discusses some of the techniques that have been or might be used to bring a measure of order to intangible losses. It starts with one important observation: zero is the one amount we know is wrong. When plaintiff really did suffer pain, an award that excludes all compensation for pain cannot pretend to put him in the position he would have occupied but for the wrong. While some despair of ever finding the right number, so far courts have not resorted to the one number they know is wrong.

1. Terminology

The terms used in dealing with harms we feel is not precise. Thus, different writers will use the terms different ways. The definitions here attempt to offer some sense of how the terms are used. Pain refers to the unpleasant (or worse) physical sensation felt as a result of a physical injury. Suffering refers to both pain and the unpleasant (or worse) thoughts that accompany a physical injury. Thus, suffering includes thoughts about the injury. This may include the anticipation of future pain, worry about supporting one's self or family, worry about how to pay doctors, despair over disabilities (related either to work or to leisure activities), and a myriad of other thoughts that may plague a victim of physical injury. Distress refers to unpleasant (or worse) thoughts unaccompanied by a physical injury to the distressed person. Thus, relatives of an injured person may suffer distress. So may individuals exposed to insults, libel, humiliation, or other indignities. Loss of joy (or lost enjoyment of life) refers to the reduced ability to experience joy. It may result from injuries that preclude awareness of the joys of life, but also applies to disabilities that prevent a person from participating in activities that previously provided joy.

2. Subjective Value

Market value is objective value—the amount a reasonable person would pay. Often, items have greater value to one person than to the market. That value to the individual is subjective value. Examples include wedding photos, pets, or the family farm. Few others would pay much for your wedding photo or your cat; for the farm, market value might be higher. But you might refuse enormous sums for any of these because these things bring you more joy than the money could provide. When defendant deprives plaintiff of property she values more than the market, compensation at the market rate may not make plaintiff as well off as she would have been but for the wrong.

Subjective value can apply to almost any property plaintiff was not actively trying to sell. The preference to keep the property may reflect a value that exceeds what plaintiff thought she could receive in exchange for the property.

a. Danger of Overcompensation

When plaintiff alleges that the property had special value to him, the claim is hard to prove or to disprove unless plaintiff recently rejected a bona fide offer for the property. Thus, an award based on subjective value may leave plaintiff better off than if the wrong had not occurred. Consider two examples.

Defendant damaged plaintiff's car, worth $10,000 before the injury but only $3,000 after. Repairs will cost $15,000, but plaintiff argues repair is justified because the car has special value to him. If allowed to recover $15,000, plaintiff might repair the car, achieving the position but for the wrong. But plaintiff might instead sell the car for $3,000 and use that money plus the award to buy an $18,000 car. If so, plaintiff is better off than if the wrong had not occurred: he should have a $10,000 car in good condition; instead he has an $18,000 car.

Defendant destroyed plaintiff's antique watch, which had a market value of $1,000. Plaintiff claims that watch was worth more to him, because it had belonged to his great grandfather. If true, awarding subjective value would compensate plaintiff. But if plaintiff really doesn't care about the watch and would have sold it if offered the opportunity, anything more than $1,000 makes plaintiff better off than if the wrong had not occurred.

Because defendant has little chance to counter plaintiff's testimony concerning subjective value, overcompensation is hard to prevent. Courts are wary of accepting every estimate plaintiff offers of the value of property, even if the claim seems credible.

b. Measuring Subjective Value

Confronted with claims that property has subjective value, courts try to measure that value in several ways. Techniques include: (a) market value; (b) cost to replace or reproduce; (c) value to the plaintiff; (d) emotional distress. The last is not really an effort to measure subjective value, but to employ a different approach to the cases.

(1) Market Value

Market value is not a measure of subjective value, but a rejection of it. The effect is to deny subjective value for any good available in the market. This will not apply to unique items, such as photographs, keepsakes, heirlooms, etc. But it might apply to claims that a car has sentimental value if the same year and model is available on the market.

(2) Cost to Replace or to Reproduce

In some cases, property with sentimental value can be reproduced. For instance, if the wedding photographer has the negatives, new prints can be made to replace those destroyed by defendant. The new prints will have a market value near zero (to anyone but the plaintiffs). Awarding the cost to reproduce the property provides better compensation. Plaintiff has what she had before (wedding pictures of her wedding, though not the original prints). Damages should not be limited to the (lower) market value the prints would have once made.

(3) Value to the Plaintiff

The value to the owner arguably means the amount for which the owner would sell, if anyone else made that offer. These estimates get outrageously high because they cannot be subjected to market scrutiny. No one will offer these amounts and plaintiff no longer has the property to sell anyway; thus, we can't put plaintiff to the test to see if he would really reject $50,000 for the wedding pictures and hold out for $1 million.

Some courts limit value to the plaintiff by awarding personal value, but rejecting sentimental value. All subjective value involves some sentiment; the line has been drawn at affected or mawkish sentimentality. This leaves some room for juries to recognize personal value, but leaves some room for courts to reject outrageously large awards.

Another approach focuses on the cost to obtain the item. Some property has a market value less than the cost to get it. In effect, parties who obtain that property lose net worth by exchanging valuable money for things that lack market value. The willingness to enter the transaction in the first place offers some evidence that the goods have subjective value that exceeds the cost to produce them. Wedding pictures must be worth at least the cost to obtain them (and to protect them in an acid free paper album, etc.) Video tapes of family must be worth at least the cost of the blank tape, plus some portion of the cost of a video camera. Compensating the cost to obtain the property provides a minimal estimate of sentimental value.

(4) Emotional Distress

In some cases, courts shift from a discussion of sentimental value into a discussion of distress. Normally, emotional distress over the loss of property would not be compensable—any more than emotional distress over injuries to family members are compensable, absent additional considerations. Courts have awarded distress over damage to property if the damage was malicious or intentional. Thus, when defendant maliciously killed plaintiff's dog, plaintiff might recover for the distress of the act. (Intentional infliction of emotional distress might be sustainable on such facts.) Some courts asked to award the subjective value of a pet—market value, with the possible exception of purebred show animals, probably is much lower than value to the owner—have moved from a discussion of subjective value into a discussion of emotional distress, thus bypassing the issue.

The RESTATEMENT THIRD OF TORTS: REMEDIES § 21 provides that emotional distress damages are recoverable for "an intentional tort that is principally directed at property rights or financial interests, committed under circumstances in which emotional harm is especially likely to result"—although it recognizes that the law is not well settled in this area. The Restatement offers the following example in Comment f:

> Annette was murdered in an apparent street crime. Anonymous sources on social media began circulating the story that Annette had been assassinated in retaliation for leaking sensitive emails from the political organization that had employed her. Her parents and the political organization both vehemently denied the story. Cable TV Network paid Dennis, a private investigator, to volunteer his services to the parents. Dennis entered into an oral contract with them, in which they promised to cooperate with his investigation and he promised to keep his investigation and findings confidential unless they approved the release of some or all of the information. The parents did not know that Network was paying Dennis. Dennis took statements from the parents, learned some facts, and made up others.
>
> Network prepared to break the story that the charges on social media were true, with Dennis as its star source of information. Network induced him to break his promise of confidentiality and to report all his findings, real and fictitious, including statements that the parents had made to him, without the parents' permission. The court found that Network had tortiously interfered with Dennis's contract with the parents. Damaging charges against their daughter, quite possibly false and if false, defamatory, publicized in connection with her untimely death, were especially likely to cause emotional distress.

3. Pain & Suffering

Juries may award a victim of physical injury an amount intended to compensate a for the pain and suffering incurred as a result of the wrong. Trial courts may reject the award if it is against the great weight of the evidence. If a trial court does not remit the award or order a new trial on damages, an appellate court may intervene only if the award is so excessive that it shocks the conscience. Another formulation of this test asks whether the award is so large that it evinces passion, prejudice, corruption, whim, or caprice on the part of the jury. The standard encourages some judges to defer to almost any amount a jury awards. Other judges seek to put more teeth into the test.

a. Consistency with Prior Awards

When an award for pain and suffering seems out of line with prior awards in the same jurisdiction, courts sometimes reject or reduce an award. Thus, when earlier cases involving worse injuries produced smaller judgments for pain, a court may feel comfortable reducing the award. While understandable, the analysis suffers several problems. First, it must account for changing times. The amount appropriate 40 (or even 5) years ago may be inadequate today, whether due to inflation or changing societal values. Second, it assumes, without basis, that the earlier awards were correct. It is just as plausible to argue they were too low and the existing jury just right. Third, it cannot account for individual differences in sensitivity to pain. Pain that some shrug off others find debilitating. Compensation for the same injury the same year might differ based on these differences among people.

b. Limit to Consciousness

Pain and suffering imply some element of awareness. Plaintiffs in a coma may be unable to recover for pain and suffering. Without some consciousness of their state, they may feel no pain and may have no thoughts courts recognize as suffering. Even conscious victims may suffer injuries that involve no pain, such as injuries that sever the nerves that convey pain to the mind. *But see* D.4, *infra*.

c. Inappropriate Arguments at Trial

Appellate courts have been asked, with limited success, to overturn large awards based on the arguments used to inspire juries to make large awards.

(1) Per Diem Arguments

Plaintiffs often suggest that compensation for pain could be calculated using a relatively small amount per day (or hour or week), then multiplying by the number of days plaintiff will suffer the pain. Arguments of this sort are called per diem arguments. Typically, they result in much larger awards for pain than would result from considering the entire period as a whole. Absent any testimony that a day of pain is worth a particular amount, the argument lacks any foundation in the evidence. Absent any market for pain, no evidentiary basis is possible. In addition, small differences in the appropriate amount per day produce large differences when multiplied by many years. On the other hand, without any basis to call one amount wrong and another right, there is no way to assess whether per diem arguments persuade jurors to award too much or prevent them from awarding too little.

Courts generally allow per diem arguments, although often tempered by an instruction to the jury that they are merely arguments and not evidence. *See* RESTATEMENT THIRD OF TORTS: REMEDIES § 20, cmt. f.

(2) Golden Rule Arguments

Plaintiffs sometimes suggest that jurors consider how much they would want if they suffered the plaintiff's injuries. This is called the golden rule argument—award unto plaintiff as you would have others award unto you. By inviting jurors step into plaintiff's shoes, it undermines their role as impartial decisionmakers, evaluating the merits of the argument. As a result, it is almost universally held improper to make golden rule arguments.

d. Statutory Limitations

Some states limit the amount recoverable for nonpecuniary (or noneconomic) losses. For example, California limits recovery in medical malpractice actions to $250,000 in noneconomic losses. (Juries may award more, but judges reduce the award as required by statute.) Other states have declared that similar statutes violate state constitutional provisions. These statutes tend to reflect a political judgment that damages for pain and distress have driven costs (for businesses and insurers) so high that the public as a whole suffers. This has no relationship to the amount of harm plaintiff suffered, but represents an exception to the rule. Without a market for pain or distress, one cannot confidently conclude whether the amounts chosen produce unrealistically low judgments or prevent unrealistically high judgments.

4. Lost Enjoyment of Life (Hedonic Damages)

Not all personal injuries involve pain and suffering. Some may cause nerve damage that prevent a person from feeling pain. For example, spinal cord injuries and injuries that induce coma may eliminate pain. These injuries, however, reduce the capacity for joy. Activities that once brought pleasure (tennis, dancing, perhaps even reading) may be impossible following the injury. To put plaintiff in the position she would have occupied if the wrong had not occurred, compensation for the joy she will not experience seems necessary. Though logical, courts have not settled on a way to handle lost enjoyment of life in damage awards.

a. Separate Element of Damages

Loss of joy is logically distinct from pain and suffering but may be harder to segregate in practice. A person in pain nonetheless may experience the same joys she always felt. An unconscious person may feel no pain but nonetheless experience none of the joys he would have felt but for the injury. But in many cases, the two will merge. A paraplegic denied the opportunity to pursue the delights of tennis may suffer anguish over that loss. Is that anguish lost joy, suffering, or both? If measured separately, the jury may double count this component of the injury. The imprecise nature of these concepts makes in nearly impossible for a court to discern whether the jury award double-counted the loss of joy, raising the possibility that awards overcompensate.

Lost enjoyment of life appears most often in cases where pain and suffering are not available, thus eliminating concerns for double counting. Early awards for lost joy involved federal claims for violation of civil rights by depriving the victim of life. (Unlike wrongful death actions, *see* D.6, *infra*, no statute precluded recovery of nonpecuniary losses.) Even if the death was painless (or continued life would have been full of pain), death deprived the deceased victim of the joy future years might have brought. Applying lost enjoyment to a living victim, whose disabilities may deprive them of some but not all of the joy the future holds, has been difficult. Measuring joy is as difficult as measuring pain—though perhaps joys have a market value. (One denied the ability to pursue tennis might take up fine wine or other joys the disability does not prevent. The cost of substitute joys is measurable.)

b. Part of Pain and Suffering

If juries consider loss of joy in evaluating pain and suffering, no separate component for lost joy may be necessary. Courts can instruct juries on lost joy and pain and suffering together, allowing the jury to assess them as a whole. Evidence and arguments concerning lost joy would remain appropriate. Combining these two components poses one danger: limitations appropriate to pain and suffering may not be appropriate to lost joy. For instance, a person with no consciousness may lose joy, even if she feels no pain. To apply the rule denying pain and suffering to lost joy may produce inadequate compensation for the plaintiff (or, more importantly, inadequate deterrence for defendants, since the unconscious plaintiff is unlikely to benefit from the award).

5. Indignity and Emotional Distress

In some cases, the primary (or perhaps only) loss will consist of indignity or distress. Torts such as intentional (or negligent) infliction of emotional distress recognize the importance of these harms. Traditional torts sometimes awarded damages even when no tangible loss could be proven, as in defamation and trespass. More recently, deprivation of constitutional rights may give rise to a cause of action, but the harm may consist of nothing more than an abstract sense of loss, resulting only in an award of nominal damages.

Awards for distress and indignity raise many of the same problems discussed under pain and suffering, with the added difficulty that they are more subjective. All jurors have experienced pain from physical injury and can devise some manner of comparing it to the plaintiff's pain. But indignity and distress relate entirely to the plaintiff's reaction. Some let insults roll off their backs, others mull over them for years (or generations). The severity of the harm is largely in the mind of the plaintiff—and, in some cases, in the control of the plaintiff.

a. Torts Involving Indignity

Where torts cause distress or indignity, courts include compensation for this injury in the award. Like pain and suffering, courts allow juries discretion to determine an appropriate amount. Like pain and suffering, courts review the amount for excessiveness. Like pain and suffering, disputes about the propriety of per diem and golden rule arguments arise. *See* D.3.c, *supra*.

(1) Actual Damages

Where the plaintiff presents evidence of distress or emotional suffering, juries may award an appropriate amount to compensate for these harms.

Distress and indignity are not measured and calculated. In affirming awards, however, courts tend to consider the outrageousness of defendant's conduct. Although objectively reasonable (a reasonable plaintiff would suffer less from a minor affront than from an outrage), the focus on defendant's conduct shifts focus away from the effects on the plaintiff. If we seek to put plaintiff in the position she would have occupied but for the wrong, the effects on the plaintiff may deserve more attention. The focus on defendants may reflect concern that plaintiffs exaggerate their emotional state, while defendants lack any means of rebutting their claims.

(2) Presumed Damages

In some torts, presumed damages are available as a substitute for actual damages. For instance, where a libel plaintiff cannot prove any loss to business or other financial interests, she may nonetheless recover presumed damages—that is, damages in an amount the jury deems will approximate the plaintiff's likely harm. Similarly, trespass often produced presumed damages, even if no harm to the property occurred. Some statutes, such as the copyright act, also allow presumed damages.

b. Contract Actions

Emotional distress in contract actions remains rare and limited. In most settings, courts limit recovery to tangible losses. Plaintiffs are expected to bear the emotional effects on their own. (It isn't personal, it's business—or, at least, it's contract.)

Damages for distress can arise from several settings: (1) where the breach also constitutes a tort; (2) where the breach causes physical injury; or (3) where the breach or the contract are of a type that makes serious emotional distress particularly likely to occur. The first are not really contract actions, at their root. The second involve pain and suffering more than emotional distress. The third merit some elaboration.

Originally, the exception was very limited. It applied to cases where the entire loss seemed emotional. One common example involved mishaps with caskets at funerals. Value as warranted minus value as delivered might be negligible or even zero. But the distress of seeing one's relative fall through the bottom of a casket justified some recovery. More recently, courts have expanded recovery for emotional distress slightly. It now includes some contracts where the plaintiff bargained for a performance that had largely emotional significance. For instance, when a vacation does not live up to the promises made, the effects are not financial, but emotional. When plastic surgery does not live up to the promises, the effects are more emotional than financial. The exception might stretch to cover breach of an insurance contact, where nonpayment seems particularly likely to cause distress. Most courts instead classify such breaches as torts.

c. Constitutional Rights

Deprivation of a constitutional right may not involve much actual loss. This is particularly true of procedural rights, where the denial of a hearing may not affect the outcome. That is, even if a hearing had been held, the same result might have ensued (*e.g.*, suspension from school, discharge from a job, denial of medical license). Where the result would have differed (for example, no discharge from employment would have occurred if a hearing had been held), damages for the substantive effects may suffice. The issue concerns whether the award should be increased for deprivation of a right.

Damages for the abstract value of a right have been rejected by the U.S. Supreme Court. *Carey v. Piphus*, 435 U.S. 247, 98 S.Ct. 1042, 55 L.Ed.2d 252 (1978). Where loss of the right is the only harm, plaintiff may recover nominal damages. Where loss of the right caused other losses, those losses should be recovered. Thus, distress caused by the loss of a right is recoverable. Evidence must link the distress to the loss of the right, not to the legal conduct of the defendant. For instance, in *Carey*, the plaintiffs proved distress, but did not prove whether the distress resulted from the wrong (lack of a hearing) or their suspension from school, which would have occurred even if the hearing had been held.

Damages for loss of the right to vote have been upheld. *Nixon v. Herndon*, 273 U.S. 536, 47 S.Ct. 446, 71 L.Ed. 759 (1927). The court distinguished these from the abstract value of rights, calling them "a particular injury-the inability to vote in a particular election-that might be compensated through substantial money damages." *Memphis Community School Dist. v. Stachura,* 477 U.S. 299, 106 S.Ct. 2537, 91 L.Ed.2d 249 (1986). *Stachura* rejected the suggestion that other substantive rights, such as the first amendment, justified damages aside from the harmful effects of the deprivation.

6. Wrongful Death and Survival Actions

Traditionally, most tort actions were personal to the victim. If the victim died, the right to recover for the injury died with her. Two independent methods prevent this injustice: allowing the victim's action to survive her death, or allowing the victim's survivors to bring an action for causing the death. States generally allow both, though they may differ in the line drawn between them. Survival actions allow the victim (via the victim's estate) to recover for losses suffered between the time of the injury and the time of death—in some cases even if the time is a matter of minutes. Survival actions do not allow recovery for the death itself, however. Wrongful death statutes allow close surviving relatives to recover their losses caused by the deceased's wrongful death. Some wrongful death statutes specify that survivors may recover only pecuniary losses. Originally interpreted to mean financial losses (expenses or income), the definition has expanded somewhat to cover other losses the death may cause.

The wrongful death action belongs to the survivors and measures their losses, not those of the deceased. Most states define the appropriate plaintiff by statute—spouses, children, and parents (in that order) generally qualify.

a. Out-of-Pocket Costs

Death may impose out-of-pocket costs on the survivors. Funeral expenses are the most common, though other costs may result. These costs are recoverable. (In theory, many of these costs would have been incurred eventually. Defendant caused the survivors to incur them now instead of later. That loss can be remedied by awarding the difference between the actual expenses and the present value of the expected future expenses. So much for theory.)

b. Loss of Support

Where the deceased supported the survivors, the amount of support is recoverable. Typically, courts calculate loss of support by assessing the deceased's lost income (for the entire work-life expectancy) and subtracting the amount the deceased would have consumed for purely personal purposes. Thus, shared expenses, such as housing, food, utilities, etc., would be recoverable by the survivors. Future lost support is reduced to present value and adjusted for inflation.

Loss of support provides substantial recovery when the deceased held a paying job. It offers little or no recovery if the deceased was a child, a retired person, or an adult who did not hold a paying job (such as homemakers). It may also provide no recovery if the deceased had no live-in dependents. Most expenses, in that case, would be personal consumption rather than support of others.

c. Loss of Services

If the deceased provided services to the survivors, the value of those services may be a pecuniary loss. To remain in the position they would have occupied but for the wrong, the survivors will need to obtain replacement services. Whether they pay for those services or give up other activities to perform the services for themselves, they are net worse off than before, requiring compensation. Most states allow recovery for loss of services. The cost to replace these services in the market offers a plausible measure of the loss. The types of services that might qualify vary widely. As one example, the District of Columbia allows recovery for "care, education, training, guidance, and personal advice" *District of Columbia v. Hawkins*, 782 A.2d 293, 303 (D.C. 2001).

Loss of services can be substantial, especially when deceased was a parent caring for children. Deceased children and retirees probably provided fewer services to their survivors. Similarly, deceased persons who lived alone probably provided fewer services.

d. Loss of Consortium (Society)

A majority of states allow recovery for loss of consortium, sometimes referred to as loss of society. *See* RESTATEMENT THIRD OF TORTS: REMEDIES § 23, cmt. b. Loss of consortium includes intangible contributions of the deceased, such as affection, care, comfort, companionship, love, and protection. The absence of these leaves survivors worse off than before. In some jurisdictions, the wrongful death statute limits recovery to pecuniary losses. In such jurisdictions, allowing recovery for consortium damages seems problematic. Nevertheless, courts sometimes interpret the statute broadly, allowing consortium damages as a way of preventing embarrassingly low awards for wrongful death.

e. Grief and Distress

Very few states allow recovery for grief and distress caused by the death. This is consistent with rules limiting recovery for distress over injuries to others. Some states, however, have begun to allow recovery for these components.

f. Survival Actions

The survival action covers all losses incurred between the time of injury and the time of death. It requires that the victim survive the initial impact, at least by a short time. (If death is instantaneous, no damages could accrue between injury and death.) This includes lost wages for any period before death, pain and suffering prior to death, and occasionally some property damages (as where clothing or a vehicle were damaged in the accident that injured the victim).

7. Loss of Consortium

Loss of consortium is both a remedy and a cause of action. Injuries to one person may cause losses to others who rely on that person for services and support. These losses may be pecuniary: replacing those services may involve expenses to hire a substitute provider. These expenses are not losses to the victim, who may recover for loss of income, but not for loss of the ability to serve others. (To the extent that the inability to perform services to others distresses the victim, that distress might be recoverable, but not the cost to replace the services.) As a result, these lost services will not be included in the damages defendant pays unless the other party can bring a separate cause of action for them. Loss of consortium is that cause of action. Traditionally limited to spouses, some expansion has occurred recently to allow recovery for or by children.

a. Recoverable Losses

Loss of consortium generally includes three components: services, society, and sexual relations. It usually does not encompass grief, distress, or outrage at the injuries caused to another. As with wrongful death, some states have extended consortium to distress. In others, distress may be recoverable in an action for negligent infliction of emotional distress, but most states strictly limit liability for that action.

(1) Services

Services represent pecuniary losses to the plaintiff. When injuries to one spouse prevent him from performing household tasks, others must perform those tasks. Hiring others to perform the tasks clarifies (and liquidates) the pecuniary nature of the losses. Even if the deprived spouse steps up and performs the services, the loss of time for other activities (whether remunerative or leisure) remains a real loss courts treat as pecuniary.

The cost to replace the services in the market is one measure of the loss. If the victim provided better services than those available in the market, this measure might be too low—or too high if professionals would provide better services than the victim. Even where the plaintiff does not pay to replace the services, these costs are easier to measure than the loss of leisure that plaintiff actually suffers. In theory, the plaintiff will choose the loss that is lower—will hire others if leisure is more valuable than the cost to hire others, but will perform the services himself if leisure is less valuable. In some cases, shortage of funds may explain a different choice. Issues of this nature sometimes lead courts to award more of less than the market value of services, even when it does not suspect that the hours spent on services have been exaggerated.

(2) Society

People provide each other much more than pecuniary services. Loss of society includes affection, solace, comfort, companionship, assistance, and (between spouses) sexual relations. These services are harder to evaluate, resembling emotional distress. Keeping elements of distress and grief from entering the calculation of lost society can pose difficulties for the court. In some cases—especially those not involving spouses—courts reject recovery for these intangible components.

b. Permissible Plaintiffs

A huge range of people may suffer losses as a result of tort injuries to another. Courts insist on limiting the action to a very narrow range of relatives. Traditionally, loss of consortium was available only to spouses. Some states (at least 15) now allow loss of consortium claims by children—though many limit the claim to minor children or disabled adult children who remain their parents' responsibility during adulthood. Fewer states have recognized a parent's right to seek loss of consortium for injuries to their child. Similarly, consortium claims brought by fiancés, domestic partners, roommates, and relatives outside the nuclear family have met with almost no success. The emergence of domestic partner statutes, entitling domestic partners to be treated as spouses for legal purposes, may alter this outcome. As a practical matter, states may find it difficult to deny consortium to any person who could recover for wrongful death if the injury had been fatal. Once the relationship justifies recovery for death, denying recovery for nonfatal injuries seems inconsistent.

c. Procedural Aspects

Consortium claims risk inconsistent recovery. The risk increases if the consortium claim is resolved separately from the victim's underlying tort claim. While one jury may be able to allocate the losses consistently to one plaintiff or the other, separate juries may not know which losses the other included. The risk of double recovery prompts some states to require that the consortium claim be joined with the victim's suit.

REVIEW QUESTIONS

1. Which of the following arguments is most likely to be held improper when addressing the issue of pain and suffering?

   a. "If it would be worth even $1 an hour to avoid such agony, plaintiff should recover about $193,000 for the 22 years she will suffer this way."

   b. "Would you suffer this pain in exchange for $1 an hour? If not, perhaps a higher rate would be justified. But even at $1 an hour, plaintiff deserves about $193,000."

   c. "Plaintiff is comatose. She feels nothing. An award of pain and suffering would compensate her for a loss she did not incur."

   d. "No prior awards in this county for similar injuries ever exceeded $100,000; to award nearly twice that is inappropriate."

2. Violation of one the following rights has justified substantial damage awards, even when no additional harmful consequences were shown. Which one?

a. Freedom of Speech

b. Free Exercise

c. Right To Vote

d. Procedural Due Process

e. Right To Trial by Jury

3. P's dog, Skye, was a mutt, obtained from the pound for the cost of a license. Skye was very smart and did many tricks. P's neighbor, D, wanted to enter Skye in a World's Smartest Mutt contest, which had a $20,000 first prize. P refused. P was very fond of Skye and did not want to be separated from her for the 10 days it would require to drive to the contest, compete, and drive back. D offered P half the winnings, but P refused. D offered $1,000, guaranteed up front, but P refused, stating that no amount of money would induce her to live without Skye for 10 days. D lured Skye into his car and started on the trip without P's knowledge or consent. D intended to return Skye after the competition. On the way, D (through no fault of his own) was involved in a traffic accident in which Skye was killed. What, if anything, can P recover from D in a suit for conversion? What if D never made the offer of $1,000, but all the other facts remain the same?

4. Which of the following elements of damages are recoverable in a wrongful death action? (Check all that apply)

a. The deceased's future income during her life expectancy

b. Funeral expenses for the deceased

c. The value of services the deceased provided for the survivors

d. The survivor's grief

e. The deceased's pain and suffering

ANSWERS

1. B.

2. C.

3. The cost to obtain a new dog from the pound is a minimum recovery. Emotional distress seems out of reach, because D did not act with malice. That is, D did not intend to permanently deprive P of Skye, only to borrow her for 10 days. Perhaps distress for 10 days is recoverable, since D did intend that harm.

The key is to prove subjective value. There is some evidence here. P refused an offer of $1,000 for 10 days of Skye's time. That's a rental value of $100 a day—refused by P because it was too low. P valued Skye more than $100 a day. Multiplied by Skye's remaining life expectancy, there is a decent case for that recovery. P also refused half the winnings, which might have totaled $10,000 for the 10 days (or $1,000 a day). Without any certainty that Skye would have won, it is difficult to assert that refusing that offer establishes a value to P of $1,000 a day. (But if Skye's chance of success exceeded 10%, perhaps a number greater than $100 a day could be supported.) The mere statement that no amount of money would be enough is the kind of hyperbolic statement courts reject. Uttered outside of court, it isn't completely self-serving; P did not know at the time that the statement might be needed to support a large damage award, so its sincerity seems more credible. But one may doubt whether, at $1 million, P would have said the same thing. Since this statement seems to justify an infinite award, the impracticality of assessing damages at that level also works against it.

Without the offer of $1,000. The case becomes very difficult. None of the other facts support any particular amount. Plaintiff never rejected a bona fide offer that could be treated as a value, whether for sale or rental. P might produce evidence of expenses—food, vet, toys, beds, etc.—and argue that the value of Skye exceeded the investment in Skye. While expenses like food might be rebutted by the claim that P actually had a duty (under laws forbidding animal cruelty) to feed Skye, the fact that P did not give Skye to the pound or Humane Society suggests the food was not a burden, but an investment in the pleasure of Skye's company.

4. B and C. A is excessive; the survivors recover only the portion used for their support, not the entire income. D is possible, but only in a very few states. The vast majority reject grief. E is available to the deceased's estate in a survival action, but not to the survivors in a wrongful death action.

E. Limitations on Recovery

Since the nineteenth century, judges have exhibited concern that juries might overcompensate plaintiffs. Efforts to avoid putting plaintiff in a better position than she would have occupied but for the wrong emerged, not to be stingy, but to prevent juries from becoming too generous with other peoples' money. While occasionally erring on the side of undercompensation, recent efforts tend to follow the same pattern. They start with the general rule on damages as the target.

1. Causation

To some extent, the general rule on damages builds causation into its formulation by limiting plaintiff to the position she would have occupied if the wrong had not occurred. In effect, this rejects damages not caused by defendant's misconduct, losses plaintiff would have suffered even if defendant had not committed the wrong.

Basic issues of causation—cause in fact, legal cause, etc.—tend to be covered in first year tort courses, not remedies courses. These rules relate to liability rather than damages. Here, we will focus on causation doctrines that affect damage calculation.

a. Mixed Motive

Sometimes the wrong depends on the motivation: conduct motivated by one reason is wrong, but the same conduct motivated by other reasons would be perfectly legal. Employment offers easy examples. Discharging an employee for bad work is legal, while discharging an employee because of race, gender, age or any number of other factors would be illegal. Problems arise when the action has mixed motivation.

(1) Multiple Sufficient Causes

Sometimes either of two (or more) reasons, one wrong and one acceptable, would have produced the conduct independently of the other. When the conduct would have been the same even if the wrongful reason did not exist, then the wrongful reason was not a but-for cause of the harm. For example, if an employee caught embezzling money is fired, defendant may testify persuasively that he would have been discharged regardless of any protected characteristic. Proof that the defendant also harbored a bias against people of plaintiff's description may establish a second possible reason, but is insufficient to establish but-for causation. Even if defendant was planning to fire plaintiff for wrongful reasons, if the rightful reason provides sufficient independent cause, the wrong is not a but-for cause of the harm. In the standard torts case, however, but-for causation is not required in such a case—both the legitimate and illegitimate reasons would be held to be causes of the harm. The Supreme Court in Title VII and ADEA employment discrimination cases has not chosen to follow tort law in this respect, however, holding not only that the bias of the decisionmaker was not a but-for cause, but was not a cause at all. *See University of Texas Southwestern Med. Ctr. v. Nassar*, 133 S.Ct. 2517 (2013).

The but-for requirement conceals two problems. First, was the independent cause really sufficient? If defendant might not have acted wrongfully faced with only the legal motive, then the illegal motive may in fact be the cause. Plaintiffs may try to prove that the legitimate reason is a pretext, that the wrongful reason actually caused the harm. Evidence of defendant's state of mind often is hard to rebut. Similar situations where the defendant acted differently provide some evidence of pretext. Second, an illegitimate motive may have led to discovery of the legitimate motive. For instance, an employer who observes minority employees more closely than others may discover misconduct by minority employees but not others. While plaintiff's misconduct may justify defendant's conduct independently, the different scrutiny may itself be a violation of law, which caused the discovery and hence the discharge. The issue here may involve conflicting policies: one forbidding discrimination, another permitting discharge of substandard or dishonest employees. *See* E.7, *infra*.

(2) Multiple Insufficient Causes

Sometimes neither of two (or more) reasons, one wrong and one acceptable, would have produced the conduct independently of the other. That is, the combination was essential to cause the conduct. When the conduct would have been different if the wrongful reason did not exist, then the wrongful reason was a but-for cause of the harm. For example, suppose an employer encounters employee misconduct that would not normally cause him to discharge the employee. However, because the employee also was active in organizing the union (an illegal consideration), the employer decided to fire the employee. Union activity was not sufficient to cause discharge; we can tell because the employer did not fire her just for that, before the other conduct was discovered. Neither was the misconduct; we can tell from past practice. The combination produced the conduct; the wrongful reason was a necessary factor in causing the conduct.

b. Loss of Chance

Loss of chance is one of two doctrines aimed at wrongs that increase the risk of harm, but may not cause the harm. *See also* E.1.c (Potential Harm), *infra*. Loss of chance refers to situations where plaintiff has a chance of avoiding a harm, but defendant's wrong reduces the chance. Loss-of-chance recovery has thus far been limited to medical cases, for example where the failure to diagnose a problem earlier may reduce the likelihood of treating the condition. In each case, the defendant did not cause the condition and, thus, did not cause the harms attributable to the condition. Thus, attributing the full loss to defendant is unjust. But defendant's wrong did deprive plaintiff of opportunities that might (or might not) have prevented the harm. Thus, zero recovery seems to underestimate the plaintiff's loss.

(1) Actual Causation

Medical testimony often reveals the relative chances of success of non-negligent versus negligent treatment. For example, the chance of successful treatment might have been 65% if plaintiff's condition had been diagnosed earlier, but only 40% when actually (and negligently) diagnosed. Out of every 100 patients in this situation, 40 will not suffer the harm at all (and presumably not sue). Of the 65 who suffer the harm, 35 would have suffered it regardless of the wrong, while 25 suffered it because of the wrong. In such case, plaintiff cannot prove that the harm was caused by defendant's failure to timely diagnose the illness, and plaintiff's recovery will be limited to loss-of-chance damages.

But suppose defendant's negligent delay in diagnosis caused plaintiff's chance of recovery to drop from 65% to 20%. Of the 65 patients who suffer the harm, 35 would have suffered it regardless of the wrong, while 40 suffered it due to defendant's failure to timely diagnose. In such case, plaintiff has proven more likely than not that the harm was caused by defendant's negligence (because 40% is greater than 35%), and plaintiff is not limited to loss-of-chance damages—plaintiff may recover 100% of the value of the injury.

(2) Proportional Recovery

Courts typically award proportional damages in loss-of-chance cases. That is, they **calculate the harm plaintiff suffered and multiply by the percent reduction in chance defendant caused**. On the numbers above, plaintiff might receive 25% of total loss, because reducing the chance of survival from 65% to 40% caused a 25% loss. Alternatively, courts could focus on the odds that the loss would have occurred anyway. Taking the 60% who suffered the harm, 25/60 (41.67%) would not have suffered the harm but for the wrong.

(3) Separate Cause of Action

Some courts treat loss of chance as a separate cause of action, requiring separate pleading. Because defendant's wrong does not cause the harm, actions requiring proof that the defendant's wrong caused the harm (such as wrongful death statutes) are not satisfied.

c. Potential Harm

In some cases, defendant's wrong does not immediately cause harm to plaintiff. Instead, the harm subjects plaintiff to a risk of loss. For example, exposing defendant to a harmful substance may increase the risk that plaintiff will suffer a harm, even though many people exposed will not suffer the harm—and some might have suffered the harm even if not exposed to the substance. In these cases, proof that the defendant's wrong caused the harm is problematic. While some people wronged might not have suffered injury but for the wrong, others would have suffered the harm regardless of the wrong. To compensate those who would have suffered the wrong anyway puts them in a better position than they would have occupied but for the wrong. But it may be impossible to determine which individuals were injured by the wrong and which were not.

(1) Proportional Recovery After Harm

If the plaintiffs wait and sue after they develop the harm, the issue becomes one of causation. For instance, if defendant exposed 100 plaintiffs to a toxic substance that increased the risk of cancer from 2% to 6% (a 300% increase), only six suits will be brought (by the six who develop cancer). Arguably, four should prevail and two lose, on the ground that those two would have developed cancer anyway. Assuming the two cannot be identified, all six might recover: on these numbers, the chance that the spill caused the cancer is 67% (4 out of 6), satisfying the preponderance of the evidence test, though perhaps not the reasonable medical certainty test. Alternatively, each plaintiff might recover 67% of her losses. This overcompensates two plaintiffs and undercompensates four, but assesses exactly the right costs against the defendant. Thus, deterrence will be accurate even though compensation (inevitably, given the evidence) is imprecise.

(2) Proportional Recovery After Exposure

The problems are compounded when plaintiffs sue at the time of exposure instead of at the time the harmful effects manifest. On the same numbers, 94% of the plaintiffs will develop no cancer and thus deserve no award, 2% would have developed cancer anyway and thus deserve no award. The other 4%, whose cancer was caused by the defendant's wrong, deserve full compensation, but must share their award with all 96 others, not just the 2 who suffer the harm. If total losses for the four are $4 million ($1 million each), each will receive $40,000—as will each of the other plaintiffs exposed to the chemical. In addition, the harm of the cancer (cost of treatment, pain, etc.) will be discounted to present value, reducing the award substantially. The cost to defendant provides the right deterrent—and provides it now, eliminating the risk that bankruptcy or other problems preclude future recovery.

(3) Risk of Harm Distinguished from Fear of or Testing for Harm

The claims discussed in this section are for present recovery of an increased risk of future harm. Such claims must be distinguished from claims for the present fear of, or the costs of testing for, future illness. Exposure to a toxic chemical, for example, may cause plaintiff any (or all three) of the following: (1) an increased risk of suffering a future disease; (2) the emotional distress of worrying about the increased risk; and (3) the costs of detecting future illness in time for effective treatment. The rules governing recovery of each of these harms are different. As this section explains, most courts prohibit or severely curtail recovery for the increased risk itself. Courts are more amenable to allowing recovery for fear and medical monitoring. The latter is discussed in B.5.a.1, *supra*. Courts' approach to claims for fear of future illness may be summarized as follows: Most courts allow exposure-generated emotional distress claims with a showing of current physical symptoms or harm. For instance, where a plaintiff has developed asbestosis, the plaintiff can often recover for fear of mesothelioma (a fatal, asbestos-related cancer). In exposure claims without accompanying injury or symptoms, courts typically limit recovery to cases in which the plaintiff was actually exposed (as opposed to reasonably believed to have been exposed) to a particularly horrible illness. For example, courts have been more willing to allow recovery in HIV exposure cases than in carcinogen-exposure cases, reasoning that carcinogens are more ubiquitous and cancer more treatable (at least at the time of the cases) than AIDS.

(4) Res Judicata vs. Statute of Limitations

The divided harms put plaintiff in a dilemma. If the injury has already begun, the statute of limitations may begin to run, forcing plaintiff to sue after exposure. Yet suing now precludes a later suit concerning the same misconduct; res judicata precludes a second action alleging the same underlying wrong, thus forcing plaintiff to bring all the claims for loss in the first suit. A doctrine precluding recovery of potential future harms in the first suit in effect precludes them altogether, unless the jurisdiction crafts an exception to the usual application of res judicata.

d. Harm to Others: Fluid Class Recoveries

In some cases, plaintiffs have proposed that wrongs to some people be remedied by awards to others. This can apply to damage actions, where plaintiffs ask that defendant issue rebates to future customers in light of overcharges to past customers. It can also apply to injunctions, where a court may order conduct beneficial to subsequent persons like the injured persons. These issues usually arise in class action suits, where identifying the original injured parties and calculating the loss to each might be impossible or may cost more than the loss to each victim would justify. A class of similar people might be easier to identify and compensate, even though it might compensate people who were not victims of defendant's wrong.

Courts may approve settlement agreements that benefit classes similar to those injured. Even if some victims will receive no compensation and some people who were not victims will receive compensation, a court may find that the settlement is in the best interest of the class. With rare exceptions, courts may not impose remedies to persons who were not injured by the defendant's wrong over defendant's objection.

2. Avoided Consequences

The general rule for damages—putting the plaintiff in the position she would have occupied if the wrong had not occurred—requires compensation for losses the plaintiff did suffer, but not for losses she did not suffer. Thus, any loss the plaintiff avoided should not be included in the recovery. More controversially, when a wrong bestows benefits in addition to causing losses, plaintiff should recover her net loss, after offsetting the benefits.

a. Avoided Losses Without Benefits

In many cases, plaintiffs will minimize their own loss. Plaintiffs cannot recover for losses that they do not suffer. For example, if a seller refuses to deliver goods, a buyer may find a substitute supplier and, in the process, avoid any consequential losses from the breach. Having avoided the consequential losses, the buyer does not recover them. She may recover cover price minus contract price (if the substitute goods cost more) plus the incidental costs incurred to find the substitute goods, but not the consequential damages she avoided. Similarly, when an employer wrongfully discharges an employee, the employee may find a substitute job, thus replacing the wages the first job would have paid. The employee may not recover the full amount of salary the breaching employer promised. He may recover full pay for any period between jobs, plus the cost of finding the new job, and any difference in salary between the jobs. But he can't get both salaries, only his net loss. The same applies to physical injuries. If a pedestrian is hit by a car, medical treatment may prevent permanent disability. She cannot collect for the disability because she didn't suffer one. She can collect for the cost of medical care, plus any temporary disability she suffered during medical care. In each case, awarding plaintiff damages for the losses avoided would be silly.

b. Cost of Avoiding Losses

The cost of avoiding a loss is recoverable, as illustrated by all the examples in the previous section. The phone calls (and other costs) to find a substitute supplier, the cost of printing and mailing resumes (and other job search expenses), and the cost of medical care are recoverable. They are losses caused by the breach. These costs sometimes are called incidental damages. In some cases, they are treated as the direct loss suffered, not as a cost of avoiding a different loss. But in all cases they are recoverable as an element of damages.

c. Nominal Damages

In some cases, the breach will cause no harm at all. For instance, if the price of substitute goods is lower than the contract price, a buyer may save money on the substitute contract, even after accounting for the cost of cover. In tort, a victim of fraud may find that the property purchased is worth more than the price, presenting a net gain. In these situations, no actual damages would be recoverable.

In some cases, especially tort cases, that is the end of the matter. There is a considerable split among jurisdictions regarding whether nominal damages are recoverable in tort actions. In a slight majority of jurisdictions, nominal damages are available in any tort action in which liability is proven, but where the plaintiff cannot prove compensatory damages. *See* RESTATEMENT THIRD OF TORTS: REMEDIES § 38. Even in these jurisdictions, for some actions—most notably, negligence—the plaintiff must still prove harm, even if they cannot prove an *amount* of damages with reasonable certainty. In a large minority of jurisdictions, nominal damages are available for some torts but not others. Comment d to Restatement § 38 explains:

> [N]ominal damages are generally available for intentional torts against a person, such as assault, battery, and false imprisonment, if

> the factfinder awards no compensatory damages. * * * The purposes of vindication and declaration seem especially important for such affronts to personal autonomy. Comments b and c to Restatement Second, Torts § 907 listed a number of torts for which nominal damages historically have been found to be available: assault, offensive battery, false imprisonment, conversion, defamation, trespass to land, breach of duty by a public officer, interference with the right to vote or hold public office, and tortious interference with patent rights. This list is not exhaustive, but it identifies many of the most important cases, and nominal damages would be available for these torts in most jurisdictions at the time of this Restatement. Nuisance, abuse of process, and malicious prosecution are other torts in which nominal damages are commonly available even in states that do not award nominal damages for all torts.
>
> The torts most frequently mentioned as not supporting nominal damages are negligence, trespass to chattels, fraud, tortious interference with contract or business relations, and breach of fiduciary duty. Most commonly in these cases, courts that refuse nominal damages say that for these torts, there is no tort without proof of actual harm. And if there is no tort, there can be no remedy, not even nominal damages.

Nominal damages awards, even when allowed, are rare because no one pays an attorney to bring a case if they realize the remedy will be limited to nominal damages. These cases usually arise either when plaintiffs misjudge the extent of their likely recovery, or when the plaintiff might also be entitled to punitive damages.

d. Offsetting Benefits

In some cases, a breach bestows a benefit on the defendant. Even if the breach harms the plaintiff in some ways, the net loss suffered may be reduced by the benefit bestowed, "to the extent that this is equitable." RESTATEMENT (SECOND) TORTS, § 920. While no similar rule is stated in contract law, the same principle is built into the damage rules. For instance, when a seller breaches, buyer is entitled to recover cover price minus contract price. Courts subtract contract price because, as a benefit of the breach, buyer no longer needs to pay the breaching seller. To allow buyer to collect cover price without subtracting the retained benefit would exceed the net loss buyer actually suffered.

(1) Basic Illustrations

The most common operation of the offset the benefits rule is to reduce a plaintiff's recovery by a benefit gained in mitigation. For example, suppose a plaintiff is unable to work as an iron worker for six months due to injuries suffered at the hands of defendant in an auto accident. For three of those months, plaintiff finds replacement work as a janitor. So long as plaintiff could not have done the janitor work while serving as an iron worker, plaintiff's janitor wages should be subtracted from his lost-wages award against defendant.

Consider two further examples: Suppose defendant uses explosives on her property, causing a landslide on plaintiff's property. Damage to plaintiff's land—destroyed fences, lost cattle, etc.—would be recoverable. But if the landslide also opened the entrance to a cave on plaintiff's land, it may have allowed plaintiff a new business opportunity. The value provided might be offset against the damages claimed.

Suppose government agencies falsely accuse plaintiff of a crime. Any losses to plaintiff's business or reputation would be recoverable. But if the notoriety permitted plaintiff to write a best-selling book about the experience, the benefit bestowed by the wrong might be offset against the damages claimed.

(2) Benefit to the Interest Injured

The Second Restatement and a minority of courts offset the benefits only if the benefits inure to the same interest injured. Thus, a financial benefit might offset a financial harm. But a financial benefit might not offset pain and suffering or harm to dignitary interests (such as reputation).

The same-interest limitation might explain some cases involving unwanted children. When defendant fails to sterilize a person (whether negligently or in breach of contract), the parents may suffer costs raising an additional child. The emotional benefit they may receive from raising a child does not affect their pecuniary interests. Thus, no offset might be found. On the other hand, if parents tried to prevent the birth of a child suffering from a severe genetic defect, their losses may include emotional distress raising the child. If so, emotional benefits of raising a child might offset the loss.

The RESTATEMENT THIRD OF TORTS: REMEDIES § 9 rejects the same-interest approach, explaining that it is a minority approach and that even jurisdictions that purport to adopt it often ignore the rule.

(3) To the Extent Equitable

In some cases, plaintiffs do not want the benefits. That is obvious in the birth cases, where plaintiffs paid to prevent the very benefit that defendant now seeks to offset against recovery. It might apply to the landslide; plaintiff is a farmer who may have no interest in opening a tourist attraction. The rule aims to limit plaintiffs to their actual losses—to put them in the position they would have occupied but for the wrong—not to allow defendants to foist unwanted benefits on the plaintiff. For example, if defendant paved plaintiff's farm and put up a parking lot, plaintiff would be entitled to the cost of restoring the land to farm territory, regardless of any increase in its net value. Defendant cannot push plaintiff into a different career by means of offsetting damages.

(4) Calculating the Offset

Courts that limit benefits to the interest injured face unanswered questions about how to offset benefits. For instance, if the emotional benefit exceeds the emotional harm, should the excess benefit also offset pecuniary harms? Or, once the emotional harm has been reduced to zero, do the emotional benefits cease to apply? Similarly, can plaintiff avoid offset by not pleading emotional harms, even though she suffered emotional harm? Or can defendant prove plaintiff's emotional harm in order to introduce evidence of the emotional benefit? Faced with questions like this, courts sometimes refuse to apply the benefit rule at all. And, as explained above, a majority of courts have abandoned the distinction between the interests, allowing total offset.

e. Collateral Source Exception

Benefits bestowed by sources other than the defendant do not offset the plaintiff's recovery. RESTATEMENT (THIRD) OF TORTS § 10. Defendant is entitled to a credit for benefits it provides—whether payments or other kinds of offsetting benefits under the preceding rule. But benefits provided by others do not offset defendant's liability. For example, in a wrongful death action, defendant cannot claim credit for life insurance proceeds received by the survivors. In a personal injury action, damages are not offset by health insurance benefits, aid provided by plaintiff's friends or family, or payments from a government or nonprofit program. Indeed, this rule is so strong that evidence regarding collateral benefits may not reach the purview of the jury without creating reversible error.

Tort reform proponents have attacked the collateral source rule, sometimes with success. *See, e.g.,* N.Y. Civil Practice Laws Revised § 4545(c), (d) (damages offset by insurance and social security benefits, less premiums plaintiff paid for those benefits in the preceding two years; but no offset for charitable contributions to plaintiff). When others pay the costs of plaintiff's harm, plaintiff does not suffer those losses. Thus, any recovery may leave plaintiff in a better position than she would have occupied if the wrong had not occurred: she collects full damages from the defendant, but does not suffer some of the losses because others paid them. Sometimes the argument is false. Health insurers often assert subrogation claims, collecting from the tort damages the amount recovered for costs they paid. Even when true, deterrence policies require the defendant to internalize the full cost of the harm caused by the wrong. Regardless of who bore the loss in the first instance, the correct amount of deterrence depends on the cost ultimately being shifted to the defendant.

3. Avoidable Consequences

Often called mitigation of damages, the avoidable consequences doctrine limits the amount of damage a plaintiff may recover to the amount she could not have avoided by reasonable conduct undertaken after the defendant's wrong. The rule may leave plaintiff worse off than if the wrong had not occurred. For instance, a discharged employee who makes no effort to find a new job may end up with less money than she would have received if she had not been discharged. If defendant can show that plaintiff would have found suitable work had she tried, the amount plaintiff could have earned will be subtracted from the amount defendant would have paid the plaintiff. (The cost plaintiff would have incurred to make a job search probably will be awarded to plaintiff, since the reduction could not have occurred without the expenses, for which defendant would have been liable.)

a. Rationale

Several reasons may be at work here. Where plaintiff could have avoided the loss, it is harder to say defendant caused the loss; rather, plaintiff, by not avoiding the loss, may be the legal cause. Alternatively, a policy to avoid waste urges courts to provide an incentive to prevent losses, when reasonable. The avoidable consequences doctrine provides plaintiff with an incentive to prevent the loss and thus minimize waste. The rule strives to treat avoidable consequences the same way courts treat avoided consequences. In effect, it treats plaintiff as if she did avoid the losses that she should have avoided.

b. The Rule

If the plaintiff fails to make reasonable post-injury efforts to minimize the loss caused by the defendant, the losses she could have avoided by reasonable efforts will be denied. The rule applies in tort and contract. For instance, if seller breaches a promise to supply goods to a buyer who would have earned a profit by reselling them, the buyer must try to obtain the goods from another source in order to avoid losing the resale profits. Similarly, if defendant injures plaintiff in an automobile accident, plaintiff may need to obtain medical care to prevent the injuries from becoming a permanent disability. If refusing medical care is unreasonable, defendant may owe only the cost of the medical care, not the loss caused by the disability.

In the tort context, the avoidable consequences is distinguished from comparative fault by the fact that the avoidable consequences doctrine considers conduct *after* the defendant's tort, whereas the comparative fault occurs *before or simultaneous with* it. Whereas avoidable consequences complete bars the recovery of damages the plaintiff might have avoided. Comparative fault merely reduces plaintiff's recovery according to the percentage of responsibility the jury assigns to the plaintiff. A minority of courts have abrogated this distinction by apportioning avoidable consequences between plaintiff and defendant. *See* RESTATEMENT THIRD OF TORTS: REMEDIES § 8, cmt. p.

(1) Defendant's Burden

This is an affirmative defense that defendant must plead and prove. Defendant must show not only that plaintiff's efforts were unreasonable, but also the amount of loss that reasonable efforts would have prevented. For this reason, failure to make futile efforts will not alter plaintiff's recovery. Because efforts, if made, would not have reduced losses at all (i.e., would have been futile), no reduction occurs no matter how unreasonable plaintiff was to refuse to make those efforts.

(2) Reasonable Efforts, Not Successful Efforts

If a plaintiff makes reasonable efforts to minimize the loss, no reduction in damages occurs even if those efforts failed. For example, a discharged employee who makes reasonable efforts to find a new job may fail to find substitute work. She recovers the full salary defendant would have paid, plus the cost of the efforts to find new work. In effect, where plaintiff's reasonable efforts fail, courts conclude that reasonable efforts would not have prevented the loss.

(3) Reasonable Efforts, Not the Best Choices

Faced with several different ways to minimize the loss, plaintiff may choose any reasonable way. Even if 20–20 hindsight shows that a different choice might have reduced damages more, plaintiff recovers the damages he actually suffered. In effect, if defendant wants to specify how the loss should be minimized, defendant should negotiate with plaintiff instead of simply breaching and leaving plaintiff to deal with the losses.

(4) Reasonable Efforts, Not Extraordinary Efforts

Sometimes damages can be reduced by exceptional efforts. A discharged employee might find a new job by moving to a new town or state, by retraining in a different field, or by accepting work that affronts her dignity. Where minimizing the loss requires undue risk, burden, or humiliation, no reduction of damages results.

(5) Reasonable Efforts vs. Good Faith Efforts

The rule requires reasonable efforts. Some courts, however, show remarkable reluctance to hold that a plaintiff acted unreasonably. In some cases, the court takes into account ways that the plaintiff differs from the ordinary, reasonable person. For example, a plaintiff who refused simple, safe surgery almost certain to prevent disability received full compensation for her injuries. The refusal was deemed reasonable because the plaintiff's mental disorder caused her to focus on the risks and underestimate the benefits. By taking into account the patently unreasonable aspects of plaintiff's character and concluding the decision was reasonable for her, the court in effect applied a good faith standard. Other decisions, with more justification, consider religious objections to medical procedures. The constitutionally protected status of religion make it difficult for courts to rule on reasonableness in that setting. The net result is that reasonableness may mean something different under the avoidable consequences doctrine than it means when determining defendant's liability for negligence.

c. Exceptions, Real and Imagined

(1) Lost Volume Seller

In some cases, transactions that appear to reduce the loss are not really substitute transactions. Where plaintiff could have entered two transactions—both the one defendant precluded and the one claimed in mitigation—the second transaction does not offset the harm of the first. For example, a boat dealer may be able to order as many boats from the manufacturer as he can sell. If one buyer breaches, selling that boat to another buyer may not offset the loss from the first sale. But for the breach, plaintiff could have sold two boats, not one. In addition to the second transaction, plaintiff should recover the profit lost on the first transaction (as well as any incidental costs incurred because of the breach). The same is true of a discharged employee who moonlights. If the employee would have worked both jobs—the original job with defendant and the second job—wages from the second job may not offset the wages lost as a result of defendant's breach. In each case, however, evidence that the plaintiff would not have entered the second transaction but for defendant's breach of the first suggests the second is a substitute transaction, not an additional transaction.

In the construction trades, courts often assume that contractors (or subcontractors) are lost volume sellers. By hiring more laborers, contractors can work additional jobs without increasing overhead. Thus, if defendant wrongfully throws a contractor off the job, the next job the contractor takes may not be a substitute. The contractor could have worked both jobs and is entitled to the profit from two jobs, not just one.

(2) Mitigation Before the Breach

If the plaintiff anticipates a breach, he can take precautions to minimize the harm the breach will cause. For instance, a plaintiff who buckles a seat belt may reduce the harm he will suffer if an accident occurs. Because seat belts are an eminently reasonable precaution, some courts have reduced the amount plaintiff can recover by the amount defendant can prove would have been avoided by buckling up. Statutes have rejected this rule in many states, including those that require seat belt use. In others, pre-breach precautions are governed by comparative negligence rules. (While the accident would have happened despite the seat belts, the failure to use them did contribute to causing the injury.) On the whole, avoidable consequences is not well-suited to dealing with pre-breach precautions. Thus, as explained above, in the context of tort claims, most jurisdictions reduce a plaintiff's recovery for pre-tort unreasonable conduct pursuant to the doctrine of comparative fault.

(3) Defendant's Equal Opportunity to Mitigate

Some courts have said that plaintiff's recovery should not be reduced if defendant had an equal opportunity to mitigate the loss and failed to do so. In most cases, the holding is dicta, following a conclusion that plaintiff did act reasonably. The exception makes no sense and probably will disappear even from dicta.

(4) Intentional and Reckless Torts

As is the case with comparative fault, in the torts context, damages against an intentional or reckless defendant will only be reduced if the plaintiff has intentionally or recklessly failed to mitigate their damages.

4. Foreseeability

Foreseeability can affect several issues. It may be one test for whether a wrong proximately caused an injury. It may contribute to decisions concerning whether a defendant owed a duty to the plaintiff. In addition, foreseeability can be used to limit damages. The doctrine is clearer in contract cases, but also applies to some torts, especially where damages consist of business income.

a. The Rule

Plaintiff cannot recover damages for loss that the defendant did not have reason to foresee at the time of contract formation as a probable result of the breach. Where damages flow naturally from the breach in the ordinary course of events, the rule is satisfied. Defendant should foresee these natural consequences of breach. Where consequences are less ordinary, other circumstances still may give defendant reason to know of these probable losses. Most commonly, plaintiff may reveal facts that give defendant reason to know that this type of loss is probable in the event of breach. *See Hadley v. Baxendale*, 9 Ex. 341, 156

Eng.Rep. 145 (1854) (mill was shut down pending replacement of a shaft; carrier misdirected the shaft, delaying replacement; no damages for lost profits because not foreseeable).

(1) Reason to Know

The rule requires that defendant have reason to know, not necessarily actual knowledge. A particularly dense defendant remains liable for the damages he should have foreseen.

(2) Time of Contract Formation

Foreseeability applies to the time of contract formation. This protects a defendant's ability to bargain for a different allocation of risk. For instance, a defendant may want to: (1) reject the deal altogether given the risk of loss; (2) raise the price to compensate for the risk of loss; (3) include a clause limiting or excluding recovery of some or all of the loss; (4) buy insurance to cover the risk of loss; (5) take extra precautions to reduce the risk of loss. Without reason to know that losses of this type are likely, the right to bargain for terms like this is meaningless.

(3) Breach Need Not Be Foreseeable

The rule governs the foreseeability of losses if the contract is breached. The fact that the defendant had no reason to know she would breach the contract has no bearing on the inquiry. If the defendant had considered the effects of a breach (like the one that occurred), would she have had reason to know that this loss was probable?

(4) Probable Result of Breach

The fact that loss was possible will not satisfy the rule. Parties to a contract need not bargain over every remote possibility that might follow a breach. But if the loss was a probable consequence of breach, defendant should either bargain over the loss or pay damages for the loss. In some cases, courts find foreseeability only when the loss was nearly inevitable. This probably reflects a relatively strict interpretation of the "ordinary course of events": the inevitable is ordinary; anything else is just possible or unusual. As such, it would be harder to argue that a consequence mentioned by the plaintiff should be deemed unforeseeable merely because defendant had no reason to know it was inevitable or even probable.

(5) Amount of Loss vs. Type of Loss

On one reading, defendant must have reason to know that plaintiff probably would suffer losses of the type she now claims. On this reading, if defendant had reason to know that plaintiff intended to resell the property, lost profits would be foreseeable. On another reading, however, the amount of profits must be foreseeable as a probable result of the breach. Even if defendant knew that plaintiff intended to resell the property, if the resale price was wildly higher than defendant had any reason to know, the excess profit might be deemed unforeseeable. Plaintiff could recover the amount of profit defendant had reason to expect, but not the excess.

Neither interpretation reflects the language of the Uniform Commercial Code, which allows recovery for loss "resulting from the general or particular requirements and needs of which the seller at the time of contracting had reason to know. . . ." U.C.C. § 2–715(2)(a). This does not seem to require that the amount of loss (or even that the type of loss) be foreseeable as a probable result of the breach, only that the requirements and needs of buyer have been foreseeable. Nonetheless, courts often treat the U.C.C. rule as identical to the traditional rule discussed above.

b. Consequential Damages vs. Market Value

The foreseeability rule applies to consequential damages—typically lost profits. Its application to other losses has not been as consistent. The U.C.C. specifically incorporates foreseeability into the definition of consequential damages, suggesting that it has no effect on other measures. That may be significant. When shortages develop, buyer may need to cover at a price much higher than the seller could have anticipated at the time of contract formation. Because foreseeability in the U.C.C. governs only consequential damages, it should not limit recovery in that setting. The same might be true outside the sale of goods. For instance, an insurer who refuses to provide a policy after prices skyrocket might have to pay the additional cost of obtaining a substitute policy, no matter how little reason it had to know that the prices would increase so much.

Some courts address the issue by reference to lost asset value. For any asset that has value, depriving plaintiff of that asset (even temporarily) naturally deprives her of the value of the asset. That much is not only probable, but inevitable. Thus, even if plaintiff cannot show how much profit she would have earned had the asset been delivered on time, she may be able to prove the fair market value of the asset (or the fair rental value, where she was deprived of the asset only temporarily). Where assets can be used to produce profits, the fair market value probably includes the market's estimate of the likely profits from use of the asset. This will not include any unusual profits plaintiff might have made, but will include the ordinary profits anyone could make. In this way, damages may shift from consequential losses to market losses.

5. Reasonable Certainty

A plaintiff must prove that the defendant's wrong caused harm to the plaintiff pursuant to the preponderance standard. Once causation has been established—or, put differently, once the "fact" of harm has been established—the amount of damages need only be determined with "reasonable certainty." Some jurisdictions interpret this standard to require *more* than a preponderance of the evidence. A majority, however, apply the standard as *less demanding* than a preponderance. *See* RESTATEMENT (THIRD) OF TORTS: REMEDIES § 5(b). Courts often explain this by stating that the plaintiff need not prove the amount of damages with precision; rather, "reasonable certainty" merely precludes juries from speculating about the amount of damages. Where the evidence establishes that plaintiff has suffered some damages, the jury may make a reasonable estimate of the amount.

While the jury will be instructed to apply the reasonable certainty rule, its primary effect involves judges. By requiring some degree of certainty, the rule enables courts to strike some elements of damages, or to order new trials on damages when jury awards exceed the amount the court believes the evidence will support. More often, however, this relaxed standard operates to give juries wide discretion in setting the amount of damages.

a. Applicable to Each Component Separately

The rule applies to each component of a damage award. Thus, if plaintiff can show one component (say, cost to repair a building) with reasonable certainty, but cannot show other elements (say, the profit plaintiff would have earned from operating a business from the building) with reasonable certainty, plaintiff can recover the components proven. Defendant cannot avoid all damages simply by proving that one element is uncertain.

b. The Standard Varies with the Wrong

The degree of certainty required with regard to the amount of damages varies with the nature of the wrong. Damages such as pain and suffering, emotional distress, dignitary harm are so inherently uncertain that courts do not generally curb them by application of the reasonable certainty rule. Rather, such damages are typically reversed only if "grossly excessive" or "grossly inadequate." *See* RESTATEMENT (THIRD) OF TORTS: REMEDIES § 5(c).

c. Wrongdoer Exception

Where the defendant's wrongful conduct caused plaintiff's inability to prove damages with sufficient certainty, courts usually permit the jury to estimate the amount of the loss without even the reasonable certainty limitation. *See Bigelow v. RKO Radio Pictures, Inc.*, 327 U.S. 251, 66 S.Ct. 574, 90 L.Ed. 652 (1946). Taken literally, this exception can swallow the rule. In almost every case, if defendant had not committed the wrong, plaintiff would be in the position she would have occupied but for the wrong and, therefore, could prove what that position is. Defendant's misconduct always creates the uncertainty.

Courts applying the exception generally limit it to uncertainty concerning the amount of damages, not uncertainty concerning the existence of damages. Thus, courts will still deny recovery for lost profits to a plaintiff who cannot prove by a preponderance that she would have made profits or suffered losses. But where plaintiff can prove some profits, even $1, the court will apply the wrongdoer exception to permit the jury to estimate the amount of lost profits, even if the amount cannot be demonstrated with reasonable certainty.

d. Proving Damages with Reasonable Certainty

The rule may not preclude damages very often, but it does force plaintiffs to prepare their damage evidence carefully. A plaintiff who simply relies on her own estimate of the profits her business would have made is likely to fail the reasonable certainty test. Similarly, a plaintiff whose expert witness does not attempt to estimate the amount loss may fail. *See ESPN, Inc. v. Office of the Commissioner of Baseball*, 76 F.Supp.2d 416 (S.D.N.Y.1999) (expert did not estimate amount of loss). The increasing willingness of courts to accept the testimony of accountants and appraisers, however, gives most plaintiffs some room to satisfy the rule.

New businesses still fall prey to the rule fairly often. Established businesses usually can point to some history of profits upon which to base an estimate of lost profits. Even new businesses may produce some indicia of success. For instance, a franchise might rely on the success of similar franchisees in other locations to provide some basis for concluding this business also would have succeeded. Careful market studies and projections might permit a new business to show the likelihood of profits. Certainty tends to preclude recovery only for the most speculative ventures.

e. Reducing Damages Awarded

Even if the court allows the jury to estimate the amount of damages, courts retain the ability to reject or reduce any particular award as excessive or inadequate under the certainty doctrine via the act of remittitur. Consider, for example, that even if certain in a given case that lost profits would have been at least $100, they might have been much higher. The likelihood of any given number (even the $100 minimum amount) being the right number is relatively small. This is not the relevant question, however.

Instead, the rule asks whether damages of at least this amount are reasonably certain. If so, that award satisfies the test. Thus, even if $100 is an unlikely number, as long as the court is reasonably certain that damages would have been at least that amount, a jury award of $100 would be sustained. As the amount of damages rises, the likelihood that damages would have been at least that amount declines. At some point, the likelihood of damages reaching that level diminishes below the certainty threshold. Any award greater than that amount could be rejected by the court as under the certainty doctrine.

6. The Economic Loss Doctrine

With some exceptions, tort defendants are not liable unless their misconduct physically injures the person or property of plaintiff. The rule is typically described as a limitation on defendants' duty: tort requires them to use due care to avoid injuring the person or property of others, but does not impose a duty to use due care to avoid injuring purely economic interests. If a tort injures the person or property of plaintiff, all losses, including economic losses, may be recoverable. This rule is thus similar in form and rationale (although not in its precise doctrine) to tort law's approach to claims for pure emotional distress. (*See* B.5.b.1, *supra.*)

a. Rationale

The rule serves several functions. First, it maintains the division between tort and contract law for warranty claims. Where a breach of warranty reduces the value of a product, plaintiff should proceed in breach of warranty, even if defendant's breach may have been negligent. This applies even if the product explodes. If the explosion damages other property of plaintiff, tort may lie. But if the explosion damages only the good sold, suit lies in contract.

Second, the rule limits which plaintiffs may sue in a way that courts fear to leave to decision by a jury in individual cases. Some torts affect one person directly, but have economic effects that ripple through a broad range of persons. Allowing each to sue for their economic loss allows recovery to parties far removed from the tort. In theory, rules limiting foreseeability and certainty could limit recovery for remote effects. More remote plaintiffs are less likely to present foreseeable losses or to prove them with reasonable certainty. Some courts, however, have elected to cut liability off as a matter of law rather than leaving the issue open for juries or judges to resolve by applying doctrines that depend on the facts of each case.

b. Exceptions

If a tort is inherently economic—or, at least, inherently unrelated to physical injury—courts generally allow economic losses without proof of physical injury. Fraud, attorney malpractice, defamation, invasion of privacy, and interference with contractual relations might have no damages if subjected to the physical injury requirement. Of course, fraud, invasion of privacy, and interference with contractual relations are intentional torts—and the economic loss rule only limits negligence claims (and certain strict liability claims, like product liability, that resemble negligence).

A second exception exists for negligence claims against a defendant who has provided a service for a third party for the specific benefit of the plaintiff. Classic examples are (1) an attorney who negligently drafts a will for client X that was meant to benefit the plaintiff, and (2) an accountant who performs an audit of its client company, knowing that the audit was going to be relied upon by the plaintiff (and not the general public) in considering whether to pursue a private stock offering.

Still other courts have created ad hoc exceptions that expand liability to remote plaintiffs, especially when no other plaintiff could bring a suit. These cases often involve environmental torts, where the immediate harm is to property that no one owns, such as a river or ocean. Plaintiffs who use the river, such as fishers (commercial or recreational) and boaters, have been allowed to sue. Cases of this sort often limit liability to the most direct plaintiffs (e.g., fishers), but deny liability for others affected (those who buy the fish, process them, sell them to restaurants, serve them in restaurants, or park the cars at seafood restaurants—and those who sell to the fishers, such as marinas, bait and tackle shops, and, for sport fishers, hotels, guides, etc.)

7. Public Policy

In some cases, strict application of damage rules may produce results that undermine the substantive policy objectives of one or more laws. When this happens, courts may reject or limit damages in a way that protects the policy objectives.

a. Undermining Policy Goals

Laws ban misconduct in order to prevent certain harms. In unusual cases, the rule may in fact promote the harm instead of preventing it. When damages would undermine the policy goals of a rule intended to promote those goals, courts may decide to reject or limit damages. For example, in *Brunswick Corp. v. Pueblo Bowl-O-Mat*, 429 U.S. 477, 97 S.Ct. 690, 50 L.Ed.2d 701 (1977), buyers of bowling alley equipment defaulted on payments to the seller. Instead of repossessing the equipment (which no one else wanted to buy), Brunswick bought the bowling alleys and operated them in order to collect some of the money owed. Eventually, Brunswick owned so many bowling alleys it dominated the industry. The owner of a local bowling alley sued Brunswick for antitrust violations, alleging as damages that if Brunswick had not bought a local competitor, it would have gone out of business and a share of the failed competitor's customers would have patronized plaintiff's bowling alley instead.

Because the competitor remained open, plaintiff didn't get more customers and, thus, earned less money than it could have. The trial court held that Brunswick's conduct tended to create a monopoly, in violation of the antitrust laws. On appeal, the Supreme Court held that plaintiff's damages were not recoverable. The statute was designed to protect competition, but plaintiff's damages stemmed from too much competition (Brunswick keeping a bowling alley open instead of letting it close). That kind of loss was not what the statute sought to protect.

b. Conflicting Goals

In some cases, awarding damages may undermine one policy goal, but denying them may undermine a different policy goal. In these cases, courts may decide to reject or limit damages in order to prevent undermining one of the policies at issue. No rules govern which of the conflicting policies a court should protect.

In most cases of conflicting policies, both parties are wrongdoers. Thus, awarding damages to one allows them to profit from their wrong. In some cases, this prevents liability. Both *in pari delicto* and the unclean hands defense preclude recovery. In cases where liability can be established, courts may reject damages. For instance, employers sometimes report employees who are not legally in the country to the INS when the employees try to organize a union. Discrimination against employees based on union activity violates the National Labor Relations Act. If the employees sue, the normal remedy is reinstatement and back pay. Yet it is hard to say that their rightful position includes jobs in the United States; rightfully, they should never have been in the country and, thus, never have had the jobs. Moreover, reinstatement means little to workers already deported. In effect, immigration policy requires rejecting a remedy for the workers, while labor policy demands a remedy. The Supreme Court has favored the immigration policy. *See Sure-Tan, Inc. v. NLRB*, 467 U.S. 883, 104 S.Ct. 2803, 81 L.Ed.2d 732 (1984); *Hoffman Plastic Compounds v. NLRB*, 535 U.S. 137, 122 S.Ct. 1275, 152 L.Ed.2d 271 (2002). No general rule describes how to choose among competing policies.

c. Unanticipated Implications of Rules

Some cases confront courts with unanticipated implications of otherwise good rules. Courts sometimes invoke public policy to avoid results they find unsavory. For example, medical malpractice sometimes results in the birth of an unwanted child. The elements of the tort may be clear, the application of damage rules (despite offsetting benefits) may produce a recovery. Yet courts sometimes find it necessary to rule that damages cannot be recovered for the birth of an unwanted child—in some cases, even when severe genetic defects motivated the effort to prevent the birth. *See Taylor v. Kurapati*, 236 Mich. App. 315, 600 N.W.2d 670 (1999).

Courts faced with cases of this sort sometimes invoke the public policy exception. The cases, however, do not always fit the exception well. Damages would not undermine the policy goals the rule was intended to protect. For example, deterring malpractice remains a goal, even when the consequence is birth. (At least, no court has suggested we should encourage malpractice of this sort.) These may not be cases with two wrongdoers. For example, the parents commit no wrong when they seek genetic counseling, sterilization, or even an abortion (if we confine wrongs to legally actionable wrongs). Thus, awarding damages to the parents would not encourage misconduct. Nonetheless, courts may identify and apply policies in an ad hoc manner when they find it appropriate to reject or limit damages.

8. The Mechanism for Judicial Limitations on Damages

a. Additur and Remittitur

In addition to instructing the jury on the rules governing damages, courts in many states reserve the power alter a jury's damages award by order of additur (an increase in damages) or remittitur (a reduction of damages). In some states, courts have decided that such alterations are an unconstitutional abridgment of the jury's power under state constitutional provisions similar to the Seventh Amendment to the federal Constitution. In states in which additur and remittitur are allowed, courts yet give strong deference to jury awards via the standard of review. In addition, most states and the federal courts require courts to offer the affected party the option of either accepting the adjustment or a retrial on the damages issue, either with the same or a different jury. *See, e.g.*, RESTATEMENT THIRD OF TORTS: REMEDIES § 17.

b. Standard of Review

Courts grant motions for additur or remitter pursuant to a deferential standard of review. In some jurisdictions, a court may only alter the damages verdict if it "shocks the conscience" or "suggests passion, prejudice, or corruption" on the part of the jury. In other jurisdictions, alterations are permitted only where the award falls "as a matter of law, outside the scope of the evidence." In still others, the standard of review is framed as "abuse of discretion."

REVIEW QUESTIONS

1. To establish losses with reasonable certainty, plaintiff must establish:
   a. That the amount of loss is at least the amount the jury awarded
   b. That both the existence and amount of loss are reasonably certain
   c. The amount of loss with mathematical precision
   d. That the amount of loss was reasonably certain to exceed zero
   e. None of the above, if defendant's wrong caused the inability to prove the existence of a loss
2. D, an owner of land, fired P, a building contractor, without justification. But for the breach, P would have continued working on D's project for another 6 months and earned an additional $1 million in profit. In which, if any, of the following situations should the damage award be reduced? (Check all that apply)
   a. P makes no efforts to find another contract for the remaining period of the contract
   b. P makes reasonable efforts to find additional work for the remaining period of the contract, but all work for that period has already been committed to other builders
   c. P finds another job on which P might earn a profit of $400,000, but refuses the job

d. P takes another job and earns $300,000 in profit during the six month period

e. P takes another job, but loses $150,000 in the six month period

3. D negligently damaged a barge owned by P1. P2 had leased the barge from P1. P2 had entered a contract with P3 to carry wheat on the barge. The damage forces P1 to pay $60,000 to repair the barge. In addition, P1 loses $40,000 that P2 would have paid during the period of repairs, because the lease allows credit for time the barge is not in service. P2 suffers lost profits of $20,000 because it cannot collect the price of carriage from P3. Because P2 cannot carry the wheat; P3 suffers $45,000 in lost profits (P2 is not liable due to impracticability) when it breaches a contract to sell the wheat at the port where P2 was to deliver it. Which, if any, of these parties may collect damages from D?

ANSWERS

1. D. The wrongdoer rule (E) only works if the existence of loss is certain. B is sometimes stated by courts, but most then undermine the requirement that the amount be proven with certainty by invoking the wrongdoer rule. A is a fair statement, unless you read it to require absolute certainty that the loss is at least the jury award. A judge will remit any award that exceeds the amount shown with reasonable certainty, but not necessarily any amount over the minimum award the evidence supports.

2. None. Construction contractors are treated as lost volume sellers, who could take more than one job at a time. Otherwise, in situation E, the court might increase the damage award by $150,000, since the breach not only deprived P of $1 million in profit, but also thrust P into a substitute contract on which P lost another $150,000. If not treated as lost volume sellers, D would require a reduction of $300,000. C might require a reduction of $400,000. We would need to know why P refused the work to ascertain whether that was reasonable.

3. P1 suffered property damage. He may sue D for negligence. Neither P2 nor P3 suffered property damage, but just economic loss. They may not collect from D.

If this had been a foreseeability question, we would have needed to inquire whether leases of this sort are so common that injury to P2 could be described as the ordinary course of events—or, alternatively, whether P1 mentioned the P2 lease to D. If D had a contractual relationship with P1, we might ask whether P2 was a third-party beneficiary of the contract, which might then allow economic loss to be recovered under a contract claim. Interestingly, even if P2's lease is not foreseeable, P3's loss might be. Carrying cargo on the barge should be foreseeable in the ordinary course of events. Someone must have been paying to use the barge, or so a reasonable person should assume.

F. Agreed Remedies

Parties to a contract may include terms intended to limit or to augment the remedies courts normally award. After early hostility to such provisions, courts have begun to enforce these contractual terms relating to remedies, within limits.

1. Limitations on Remedy

Limitations on remedy usually take one of two forms: (1) terms precluding recovery of some element of damages, such as consequential damages; or (2) terms substituting a different remedy for the ones provided in the code, such as the cost to repair or replace promised property. A term providing a substitute remedy may preclude consequential damages implicitly: if plaintiff can recover only the cost of repair, consequential damages are excluded. Some contracts include both kinds of provisions. Article 2 of the Uniform Commercial Code (covering sales of goods) adopts different standards for these two kinds of limitations.

a. Excluding Consequential Damages

A term precluding recovery of consequential damages is valid unless unconscionable. U.C.C. § 2–719(3). The code includes a rebuttable presumption that a clause limiting consequential damages when consumer goods cause personal injury is unconscionable. *Id.* Clauses limiting commercial consequential losses are expressly authorized. Unconscionability probably means the same thing in this section that it means in section 2–302. Unconscionable is not defined in the code. Thus, courts use varying tests to determine whether a term is unconscionable. A term almost certainly will be held unconscionable if two elements are satisfied: (1) **unfair surprise**; and (2) **oppression**, sometimes stated as terms unreasonably favorable to the person who proposed them.

(1) Unfair Surprise

Unfair surprise implies that one party: (1) was unaware of the existence or effect of the terms; and (2) that party had no fair chance to determine the existence or effect of the terms before entering the contract. It may not be enough to prove the party did not read the contract and thus did not know the terms were there. If reading the contract would have alerted her to the terms, then the surprise is not unfair. But if the terms were concealed in a manner that would have prevented her from recognizing their existence or effect—fine print, language calculated to confuse, misleading headings, etc.—perhaps the failure to discover and understand them is excusable and the surprise unfair.

(2) Oppression

Oppression (or unreasonably favorable terms) implies that one party: (1) receives an advantage from having the terms in the contract; and (2) the advantage is unreasonable. Thus, it may not be enough to prove that the terms favor one party; all terms eventually favor one party or the other. But if the terms provide an advantage that lacks a commercial justification, the term may be unreasonably favorable.

(3) Alternative Formulations of Unconscionability

The definition of unconscionability described here is relatively strict and hard to satisfy. Courts have considered other factors to find limitations of remedy unconscionable. Some courts apply this test, but require either element instead of both. Thus, an unreasonably favorable term would establish unconscionability without unfair surprise, and perhaps (though less commonly) unfair surprise would establish unconscionability even if the term was reasonable.

Other courts state or interpret the elements differently. Unfair surprise sometimes may become lack of reasonable choice. A party who does not realize a term is in a contract certainly lacks any ability to bargain for a different term (because she does not realize there is any need to bargain for a different term). But this formulation tends to expand to include other constrained choices, such as unequal bargaining power. Thus, a court may find unconscionability when a party would not have been able to persuade the other to change or delete the term if she had tried to bargain. This approach, in effect, allows the weaker party to force terms on the stronger party-a result inconsistent with contract theories based on mutual assent. Courts using this definition always require some showing of oppression in addition to lack of reasonable choice—otherwise, no term of any form contract would ever be enforceable.

Other courts redefine oppression to focus on the harmful effects to the plaintiff rather than the reasonableness of the term. Thus, a term that has harsh effects satisfies the oppression requirement, even if the other party had very good commercial reasons for insisting on that term. This approach is inconsistent with the U.C.C. requirement that unconscionability be determined at the time of contract formation; at the time of formation, the effects are unknown, while the commercial justification of the term makes it seem reasonable, not overreaching by the proponent.

b. Substituted Remedies

The U.C.C. allows parties to substitute remedies for those provided in the code. U.C.C. § 2–719(1)(a). The remedies may expand rather than limit recovery. For instance, contracts that permit the prevailing party to recover attorneys' fees expand recovery. More commonly, contracts seek to limit recovery, often by specifying plaintiff's remedy is limited to repairs.

The substitute remedy may be either exclusive or optional. If optional, the plaintiff may elect to pursue remedies under the code instead of the substitute remedy. If the substitute remedy does not specify that it is exclusive, then it is optional. U.C.C. § 2–719(1)(b). Most contracts seeking to limit remedies specify that their remedies are exclusive.

An exclusive remedy precludes recourse to remedies under the code, unless the exclusive remedy fails of its essential purpose. U.C.C. § 2–719(2). For instance, if the exclusive remedy limits the buyer to repair, the inability to repair the goods after sufficient opportunity to do so may be treated as a failure of the essential purpose of the limited remedy. The mere fact that the remedy is not as generous as those provided in the code is not sufficient to justify rejecting the contractual remedy. But the utter failure to provide the plaintiff with the benefit for which they bargained may permit the court to reject the limited remedy provided in the contract.

c. Double Limitations

Some contracts contain both limitations: they limit the remedy to repairs and they expressly exclude consequential damages, often in two separate provisions. In those cases, courts must determine how the failure of one clause relates to the other. Specifically, when repairs are impossible, negating the substituted remedy, what happens to the exclusion of consequential damages. Some courts hold that the two clauses are independent: as long as the express term excluding consequential damages is not unconscionable, it is enforceable, without regard to the fate of the substituted remedy. Others find that the failure of the substituted remedy should allow the plaintiff recourse to consequential damages: in effect, the failure of one limitation is the failure of both limitations. This view probably gives too little weight to the contract the parties made. Nonetheless, the animosity courts sometimes show to limitations that preclude effective remedies—those that put the plaintiff in the position she would have occupied if the wrong had not occurred—produce this result.

2. Liquidated Damages

Some contracts specify an amount of damages, either as a fixed amount or by a formula. Provisions of this sort are called liquidated damages clauses. Arguably, these are not substituted remedies: they do not reject the principles governing calculation of damages, but simply attempt to perform the calculation in advance. Nonetheless, a liquidated damages clause can specify a different measure than used in the code and thus could be treated as a substitute remedy.

Liquidated damages clauses have achieved general acceptance, but penalty clauses remain void as against public policy. Deciding whether a clause is a penalty or merely liquidates damages can be difficult. The substance of the clause determines its classification: merely calling a clause liquidated damages (or a penalty) will not ensure that the courts will treat it as such.

a. Liquidated Damages Clauses

A liquidated damages clause is enforceable if it is reasonable. Factors considered in determining the reasonableness of a clause include the anticipated or actual harm caused by the breach, the difficulties of proof of loss, and the inconvenience or infeasibility of otherwise obtaining an adequate remedy (say, through injunctive relief or restitution). U.C.C. § 2–718(1); RESTATEMENT (SECOND) OF CONTRACTS § 356.

Note: Amendments to the U.C.C., not yet widely adopted, propose to limit the second two factors to consumer contracts. Thus, the relation between the clause and the anticipated or actual harm would be pertinent to any contract, consumer or commercial. But difficulty of proof of loss would no longer be pertinent in evaluating liquidated damage clauses in commercial contracts. The goal seems to be to make clauses more easily enforceable in commercial settings by eliminating the argument that damages could easily be calculated after the breach and, thus, need not be estimated in the contract.

(1) Anticipated or Actual Harm

Clauses are enforceable if the amount "is reasonable in light of the anticipated or actual harm caused by the breach." U.C.C. § 2–718(1). Thus, a clause may be valid even if it wildly exceeds the actual harm, so long as it is reasonable in light of the anticipated harm. Similarly, a clause may be valid even if it wildly exceeds the anticipated harm, if it is reasonable in light of the actual harm. Thus, a clause the parties thought would be a penalty (because they underestimated how large the actual harm would be) may be enforceable.

Caution: the test specifies the anticipated or actual *harm*, not the anticipated or actual *damages*. If the harm caused by the breach is great, it does not matter that the damages a plaintiff might recover under the rules of the code are relatively small. The liquidated damages clause allows the parties to include recovery for losses that the code otherwise would not allow, especially damages that might otherwise be unforeseeable or damages that might be impossible to prove with the requisite degree of certainty. Thus, arguing that the clause is too large because the damages awarded would be lower is unlikely to succeed; instead, you must argue that the clause exceeds the amount of harm caused by the breach.

(2) Difficulty of Proof of Loss

At one time, this was a separate element. If loss would be relatively easy to measure after the breach occurred, courts refused to enforce liquidated damage clauses regardless of their reasonableness. That view has disappeared. Difficulty of proof of loss is simply one factor to discuss in evaluating reasonableness—and probably a secondary factor. It primarily effects the degree of accuracy a court will require. Where damages are relatively difficult to assess after a breach—as where profits are hard to estimate—a clause may be enforceable even if it seems relatively large in comparison to the actual loss the court believes occurred. The margin for error is larger. On the other hand, if damages are relatively easy to calculate—as where cover price and contract price are readily ascertainable in the market—a clause estimating damages may need to be relatively close to the actual or anticipated loss before a court will enforce it.

(3) Inconvenience or Infeasibility of Other Remedies

Where a plaintiff foregoes other remedies in favor of a liquidated damage clause, the court may suspect that the liquidated damage clause is excessive. Thus, a court may be tempted to call the clause a penalty unless the decision to forego other remedies is reasonable. Where other remedies are unavailable or relatively inconvenient, the choice of the liquidated damage clause may be reasonable. Thus, where specific performance is impossible—maybe because it would come too late to prevent the harm, maybe because other technicalities prevent it—the choice to seek liquidated damages instead may be acceptable. In some cases, a liquidated damage clause itself may preclude other remedies by specifying that it is plaintiff's exclusive remedy. The argument is somewhat circular and may not prevail.

b. Bonuses

In some situations, parties can achieve the same effect by writing a bonus clause instead of a liquidated damage clause. Consider two terms:

(1) A $20 million construction contract required completion by October 31, but provided that the contractor will receive a bonus of $100,000 per day for each day completion was early, up to a maximum of $3 million.

(2) A $23 million construction contract required completion by October 1, but included a liquidated damage provision calling for damages of

$100,000 per day for each day completion was delayed, to a maximum of $3 million.

No matter which day in October the construction is completed, these two provisions provide the same payment. The second clearly could be called a penalty, unless $100,000 a day is reasonable in light of the actual or anticipated harm. The first clause, however, does not specify damages for breach at all. There is no breach on any day (until after October 31), so no clause attempts to specify the damages for breach. Even analyzing the clause under this rule seems a stretch.

Some authorities urge that the rules governing penalties here should be applied to contract provisions that seek to circumvent the limitations. Thus, they suggest treating the bonus clause as if it is a liquidated damage clause, despite its completely different nature. While the rationale is suspect, a complete analysis of these clauses might need to include a discussion of this possibility.

c. Alternative Performance

Some contracts specify alternative performances: that is, they allow one party to perform in either of two ways, one of which may be more onerous than the other. For instance, a loan may allow the borrower to pay over the full life of the loan or to pay the full amount early, provided a fee for early payment is included. This is not a liquidated damage clause. There is no breach, so no damages for breach. Unless the additional charges are triggered by a breach of contract, the analysis here does not apply. *See Ridgley v. Topa Thrift and Loan Association*, 17 Cal.4th 970, 953 P.2d 484, 73 Cal.Rptr.2d 378 (1998) (prepayment fee waived if payments were timely converted fee into a penalty for breach).

Similarly, courts have not employed penalty analysis to take-or-pay clauses in oil and gas contracts. These provisions require the buyer to pay for gas whether or not she accepts delivery of the gas. Refusing delivery (arguably) is not a breach; refusing to pay is a breach. (As long as seller is paid, she cares little what you do with the package when it arrives. You can give it to the delivery person or leave it on the porch forever; it's yours to deal with as you please.) In effect, these provisions shift responsibility to resell unwanted gas from seller to buyer.

3. Agreements Regarding Equitable Remedies

Agreements sometimes provide that specific performance or other equitable relief should be awarded in the event of breach. Because equity is discretionary relief, courts generally do not give these clauses binding effect. Rather, courts view these clauses as invitations to use their discretion that way and maybe as a waiver of some objections a party might raise.

REVIEW QUESTIONS

1. P, a small business owner, pays D $1,000 to print an ad in D's phone directory. The contract between them includes a provision expressly excluding consequential damages. The provision is preprinted on the back of a form drafted by D, in paragraph number 17 (of 31 total paragraphs), in print the same size as all the other terms on the back, but a little smaller than the terms on the front (which include price, size, text, layout, dates of performance, and other negotiated items). D misprints P's phone number and address in the add, so customers cannot find P. P sues alleging lost profits of $18,000. Can P recover the lost profits?

a. Yes, because the clause excluding consequential damages failed of its essential purpose.

b. No, because commercial consequential damages can be excluded under the UCC.

c. Yes, because the clause was in fine print buried in the middle of a long contract, making it unconscionable.

d. No, because the term serves a reasonable commercial purpose and was available for P, a business person, to read.

e. Yes, because the exclusion did not expressly state it was exclusive and, therefore, plaintiff had the option to pursue other remedies.

2. P agreed to buy a house from D, making a deposit of $10,000. The contract stated that, in the event P breached the contract by refusing to pay the full price on the date of closing, D could retain the full $10,000 as liquidated damages. At the time the contract was signed, housing prices in the area had been rising steadily and significantly for several years. Thus, it seemed likely that breach by P would benefit D, allowing D to sell for an even higher price. P breached the contract. D kept the $10,000. When D tried to resell, the housing market had slowed down. D sold to another buyer for $2,000 less than P had promised. If P sues seeking return of the deposit alleging that the clause was a penalty, what is the likely result?

   a. P will win, because $10,000 was much more than the damages the parties anticipated at the time they entered the contract, showing they intended a penalty.

   b. D will win, because $10,000 is reasonable in light of the actual loss suffered.

   c. P will win, because the loss D suffered is easily ascertainable, making the liquidated damage clause unnecessary.

   d. D will win, because forfeiting $10,000 is an alternative performance, not governed by the provisions on liquidated damages.

   e. P will win, because courts don't want parties interfering with judicial functions such as assessing damages.

ANSWERS

1. D is the best answer. B isn't wrong, as far as it goes. The U.C.C. does authorize clauses like this—but includes a defense if they are unconscionable. In addition, the U.C.C. will not apply to this case. B implies that all such clauses are authorized, not just those that pass the unconscionability test. That is wrong. A and E are wrong because each refers to language applicable to substitute remedies, not to exclusions of consequential damages, the clause at issue here. C could be part of a good answer. Without some comment on the oppression of the clause, merely showing it was in fine print may not suffice—especially against a business person, who should know to read what she signs. Because some courts apply unconscionability pretty loosely, D is not a certainty. C might prevail.

2. B. A is wrong because the clause need only be reasonable in light of the anticipated or actual loss. While the clause is five times the lost profit, the cost of advertising the house longer, of paying insurance on it longer, of paying for a second set of escrow documents, and similar expenses of sale almost certainly raise the damages a bit, putting them in the ballpark of $10,000, even if they don't fill the park.

G. Punitive or Exemplary Damages

Punitive Damages are not damages in the usual sense. They are a monetary recovery, but they are not based on the loss or damage the plaintiff suffered. Rather, they assume that compensatory damages have covered those losses completely and seek to impose an additional burden on defendant over and above the cost of compensating the plaintiff.

1. Rationale

Two rationales have been offered for punitive damages: (1) retribution and (2) deterrence. Calling the recovery exemplary damages suggests making an example of defendant, so that others seeing the results will adjust their conduct, a deterrence rationale. The name punitive damages suggests a retributive motive, aimed not at others but at the defendant alone. The choice of theory may have some implications for how these damages are implemented. For example, vicarious liability for punitive damages (under, for example, *respondeat superior*) is harder to justify if they are deemed retributive than if they are intended as a deterrent. *See* RESTATEMENT THIRD OF TORTS: REMEDIES § 40 (describing the limited circumstances in which a vicariously liable defendant may be subject to punitive damages).

2. Standard for Awarding

Punitive damages are not limited by the cause of action brought by the plaintiff, but by the level of culpability of the defendant. Thus, for example, although intentional torts are the quintessential actions in which punitive damages are available, punitives might also be available for actions in restitution, replevin, ejectment, quiet title, or even negligence if defendant's conduct constitutes recklessness.

Generally, intentional or malicious misconduct justifies punitive damages, while mere negligence or strict liability (including breach of contract) do not. The exact boundary varies among the states. All states that allow punitive damages allow them for **actual malice, where defendant intends the harm.** Generally, that includes imputed intent—not just the purpose to cause the harm, but also knowledge to a substantial certainty that harm will result. Most allow punitive damages where defendant's conduct implies malice—for example, if conduct is so outrageous that it seems likely defendant knew harm would result. *See Tuttle v. Raymond*, 494 A.2d 1353 (Me. 1985). Similarly, conscious disregard of an "unjustifiably substantial risk of significant harm" may justify an inference of malice. *See Linthicum v. Nationwide Life Ins. Co.*, 150 Ariz. 326, 723 P.2d 675, 680 (1986). Many states also allow punitive damages for reckless disregard of a known risk, at least where the risk of harm is great. Whether the risk must be significant, probable, or substantially likely to occur varies among the states. Some states—fewer today than before—allow punitive damages for *gross negligence*, though the line between negligence and gross negligence is hard to describe in a rule. In effect, this allows juries to decide whether the conduct was bad negligence instead of mere negligence, a rather subjective approach to defendant's culpability.

In most jurisdictions, a plaintiff must establish the relevant state of mind by clear-and-convincing evidence. *See* RESTATEMENT THIRD OF TORTS: REMEDIES § 39.

3. Measuring the Amount

No precise standard for measuring punitive damages has achieved general acceptance. Instead, states tend to list a number of factors juries may consider when determining how much to award. These factors include: (1) reprehensibility of the conduct; (2) defendant's wealth (*but see* G.4, *infra*); (3) amount of compensatory damages; (4) amount likely to deter similar conduct by defendant and others; and (5) the aggregate amount of all civil and criminal sanctions awarded against the defendant for the conduct at issue. RESTATEMENT THIRD OF TORTS: REMEDIES § 41(a).

A court may review the amount of punitive damages for gross excessiveness or inadequacy, so long as there is a strong basis in the record for so concluding. *Id.* § 41(b).

4. Limitations

Punitive Damages have come under attack both in legislatures and in courts. As a result, a number of limitations have been imposed on the availability and amount of punitive damages.

a. Contract

Long before tort reform, courts held that punitive damages could not be recovered for breach of contract. (The traditional exception for breach of promise of marriage has been mooted by statutes repealing that cause of action in most states.) Litigants sometimes find ways around this limitation. For instance, if conduct breaches a tort duty, the fact that it also breaches a contractual duty will not preclude punitive damages (or any other tort damages). In some cases, breaches of contract have been redefined as torts. Most notably, breach of an obligation of good faith and fair dealing in an insurance contract has been deemed a tort. Sometimes, wrongful discharge of an employee will justify punitive damages, such as where the employer retaliates against an employee who reported the employer's illegal conduct, who refused to commit perjury to conceal that conduct, or who filed a worker's compensation claim. In other cases, denying liability under a contract without a good faith belief that the defense is valid may justify punitive damages. The last probably should be treated as the tort of abuse of process (filing a frivolous defense, similar to filing a frivolous complaint), rather than as punitive damages for breach of contract.

b. Actual Damages

Some states refuse to award punitive damages unless the plaintiff can prove some actual damages resulted from the misconduct. Most states allow punitive damages even if plaintiff receives only nominal damages. These decisions can be reconciled, at least in theory. In any case where the state would not award any damages without harm to the plaintiff, it should not award punitive damages to the plaintiff. Punitive damages should not trump the liability rule requiring some evidence of injury. In any case where the state elects to award some damages without evidence of harm (nominal damages), it also should consider punitive damages. Allowing punitive damages does not circumvent a liability rule in these cases.

c. Statutory Limitations

Statutes may limit two aspects of punitive damages: (1) how much may be awarded; and (2) who receives the award. Limits on the amount of punitive damages may resemble limits on the amount of pain and suffering or other nonpecuniary damages recoverable in litigation. Statutes sometimes specify that some portion of any punitive award be paid to the state. At the extreme,

Nebraska requires that all penalties collected under state law (but not federal causes of action in state courts) be paid to counties for the use supporting schools. *See* NEB. CONST. art. 7, § 5. As a result, plaintiffs' attorneys waste no time pleading and proving punitive damages. Other states impose more modest sharing schemes, allowing plaintiffs to keep enough to cover costs and attorneys' fees, but collect a portion (50–75%) of the remaining punitive damages for the state. *See, e.g.*, FLA. STAT. § 768.73(2) (75%); IOWA CODE § 668A.1(2) (60%); *Dardinger v. Anthem Blue Cross & Blue Shield*, 98 Ohio St.3d 77, 781 N.E.2d 121 (2002). At least one court has rejected a sharing statute. *See Kirk v. Denver Pub. Co.*, 818 P.2d 262 (Colo. 1991).

d. Constitutional Limitations

The United States Supreme Court has ruled that an award of punitive damages may be so excessive that it violates the due process clause of the fourteenth amendment. Due process requires that "a person receive fair notice not only of the conduct that will subject him to punishment, but also of the severity of the penalty that a State may impose." *BMW of North America, Inc. v. Gore*, 517 U.S. 559, 574, 116 S.Ct. 1589, 1598, 134 L.Ed.2d 809 (1996). To determine whether an award satisfies that standard, the Court identified three factors the court should consider:

> "(1) the degree of reprehensibility of the defendant's misconduct; (2) the disparity between the actual or potential harm suffered by the plaintiff and the punitive damages award; and (3) the difference between the punitive damages awarded by the jury and the civil penalties authorized or imposed in comparable cases."

State Farm Mutual Automobile Ins. Co. v. Campbell, 538 U.S. 408, 418, 123 S.Ct. 1513, 1520, 155 L.Ed.2d 585 (2003). Note the similarity between these factors and the factors state courts often employ in deciding how much to award. *See* G.3, *supra*. In effect, the Constitutional rule simply allows the federal courts to review state court decisions regarding whether damages are excessive under the circumstances, perhaps coming to a different conclusion. In addition, courts must review the constitutionality of a punitive award de novo, rather than applying an abuse of discretion test. *Cooper Industries v. Leatherman Tool Group*, 532 U.S. 424, 121 S.Ct. 1678, 149 L.Ed.2d 674 (2001).

In *State Farm*, the Court appeared to reject evidence of defendant's wealth, a factor commonly used by state courts. When reviewing the constitutionality of a punitive damage award, "the wealth of a defendant cannot justify an otherwise unconstitutional punitive damages award." *State Farm*, 538 U.S. at 427, 123 S.Ct. at 1525. This language does not preclude a state from admitting evidence of defendant's wealth or allowing the jury to rely on that evidence. A court reviewing the jury award, however, cannot rely on evidence of defendant's wealth to establish that the award satisfies constitutional limits. Unless the other factors establish the constitutionality of the award, it will need to be reduced.

(1) Reprehensibility

Courts consider the nature of the harm (physical injury vs. economic loss), the defendant's state of mind (malice or indifference to the safety of others vs. mere accident), the financial vulnerability of the plaintiff, the frequency of the misconduct (repeated actions vs. isolated incident). These factors are similar to those states use in determining the availability of punitive damages. *See* G.2, *supra*. Realistically, any argument that makes the harm or the conduct seem more severe may contribute to the reprehensibility of the conduct. The factor is likely to give rise to rhetoric more than analysis.

The Supreme Court in *Philip Morris USA v. Williams*, 549 U.S. 346, 127 S.Ct. 1057 (2007), held that reprehensible conduct by the defendant against anyone other than the plaintiff may not be considered by the jury in assigning punitive damages. Evidence of general reprehensible conduct may, however, be admissible to show that the conduct that harmed the plaintiff also posed a risk to the general public and was therefore particularly reprehensible. It seems unlikely that a jury will find it easy to parse such a distinction.

(2) Proportionality

Courts consider the relationship between the compensatory damages and the punitive damages. The factor can work two ways. First, the smaller compensatory damages are, the more likely that a large punitive award will seem excessive relative to the harm caused. In *State Farm*, the Court rejected any formula but hinted that few awards could survive scrutiny where the ratio of punitive damages to compensatory damages was 10:1 or higher. 538 U.S. at 425, 123 S.Ct. at 1524. (On remand, the Utah Supreme Court ignored the U.S. Supreme Court's suggestion that $1 million would be an appropriate award, instead allowing Campbell $9 million in punitive damages-a ratio of 9:1. *See* 98 P.3d 409 (Utah 2004), *cert. denied*, 543 U.S. 874, 125 S.Ct. 114, 160 L.Ed.2d 123 (2004).) In calculating this ratio, courts may use the potential harm of defendant's misconduct rather than actual harm. Thus, a defendant whose nefarious scheme fails (perhaps due to injunctive relief) still may face a substantial punitive award.

Second, the larger the compensatory award, the more likely it is that compensatory damages alone will deter the misconduct adequately. Thus, punitive damages may be unnecessary or, if justified, a relatively low ratio (say, 1:1) may suffice.

Rules of proportionality do not strictly apply to claims for nominal damages, although it seems likely that a large punitive damages award attaching to nominal damages would not likely be upheld.

Since the *State Farm* decision, scholars have found that the proportionality requirements have not led to reduced punitive damages awards in typical cases, although they possibly have had a downward impact in blockbuster cases. For a useful summary of the literature, see Benjamin J. McMichael, *Note Constitutional Limitations on Punitive Damages: Ambiguous Effects and Inconsistent Justifications*, 66 VAND. L. REV. 961 (2013).

(3) Other Sanctions

Courts consider other sanctions—usually criminal penalties, but sometimes from other statutes—that might apply to the misconduct. The larger the other sanctions, the more likely a large punitive damage award will survive. The large statutory sanctions serve to put defendants on notice that the government takes misconduct of this type seriously, thus serving the purpose of the due process clause. Where penalties are smaller, the defendant lacks warning of the severity of the penalty that a state may impose. Deference to legislative decisions about the appropriate magnitude of a sanction may be appropriate. This approach may limit the usefulness of punitive damages as a means to rectify the legislature's failure to impose sanctions large enough to deter misconduct.

5. Punitive Damages in Arbitration

When arbitrators award punitive damages, courts confront questions concerning the propriety of those awards. The challenges take different forms. Some argue that arbitrators should not be allowed to award punitive damages at all, that this power should be reserved for the government (that is, judges and juries). Others argue that arbitrators should not be allowed to award punitive damages unless a court would have been able to award punitive damages in the type of case. Thus, an arbitrator might lack authority to award punitive damages in a contract case, but retain that authority in tort cases. Each argument runs up against the general rule that arbitrators are not constrained by the rules that limit courts, they may award punitive damages in situations where a court would not. Other challenges focus on the arbitration agreement, seeking to establish that it does not authorize the arbitrator to award punitive damages.

a. Federal Arbitration Act

The Federal Arbitration Act (FAA) governs arbitration clauses in contracts involved in interstate commerce. Federal courts have enforced arbitration awards that include punitive damages under this act. Almost all such awards involve some element of tort. Even those based on contract usually include allegations of fraud. Thus, it appears that under federal law, courts will enforce arbitration awards that include punitive damages as long as a court could have considered punitive damages had the case been litigated in court. Thus, in tort cases, an arbitration award including punitive damages seems likely to be enforced, but pure contract cases (where no tort is alleged) may not receive similar treatment.

Judicial review of arbitration awards usually does not include a review of factual findings. Thus, the arbitrator's conclusion that the defendant acted with malice—or even a decision to award punitive damages based on a lesser finding of culpability—is unlikely be reviewed in court. This may pose problems for courts seeking to apply constitutional limitations on awards of punitive damages. It remains to be seen whether the instruction to review the constitutionality of punitive damage awards de novo applies to district courts reviewing arbitration awards or only to appellate courts reviewing trial awards.

b. State Laws

Contracts not governed by the FAA may include arbitration clauses permitted under state arbitration actions. Many state courts have affirmed arbitration awards including punitive damages. As with the FAA, most of these cases include some allegation of tort. Reported cases rarely involve arbitration awards of punitive damages in cases of pure breach of contract. Some courts expressly note that in court plaintiff could have recovered punitive damages.

(1) Authorizing the Arbitrator

The issue often involves whether the arbitration clause authorized the arbitrator to award punitive damages. If the parties agreed to allow the arbitrator to award punitive damages, the state's interest in protecting people from their own agreement diminishes. Arbitration clauses can be an important part of contracts, keeping the price down by keeping the cost of resolving disputes down. Denying them their intended effect can undermine the parties' agreement—and future agreements between similar parties.

To this end, courts sometimes focus on whether the clause allows arbitrators to award punitive damages. Several approaches emerge: (1) a broad clause authorizes punitive damages unless it expressly excludes them; (2) a clause authorizes punitive damages only if it expressly includes them; (3) any indication that the parties intended to authorize arbitration of punitive damages will suffice. The last approach often involves cases where one party submits a request for punitive damages and the other party does not contest the request in the arbitration proceeding. Whether viewed as course of performance (showing that the parties believed the clause permitted punitive damages from the beginning) or an implied modification of the clause (where the parties' conduct suggests mutual assent to arbitrating the issue of punitive damages), courts have enforced arbitration awards in these circumstances.

A strict focus on intent of the parties might generate a two-prong rule, allowing punitive damages when tort claims are arbitrated, but not when contract claims are arbitrated. In tort cases, denying punitive damages in arbitration would convert the arbitration clause into a waiver of punitive damages. The clause itself probably gave plaintiff no notice of that implied waiver. In contract, however, allowing punitive damages would convert the arbitration clause into a consent to punitive damages, without notice to defendant that the clause would have that effect. Giving either effect to an arbitration clause amounts to a trap for the unwary, giving the party who understands the legal effects an advantage in negotiations. It seems fairer to assume the arbitration clause authorized a different forum, but did not include a change in the rules governing damages—unless the clause expressly alters the normal remedies courts award (that is, expressly authorizes punitive damages in contract or expressly rejects punitive damages in tort).

(2) Public Policy

One famous case appears to hold that arbitrators can never award punitive damages. *Garrity v. Lyle Stuart, Inc.*, 40 N.Y.2d 354, 386 N.Y.S.2d 831, 353 N.E.2d 793 (1976). The court stated that it violated the public policy of New York for private decisionmakers (arbiters), as opposed to public officials (judges), to award punitive sanctions—even if the parties expressly authorized the arbitrator to do so. While portions of the opinion are dicta, the breadth of the stated rationale casts doubt on any punitive award from an arbitrator. On the other hand, the opinion distinguished (but did not overrule) an earlier opinion enforcing an arbitrator's award of treble liquidated damages. Because treble liquidated damages amount to three times the estimated actual damages, the award is inherently punitive.

Perhaps the fact that the parties agreed on the formula for calculating the damages (three times the liquidated amount) as well as the availability of damages in excess of compensation assuaged the court's doubts about private penalties. Nonetheless, the opinions are difficult to reconcile. *Garrity* generally has been criticized in other jurisdictions.

REVIEW QUESTIONS

1. The standard of review for appellate courts considering the constitutionality of punitive damage awards is:
   a. Abuse of Discretion
   b. Bad Faith
   c. Clearly Erroneous
   d. De Novo
2. True or False: The Supreme Court has ruled that evidence of a defendant's wealth cannot be admitted in trials where plaintiff seeks punitive damages.
3. Most courts enforce arbitration awards that include punitive damages, as long as:
   a. The clause expressly authorizes the arbiter to award punitive damages and specifies a formula for calculating the damages
   b. The parties expressly authorized the arbiter to award punitive damages
   c. The parties expressly or implicitly authorized the arbiter to award punitive damages
   d. The case arises under the Federal Arbitration Act
   e. The case involves a tort claim

ANSWERS

1. D, de novo.
2. False. The court ruled that, in assessing the constitutionality of a punitive award, defendant's wealth cannot justify an award that would otherwise be excessive. But nothing stops trial courts, as a matter of state law, from admitting the evidence and instructing the jury how they may consider it.
3. E.

H. Attorneys' Fees

The American Rule rejects recovery of attorneys' fees, leaving each party to pay their own counsel—even though other court costs are assessed against the losing party. It contrasts with the British Rule, in which the loser pays the winner's attorney, though fees assessed often do not equal actual fees incurred. The American Rule protects the ability of people of modest means to bring claims. Faced with the risk that they might need to pay defendant huge amounts for attorneys' fees, even a fifteen percent chance of losing might deter many plaintiffs. The rich might be able to take these chances, as might the poorest members of society, who have no property on which defendant could execute a judgement for fees.

Controversy arises because the rule leaves the plaintiff worse off than if the wrong had not occurred. If damages accurately assess the plaintiff's loss, reducing them by 33–50% to cover the attorneys' share (perhaps more to cover expert witness fees and other expenses) leaves plaintiff well short of the rightful position. In equitable actions, the problem is more stark. Even if the injunction prevents the wrong, the cost of an attorney falls entirely on the plaintiff, leaving her net negative.

As a result, numerous exceptions to the American Rule allow prevailing parties to recover their attorneys' fees.

1. Statutory Exceptions

A number of statutes permit the prevailing plaintiff to recover attorneys' fees. Alaska allows partial fee-shifting in all cases, in effect the British Rule. Alaska R. Civ. P. 82. Other states allow fee shifting in contract cases but reject or limit fee shifting in tort cases. Ariz. Rev. Stat. § 12–341.01; Texas Civ. Prac. & Rem. Code §§ 37.009, 38.001. Many state consumer protection statutes allow fees in suits for unfair business practices. Federal civil rights laws commonly allow fee-shifting, including employment discrimination suits and actions under 42 U.S.C. § 1983. Antitrust suits and claims under the Racketeer Influenced and Corrupt Organizations Act (RICO) allow treble damages plus attorneys' fees to a prevailing plaintiff (but none for prevailing defendants). The Equal Access to Justice Act allows fees to some parties (individuals and small corporations) litigating against the government, if their net worth falls below specified levels (in the millions). Fees are denied, however, if the government's position was substantially justified. Thus, instead of drawing the line between winning and losing, it probes the reasonableness of litigation, almost a claim for negligent litigation.

a. Asymmetrical Fee Shifting

Most fee-shifting statutes allow the prevailing plaintiff to recover fees as a matter of course. A denial of fees to a prevailing plaintiff would be an abuse of discretion, barring unusual circumstances. Prevailing defendants, however, often face a stricter standard: they may recover their fees only if the plaintiff's action was frivolous. In effect, this equates defendants' rights to fees to a malicious prosecution action. Courts explain the ruling as consistent with these statutes' purpose of encouraging plaintiffs to help the government enforce these statutes by bringing claims. The approach is equally consistent with compensating plaintiffs for the loss caused by the wrong, which includes attorneys' fees. Defendants' fees, however, are not caused by plaintiff's wrong unless it is wrong to bring the suit—applicable for malicious prosecution, but not for merely bringing a claim that loses.

b. Prevailing Party

Most statutes provide fees to the prevailing party. When a party wins a judgment in court on all counts, no problem arises. Difficulties arise whenever a lesser success occurs.

(1) Partial Success

Successful plaintiffs may succeed on some but not all of their claims or against only some of the defendants named. In these situations, courts must decide whether to reject fees associated with the unsuccessful claims.

Sometimes all hours spent on the case deserve compensation, as where defendants' conduct prevented plaintiff from discovering which of them was liable or where the unsuccessful claims were necessary to cover contingencies that otherwise might allow defendants to escape liability. In other cases, plaintiff may be limited to the fees incurred pursuing the successful claims, especially where the other claims bordered on the frivolous.

(2) Settlement vs. Consent Decrees

Where the parties agree to resolve the litigation, they may embody the agreement in one of two ways. A settlement agreement is a contract between the parties. Failure to perform allows the nonbreaching party to sue the breaching party in contract. Alternatively, the parties may ask the court to embody their agreement in a consent decree. This converts the agreement into a court order, breach of which is contempt of court. A consent decree is a judgment of the court, thus qualifying the plaintiff as a prevailing party. A settlement agreement, however, does not permit attorneys' fees. Settlements contain no indicia that the court approved the award. In fact, many settlements involve defendants paying to avoid nuisance suits, not paying to liquidate their liability for a wrong. Settling parties may include their fee arrangement in the settlement agreement.

(3) Catalyst

In some cases, filing a suit will induce defendant to change its ways. When the relief requested is injunctive, the change may moot the suit. In these situations, plaintiffs have sought fees, alleging that their suit obtained the relief sought, even though no court order was entered. The U.S. Supreme Court has ruled that catalysts are not prevailing parties under federal fee-shifting statutes. *Buckhannon Board and Care Home v. West Virginia Dept. of Health and Human Services*, 532 U.S. 598, 121 S.Ct. 1835, 149 L.Ed.2d 855 (2001).

c. Lodestar

Courts interpreting fee-shifting statutes start by calculating a number called the lodestar: the number of hours reasonably spent on the action times the reasonable hourly fee. This makes accurate time records important even for attorneys who do not generally charge by the hour. The reasonable number of hours will vary with a number of factors, including the novelty and difficulty of the case, the time required, the amount at issue, and the results obtained. The reasonable hourly fee will vary with the skill required, the ability of the attorney to accept other work, the customary fee for similar work in the community, whether the fee is fixed or contingent, time limitations imposed by other clients, the attorneys' experience, reputation, and ability, the undesirability of the case, and the nature and length of the attorney-client relationship.

These factors, collected in *Johnson v. Georgia Highway Express*, 488 F.2d 714, 717–19 (5th Cir. 1974), *overruled on other grounds*, *Blanchard v. Bergeron*, 489 U.S. 87, 109 S.Ct. 939, 103 L.Ed.2d 67 (1989), sometimes are suggested as reasons to deviate from the lodestar amount rather than as factors that affect the appropriate number of hours or appropriate hourly fee. Enhancement for contingency under federal statutes was rejected in *City of Burlington v. Dague*, 505 U.S. 557, 112 S.Ct. 2638, 120 L.Ed.2d 449 (1992). States remain free to interpret their own statutes.

The hardest aspect of the lodestar is the appropriate hourly fee. Because plaintiff's attorneys typically work on contingency, it may be difficult to ascertain the customary fee for similar litigation. Hourly fees might be higher when the chance of collecting them is lower, fees might be higher for high-risk litigation than for low-risk litigation (where plaintiff is more likely to recover money to pay them or where the chance of collecting from defendant is greater). In this way, contingency enhancement may continue to play a role within the lodestar, though not as an independent enhancement.

2. Common Funds

The American Rule allows plaintiffs to collect attorneys' fees when their litigation created a fund that benefits a group of persons. The exception does not actually allow fee shifting to the defendant. Rather, the fee comes from the award; the portion each claimant receives is reduced to account for the fees of the attorneys who created the fund. The exception shares the fees among the beneficiaries of the litigation but does not shift them to defendant. Shareholder derivative suits are a common example of litigation that creates a common fund. **In common fund cases, courts sometimes award a percentage of the fund rather than applying lodestar**. The common fund exception is a judicial creation, not a statutory provision.

3. Other Exceptions

a. Contract

If the parties to a contract agree that the prevailing party may recover attorneys' fees, courts will honor those provisions. Clauses of that nature are common in loan agreements and some leases. Terms occasionally favor only one party, such as the lender or landlord. By statute, at least one state enforces these clauses as mutual, even if their terms favor only one party.

b. Contempt

When a party's violation of a court order forces the opponent to bring contempt proceedings, courts allow recovery of the fees incurred in connection with the contempt.

c. Family Law

In family law cases, courts often order the party with greater means to pay the other's attorney. In effect, orders of this nature simply distribute family resources among the parties, much the way the division of property distributes assets from one spouse to another. In this way, the rule resembles the common fund rule, in that the assets available to the parties diminish to pay the attorneys.

d. Collateral Litigation

In some cases, defendant's wrong forces plaintiff to incur expenses in litigating against third parties. In these situations, expenses incurred in the collateral litigation are recoverable as an ensuing loss, like medical expenses or any other consequential damage. For example, a party buying goods might bargain for a warranty that the goods do not infringe anyone's intellectual property rights. If sued for patent infringement, the buyer might sue the suppler for breach of warranty and recover the fees it incurs defending the infringement action as part of the damages. Fees incurred suing the supplier fall under the American Rule, but fees incurred in the collateral litigation are recoverable. Similarly, the RESTATEMENT THIRD OF TORTS § 16 provides that attorneys' fees are recoverable if a "tort caused the plaintiff to incur attorneys' fees to investigate, negotiate, or litigate a dispute with a person other than the defendant."

e. Litigation Misconduct

When a party conducts litigation without a good faith belief that it has merit, courts may award the other party fees for opposing the move. This can be a tort, such as malicious prosecution or abuse of process. In other cases, court rules provide sanctions for bad-faith litigation. Fed. R. Civ. P. 11. The wrong can involve the entire suit, or it might involve a single motion filed in bad faith.

f. Bad Faith Conduct by an Insurer

Attorneys' fees are commonly awarded in suits alleging the tort of bad-faith conduct by an insurer. *See* RESTATEMENT THIRD OF TORTS: REMEDIES § 16(b)(2).

REVIEW QUESTIONS

1. True or False: Plaintiff is a prevailing party entitled to attorneys' fees if the settlement agreement contains substantial damages, rather than just nuisance value for the suit.
2. True or False: Under the common fund exception, defendant must pay plaintiff's attorneys' fees in addition to the damages it owes plaintiffs.
3. True or False: Once a court determines the appropriate hourly fee and number of hours, it may adjust the award up or down based on the risks involved in the litigation.

ANSWERS

All three statements are false.

Appendix A

Glossary

American Rule. The requirement that each litigant must pay its own attorney's fees, even if the party prevails in the lawsuit. The rule is subject to bad-faith and other statutory and contractual exceptions.

Arbitration. A method of dispute resolution involving one or more neutral third parties who are usu. agreed to by the disputing parties and whose decision is binding.

Asset Value. The amount a person would pay for a right to receive a future stream of income, usually generated by a right. The asset may be physical property or an intangible, such as a contract right or patent. (See also capitalization of earnings)

Attorney Fees. The charge to a client for services performed for the client, such as an hourly fee, a flat fee, or a contingent fee.

Avoidable Consequences Doctrine. The principle requiring a plaintiff, after an injury or breach of contract, to make reasonable efforts to alleviate the effects of the injury or breach. If the defendant can show that the plaintiff failed to mitigate damages, the plaintiff's recovery may be reduced.

Benefit-of-the-Bargain. A measure of damage for misrepresentation, seeking to place the deceived party in the position she would have occupied if the misrepresentation had been true. In effect, this converts a representation into a warranty.

Benefit Rule. A doctrine requiring that plaintiff's tort recovery be reduced by the amount of any special benefit defendant's tort conferred upon the plaintiff, if the benefit accrued to an interest the tort harmed and if offset is equitable. RESTATEMENT, TORTS, § 920.

Capitalization of Earnings. A method of determining the value of an item based on the income it will produce over its lifetime. It is calculated by taking the current annual income and adding it to the value of each remaining year's income, discounting future income by an appropriate percentage.

Causation. The requirement that the plaintiff must demonstrate that the losses resulted from the defendant's wrong. It includes both cause in fact (but for causation) and legal (or proximate) causation.

Certainty. The requirement that at least the existence of damages, and sometimes the amount of damages, be proven with reasonable certainty before allowing a finder of fact to assess the amount of damages.

Chancery. A court of equity; collectively, the courts of equity.

Civil Action. An action brought to enforce, redress, or protect a private or civil right; a noncriminal litigation.

Civil Contempt. A civil-contempt proceeding is coercive or compensatory in nature. Coercive sanctions confine the contemnor until he or she complies with the court order of fines her a sum per day until she complies. Compensatory contempt assesses the losses the other party suffered as a result of the contempt.

Collateral Bar Rule. A rule prohibiting a contemnor from challenging the legitimacy of an injunction in a proceeding for criminal contempt. Challenges to an order must be brought by appeal or by a motion to stay or vacate the injunction, not in a contempt hearing.

Collateral Source Rule. A doctrine denying any offset against plaintiff's recovery in tort for benefits the plaintiff received from a source independent of the tortfeasor. Insurance proceeds are the most common collateral source. Also termed *collateral benefit rule.*—Black's

Comity. Courtesy among political entities involving esp. mutual recognition of legislative, executive, and judicial acts.

Compensatory Damages. Damages sufficient in amount to indemnify the injured person for the loss suffered. Fundamentally, compensatory damages seek to place the plaintiff in the position she would have occupied if the wrong had not occurred, to the extent that money can do so.

Consequential Damages. Losses that do not flow directly and immediately from an injurious act, but that result indirectly from the act. Usually consequential damages relate to how the plaintiff would have used the damaged right, rather than to the value of the damaged right itself

Constructive Trust. A trust imposed by a court on equitable grounds against one who has obtained property by wrongdoing, thereby preventing the wrongful holder from being unjustly enriched. Such a trust creates no fiduciary relationship.

Contemnor. A person who is guilty of contempt before an instrumentality of government, such as a court or legislature.

Contempt. Conduct that defies the authority or dignity of a court or legislature. Because such conduct interferes with the administration of justice, it is punishable by fine or imprisonment.

Cost to Repair. The cost of repairing and restoring an asset to its original condition (and, if possible, to its original value).

Court of Equity. A court that (1) has jurisdiction in equity, (2) administers and decides controversies in accordance with the rules, principles, and precedents of equity, and (3) follows the forms and procedures of chancery.

Court of Law. A court that proceeds according to the course of common law, and that is governed by its rules and principles.

Cover. The purchase on the open market of a substitute for a performance promised but not delivered. Sometimes limited to buyer's purchase of substitute goods after seller breaches, U.C.C. § 2–712, it can be used more broadly.

Criminal Contempt. A contempt proceeding to punish the contemnor for a past violation of a court order.

Declaratory Judgment. A binding adjudication that establishes the rights and other legal relations of the parties without providing for or ordering enforcement.

Direct Contempt. Contempt that is committed in open court, as when a lawyer insults a judge on the bench.

Direct Loss. A loss that results immediately and proximately from an event. Usually direct loss involves the value of the right itself, not the value of how the plaintiff intended to use the right.

Economic Loss. See Pecuniary Loss.

Economic Loss Doctrine. The principle that a plaintiff cannot sue in tort to recover for purely monetary loss—as opposed to physical injury to person or property—caused by the defendant.

Emotional Distress. A highly unpleasant mental reaction (such as anguish, grief, fright, humiliation, or fury) that results from another person's conduct; emotional pain and suffering. Emotional distress, when severe enough, can form a basis for the recovery of tort damages.

Ensuing Loss. Loss indirectly or remotely caused by misconduct. See also Consequential Damages.

Equitable Clean-Up Doctrine. The jurisdictional principle that once an equity court has acquired jurisdiction over a case, it may decide both equitable and legal issues as long as the legal issues are ancillary to the equitable ones.

Equitable Estoppel. A defensive doctrine preventing one party from taking unfair advantage of another when, through false language or conduct, the person to be estopped has induced another person to act in a certain way, with the result that the other person has been injured in some way. *Cf. Promissory Estoppel.*

Equitable Lien. A right, enforceable only in equity, to have a demand satisfied from a particular fund or specific property, without having possession of the fund or property.

Equity. The system of law or body of principles originating in the English Court of Chancery and superseding the common and statute law when the two conflict. In appealing to the equity of the court, a party was appealing to the "king's conscience".

Ex Parte. Done or made at the instance and for the benefit of one party only, without notice to or argument by a person adversely interested.

Expectation Interest. The position the nonbreaching party would have occupied if a promise had been performed. More generally, the position a party would have occupied if no breach of duty had occurred.

Express Trust. A trust created with the settlor's express intent, usu. Declared in writing.

Fair Market Value. The price that a seller is willing to accept and a buyer is willing to pay on the open market and in an arm's-length transaction, each being reasonably informed and neither being under any compulsion to deal. The point at which supply and demand intersect.

Fluid Class Recoveries. Remedies awarded to one group of people based on defendant's wrong against a different (usually similar) group of people. For example, an order to discount future electricity bills because of overcharges in the past. will benefit some people who never paid the overcharges and will not benefit some people who did pay past the overcharges.

Forum non conveniens. The doctrine that an appropriate forum—even though competent under law—may divest itself of jurisdiction if, for the convenience of the litigants and the witnesses, it appears that the action should proceed in another forum in which the action might originally have been brought.

Foreseeability. The quality of being reasonably anticipatable. Foreseeability, along with actual causation, is an element of proximate cause or duty in tort law, but a direct limitation on damages in contract law.

General Damages. (1) Damages that may be pleaded generally, without specific details; (2) Damages that the law presumes follow from a specific type of wrong; (3) In tort, damages that are not easily quantifiable, such as emotional distress, pain and suffering, etc.; (4) In contract, damages are easily quantifiable, such as the cover price, market price, or resale price of property. See also Special Damages

Hedonic Damages. See Lost Enjoyment of Life.

Incidental Damages. Losses reasonably associated with or related to actual damages.

Indirect Contempt. Contempt that is committed outside the court, as when a party disobeys a court order. *Also termed consequential contempt; constructive contempt.*

Injunction Bond. A bond required of an injunction applicant to cover the costs incurred by a wrongfully enjoined party. Fed. R. Civ. P. 65 (c).

In pari delicto. A legal defense available when both parties are equally at fault.

In personam. Involving or determining the personal rights and interests of the parties.

In rem. Involving or determining the status of a thing, and therefore the rights of persons generally with respect to that thing.

Irreparable-Injury Rule. The principle that equitable relief is available only when no adequate legal remedy exists.

Intangible Property. Property that lacks a physical existence. Examples include bank accounts, stock options, and business goodwill.

Interest. A legal share in something; all or part of a legal or equitable claim to or right in property.

Joinder. The uniting of parties or claims in a single lawsuit. Fed. R. Civ. P. 19.

Judicial discretion. The exercise of judgment by a judge or court based on what is fair under the circumstances and guided by the rules and principles of law; a courts power to act or not act when a litigant is not entitled to demand the act as a matter of right.

Laches. The equitable doctrine by which a court denies relief to a claimant who has unreasonably delayed or been negligent in asserting the claim, when that delay or negligence has prejudiced the party against whom relief is sought.

Limitations (Contractual) on Remedies. A contractual provision that restricts the remedies available to the parties if a party defaults. Under the UCC, such a clause is valid unless it fails of its essential purpose or it unconscionably limits consequential damages.

Liquidated. Capable of being ascertained with some degree of certainty. For example, when damages are a fixed amount (say, the price) or calculable by a simple formula (say, contract price minus market price, times the quantity), they are liquidated. Some rules, such as prejudgment interest, apply to liquidated damages, but not to damages that are harder to ascertain (say, distress).

Liquidated Damage Clause. A provision in a contract specifying the amount or, more often, a formula used to calculate the amount of damages a non-breaching party may recover as compensation for a breach.

Loss in Value. Index but not glossary

Loss of Chance. A rule in some states providing a claim against a doctor who has engaged in medical malpractice that, although it does not result in a particular injury, decreases or eliminates the chance of surviving or recovering from the preexisting condition for which the doctor was consulted.

Loss of Consortium. A loss of the benefits that one spouse is entitled to receive from the other, including services, society, companionship, affection, and sexual relations. Loss of consortium can be recoverable as damages from a tortfeasor in a personal injury action.

Loss of Use. Losses suffered when a party could not use property (tangible or intangible) for a period of time because of defendant's wrong. See also Consequential Damages.

Lost Earning Potential. A person's diminished earning power resulting from an injury. See Lost Income.

Lost Enjoyment of Life. Tort damages available where another's negligent act results in the loss of capacity to enjoy life.

Lost Income. Wages, salary, or other income that a person would have earned but for defendant's wrong, typically resulting from loss of a job, a disabling injury, or death.

Lost Volume Seller. A seller who could have sold a larger total number of goods (or services, etc.) if defendant had not breached. Usually raised after a buyer has breached a sales contract and the seller resells the goods to a different buyer who would have bought identical goods from the seller's inventory even if the original buyer had not breached. Such a seller is entitled to lost profits, rather than contract price less market price, as damages from the original buyer's breach. U.C.C. § 2–708(2).

Mandatory Injunction. An injunction that orders an affirmative act or mandates a specified course of conduct.

Market Value. See Fair Market Value

Medical Costs. Costs incurred as a result of seeking medical attention for injuries.

Mitigation of Damages.—see avoidable consequences doctrine

Nominal Damages. A trifling sum awarded when a legal injury is suffered but when there is no substantial loss or injury to be compensated.

Noneconomic Loss. See Nonpecuniary Loss.

Nonpecuniary Loss. A loss of something not replaceable in the market. Typically, pain, suffering, grief, lost enjoyment of life, and emotional distress are nonpecuniary losses.

Officious Intermeddler. A person who confers a benefit on another without being requested or having a legal duty to do so, and who therefore has no legal grounds to demand restitution for the benefit conferred.

Order to Show Cause. An order directing a party to appear in court and explain why the party took (or failed to take) some action or why the court should or should not grant some relief.

Out-of-Pocket Loss. A measure of damage for misrepresentation, seeking to place the deceived party in the position she would have occupied if the defendant had told the truth.

The difference between the value of what the buyer paid and the market value of what was received in return. In breach of contract cases, out-of-pocket loss is used to measure reliance damages.

Pain and Suffering. Physical discomfort or emotional distress compensable as an element of damages in torts.

Pecuniary Loss. A loss of money or of something having monetary value

Physical Injury Requirement. (see economic loss doctrine)

Potential Harm. Harm capable of coming into being. Usually refers to wrongs that increase the risk that the plaintiff will suffer a future harm, such as exposure to toxic chemicals.

Prejudgment Interest. Statutorily prescribed interest accrued either from the date of the loss or from the date when the complaint was filed up to the date the final judgment is entered. Prejudgment interest is usu. calculated only for liquidated sums. Depending on the statute, it may or may not be an element of damages.

Preliminary Injunction. A temporary injunction issued before or during a trial to prevent an irreparable injury from occurring before the court has a chance to decide the case. A preliminary injunction will only be issued after the defendant receives notice and an opportunity to be heard.

Prerogative. An exclusive right, power, privilege, or immunity.

Present Value. The sum of money that, with compound interest, would amount to a specified sum at a specified future date; future value discounted to its value today.

Preventive Injunction. An injunction designed to prevent a loss or injury in the future.

Procedural Unconscionability. Unconscionability resulting from improprieties in contract formation. This type of unconscionability suggests that there was no meeting of the minds.

Prohibitory Injunction. An injunction that forbids or restrains an act.

Promissory Estoppel. The principle that a promise made without consideration may nonetheless be enforced to prevent injustice if the promisor should have reasonably expected the promisee to rely on the promise and if the promisee did actually rely on the promise to his or her detriment. *Cf. Equitable Estoppel.*

Public Policy. Broadly, principles and standards regarded by the legislature or by the courts as being of fundamental concern to the state and the whole of society.

Punitive Damages. Damages awarded in addition to actual damages when the defendant acted with recklessness, malice, or deceit. Punitive damages, which are intended to punish and thereby deter blameworthy conduct, are generally not recoverable for breach of contract.

Quasi-Contract. An obligation imposed in law because of the conduct of the parties, or some special relationship between them, or because one of them would otherwise be unjustly enriched. *Also termed implied-in-law contract.*

Real Estate. Land and anything growing on, attached to, or erected on it, excluding anything that may be severed without injury to the land.

Reliance Interest. The position the nonbreaching party would have occupied if a promise had not been made. More generally, the position a party would have occupied if no breach of duty had existed.

Reparative Injunction. An injunction requiring the defendant to restore the plaintiff to the position that the plaintiff occupied before the defendant committed the wrong.

Replacement Cost Less Depreciation. A method that fixes an asset's value by the price of a new substitute, decreased appropriately to reflect the age and condition of the asset actually lost. Usually, depreciation multiplies the value of the new asset by the percentage of useful life remaining in the original asset.

Restitution. (1) A recovery based on the amount of gain to the defendant as a result of the wrong; (2) A cause of action for Unjust Enrichment.

Restitution Interest. The position the breaching party would have occupied if a promise had not been made (or the benefit from plaintiff had not been received). Usually this involves refunding any benefit defendant received by the other party's performance.

Rightful Position. The position an injured party would have occupied if the defendant had not committed the wrong.

Sales of Goods. The transfer of moveable personal property for a price.

Special Damages. (1) Damages that must be pleaded with specificity; (2) Damages that the law will not presumes follow from a wrong without additional evidence of the causal chain; (3) In tort, damages that are easily quantifiable, such as medical expenses, lost income, cost to repair property, etc.; (4) In contract, damages are not easily quantifiable, such as lost profits. See also General Damages.

Specific Performance. A court ordered remedy that requires precise fulfillment of a legal or contractual obligation when monetary damages are inappropriate or inadequate, as when the sale of real estate or rare article is involved.

Status Quo Ante Litem. The situation that existed before the litigation.

Statute of Limitations. A statute establishing a time limit for suing in a civil case, based on the date when the claim accrued.

Stay. An order to suspend all or part of a judicial proceeding or a judgment resulting from that proceeding.

Structural Injunction. An injunction affecting institutional reform or public law.

Sua sponte. Without prompting or suggestion; on its own motion.

Subjective Value. Value to an individual owner, usually exceeding the value that others in the market would be willing to pay for particular property. Often based on an individual's perceptions, feelings, or intentions, as opposed to externally verifiable phenomena.

Subrogation. The substitution of one party for another whose debt the party pays, entitling the paying party to rights, remedies, or securities that would otherwise belong to the debtor.

Substantive Unconscionability. Unconscionability resulting from actual contract terms that are unduly harsh, commercially unreasonable, and grossly unfair given the existing circumstances.

Substitution. The process by which one person or thing takes the place of another person or thing. Fed. R. Civ. P. 25.

Survival Action. A lawsuit brought on behalf of a decedent's estate for injuries or damages incurred by the decedent immediately before dying. A survival action derives from the claim that a decedent would have had—such as for pain and suffering—if he or she had survived. In contrast is a claim that the beneficiaries may have in a wrongful-death action, such as for loss of consortium or loss of support from the decedent.

Temporary Restraining Order (TRO). A court order preserving the status quo until a litigant's application for a preliminary or permanent injunction can be heard. A temporary restraining order may sometimes be granted without notifying the opposing party in advance.

Tracing. The process of tracking property's ownership or characteristics from time of its origin to the present.

Unclean Hands. An equitable defense alleging that the party seeking equitable relief should be denied a remedy because that party has acted inequitably, such as by violating a law or by acting in bad faith.

Unconscionability. The principle that a court may refuse to enforce a contract that is unfair or oppressive because of procedural abuses during contract formation or because of overreaching contractual terms, esp. terms that are unreasonably favorable to one party while precluding meaningful choice for the other party. *See also procedural unconscionability and substantive unconscionability.*

Writ. A court's written order, in the name of a state of other competent legal authority, commanding the addressee to do or refrain from doing some specified act.

Wrongful Death. A cause of action brought by a decedent's survivors for the losses the survivor's suffered as a result of a tortious injury that caused the decedent's death.

Appendix B

Sample Exams

ESSAY QUESTION: Damages Only. Originally 75 minutes long.

You have been consulted by Terry Thomas, a person of modest means. Terry has encountered difficulty with Reproductive Services, Inc. (RSI).

In 2002, Terry was married to Chris Thomas, now deceased. After encountering reproductive difficulties, they sought the aid of RSI. RSI produced a number of embryos from egg and sperm harvested from the Thomas'. One of these embryos became the Thomas' first child, Leslie, in 2003. Unused embryos were stored in a frozen state for possible later use. In 2004, Chris died in a tragic accident. In January 2005, RSI confirmed (in response to Terry's inquiry) that embryos created in 2002 remained viable for implantation. In February 2005, at an appointment for implantation of another embryo, RSI informed Terry that the embryos created in 2002 were missing and, apparently, had been destroyed inadvertently in 2003. RSI offered to create an equal number of new embryos—which, under their contract, was Terry's exclusive remedy for RSI's failure to provide embryos upon demand. Terry explained that Chris was no longer available to provide genetic material.

Terry seeks your advice regarding a suit against RSI. RSI has breached its contract with Terry, probably has committed the tort of conversion (destroying property belonging to Terry), and may be liable for wrongful death, at least if they were negligent in discarding the embryos. (Assume state law provides life begins at conception and that this covers embryos outside the womb, not just embryos in a womb.) Assume Terry might prevail on all three counts. Identify the potential damages Terry might claim from RSI. Consider any arguments RSI might raise in response to those claims and any reply Terry might make to those objections, including your prediction of how each argument will be resolved. Assume state law follows the rules we have studied in class, including the Uniform Commercial Code (which may apply, but may not), the Restatement (Second) of Contracts, and the Restatement (Second) of Torts.

SAMPLE ANSWER

A wrongful death action seems unlikely to produce much recovery. Pecuniary losses normally include funeral expenses, loss of support, loss of services, and, in some states, loss of companionship. Grief usually is not available. Here, there were no funeral expenses; the embryos were discarded, not buried. A memorial service by Terry (T) might produce some expenses. The avoidable consequences doctrine, however, might preclude recovery, since it might be reasonable for T not to increase the loss by holding such a service. Unless services for lost embryos are more common in society than I realize, the costs may be unrecoverable. Even if recoverable, they are unlikely to be large. Loss of support faces two problems. First, it is not clear that the embryos would have been born alive. Implantation fails a large percentage of the time. Second, if born, the children might not earn much before becoming adults. Since they have no obligation to support Terry after age 18, damages here seem very unlikely. Similarly, the services the children might provide, if born alive, are unlikely to be very valuable. If companionship is limited to pecuniary companionship—the kinds of advice that people pay for, like help with taxes and investments—the benefit will be negligible until T's waning years. Reduced to present value, little recovery is likely. In addition, T saved the cost of raising the children. That pecuniary benefit offsets any pecuniary losses T claims. In a state that does not allow recovery for nonpecuniary losses in wrongful death actions, damages may not exist. Even grief may not produce a large recovery. Grief over the death of children could be large, but the grief in this case seems more akin to the grief over a miscarriage. While that would probably produce some recovery—especially because pecuniary benefits would not offset nonpecuniary losses under the Restatement's version of the benefit rule—it may not produce as great a recovery as other actions might produce.

The other two possible claims (contract and conversion) face an immediate obstacle: each arguably treats the embryos as property rather than as human beings. That may violate a public policy of this state, which declares life begins at conception. If a court holds that it violates the public policy of the state to consider the embryos as property, then the court may reject these actions and limit plaintiff to the wrongful death claim.

One way around this would be to treat the contract claim as a contract for reproductive services rather than a contract for the sale of goods (even though the UCC's definition of goods includes the unborn young of animals). We may still persuade the court to apply some U.C.C. rules by analogy, even though the case does not involve a sale of goods.

The basic remedy in contract is to put the plaintiff in the position she would have occupied if the contract had been performed—the expectation interest. Immediately, however, RSI will raise the contractual remedy limiting recovery to replacement of the embryos. T does not want this remedy, because the embryos would not have the genetic material of C, her late spouse. To negate this contractual remedy, T must argue that it fails of its essential purpose. (This would be the statutory test if the court applies the U.C.C. to this contract, treating it as a sale of goods. Applying this test to a service contract is less likely.) Here, the essential purpose was to allow T to attempt to have children despite difficulties with natural childbirth. Substitute embryos, which could have T's genetic material, provide a very large portion of that benefit. They are not exactly as good as the original performance, but substituted remedies need not be (and probably rarely are) exactly as good as the remedies provided at law. (T might be persuaded to prefer the substitute, since it would allow T to use the genetic material of any future spouse instead of C. We can raise this possibility with her, but this analysis will assume T will not change her mind.) Unless we can persuade a court that the essential purpose includes the exact genetic identity of the embryos, the clause may stand.

We could try to argue that it was unconscionable. This seems unlikely to succeed. The clause probably will come as a surprise to T, who may not have considered the remedies from breach when entering the contract. Whether the surprise is unfair surprise may depend on how the term was presented. If T simply didn't pay attention, the surprise may not be unfair. The term, however, does not seem unreasonably favorable to RSI. It limits their liability in a manner that, initially, probably seemed quite reasonable. Unless parties expected one spouse to die soon—and no one suggests either party had reason to know of C's impending demise—the replacement remedy would seem like a workable solution. It avoids the difficulty of evaluating the losses someone would suffer from breach by substituting new performance, avoiding the losses instead. The unusual circumstances that prevent the remedy from working here hardly make the term unconscionable at the time the contract was formed.

Assuming the clause can be avoided, however, damages might be quite large. We may start with the value of implanted embryos. T does not want to cover with substitute embryos because they will not have C's DNA. But substitute embryos probably have a market value, an amount that people seeking children but unable to produce their own embryos would pay. This will not fully compensate T. T values the embryos as children, not as a source of income. But it would provide a minimum estimate of the loss T suffered. T can try to augment this amount by showing the subjective value of the embryos to T or the consequential losses T suffered by losing the opportunity to have children using these embryos.

Subjective value of the embryos may be hard to establish. First, subjective value rarely is used unless neither market value nor cost to replace will suffice. These embryos probably have significant market value, running some risk that the court will reject subjective value out of hand. A court, however, seems likely to realize that embryos are uniquely subjective—more than dogs, wedding photos, heirlooms, or other intensely personal property. Thus, it may find that there is no market for embryos, not because there is none, but because T should not have to settle for the price others would pay for embryos that are worth much more to her than to anyone else.

The cost to replace also poses an obstacle. Arguably, the embryos are irreplaceable at any price. Alternatively, we can use the amount it would cost to replace these embryos if replacement were possible. This will not permit cover, but it will provide another minimum measure of value to plaintiff. Having agreed to pay for these services, the payment seems a minimum estimate of their value. (Of course, some value has already been recouped by the successful birth of Leslie.) RSI seems unlike to object to this measure, since it would need to invest about the same amount in creating substitute embryos as in paying the cost of replacement. It allows T the value of replacement without foisting off on her genetically unwanted embryos. Still, the remedy seems likely to underestimate the value of the embryos to T. They were worth more than the cost, not exactly equal to the cost. Thus, subjective value to the plaintiff may be awarded. Calculating that amount without indulging in mawkish or affected sentimentality may pose a difficulty, but one courts have confronted with family films. Perhaps this is another setting where the issue must be faced and resolved.

To the extent that we seek consequential damages, many of the problems related to wrongful death apply. We cannot establish with certainty that any loss of children occurred because miscarriage is very likely. The pecuniary losses remain quite modest. In addition, RSI might argue damages can be reduced by having a child without C's genetic material. While not quite as good as the promised embryos, they may come close, thus reducing the loss. Only the differences between these children and C's children need be awarded. It seems unlikely that a court would find it unreasonable to refuse to have children by another donor

One last possibility emerges. While the nonpecuniary benefits of children are not recoverable in wrongful death, they may be recoverable in contract. Emotional distress is available if the breach produces a physical injury or if the contract or breach are of a type that makes serious emotional disturbance particularly likely to occur. T did not suffer physical injury; the embryos have no claim because they were not subsequently born alive. But contracts for reproductive services seem particularly likely to produce distress if breached. If cases award distress when a contract for a cute nose is breached, it seems a short step to awarding distress for breach of a promise to preserve and implant embryos.

If a court does not accept a public policy defense, conversion offers an alternative route to recovery. The normal remedy would be the value before the injury less the value after. Here, the value after is zero, given that the embryos have been destroyed. The value before presents exactly the same difficulty here as in the contract action. The market value seems likely to underestimate the value to T, as does replacement cost. The arguments will rise or fall on exactly the same analysis. Loss of use raises the same difficulty of assessing the value of a chance to have children with C's genetic makeup.

One normally considers emotional distress as a normal remedy in tort. This may not apply to the tort of conversion. Distress at the loss of property seems anomalous, especially in a jurisdiction that refuses to award distress when parents lose their children in a tort. Some cases hold that distress might be available if the tort was intentional. Here, RSI claims the loss was accidental. We should inquire into exactly what that means and whether it is true. One can imagine accidents—the refrigeration failed in this unit or these embryos were mistaken for others that were to be discarded. But one can imagine less innocent breaches, too. If an intentional tort emerges, we might recover not only distress, but also punitive damages. Further investigation is appropriate.

ESSAY QUESTION: Entire Course. Originally 105 minutes long.

On May 11, 2005, Ms. Sophee Stree, an influential partner at your firm, called you into her office. There she introduced you to Dr. Chris Heiser, a research biologist. Chris seeks your firm's assistance concerning a dispute with Phog Pharmaceuticals (Phog), Chris's employer. Chris relates the following facts.

In May 2003, Chris left a lucrative position at Eli Tulips & Co. (Tulips), a pharmaceutical company in Illinois, and moved to California to take a position with Phog. Phog promised Tulips $300,000 per year, 50% more than Tulips paid, plus substantial increases in research budget, staff, fringe benefits, and other perks. The contract guaranteed employment for five years. In addition, the contract specified that Chris would receive 20,000 shares of Phog stock (worth $2 million in 2003) when Phog successfully patented the arthritis treatment it hired Chris to develop. (A successful product probably would produce more than $40 million in profit for Phog.) Before accepting, Chris told Phog that the employment contract with Tulips contained a noncompetition agreement, forbidding Chris from working for another pharmaceutical manufacturer for one year after leaving Tulips. (Other jobs, such as teaching at a University or working for a public health agency would not violate this agreement.) Phog told Chris that agreements like that were void as against public policy under California law (which is true), so that as long as Chris moved to California, it would not violate any valid agreement to work for Phog. (Ms. Stree mentions that Illinois law probably governs the Tulips-Chris agreement, so Phog's conclusion might be wrong.)

Chris recently made a breakthrough in the research. While some technical issues remain to find an efficient way to mass produce the drug, Chris's work has made it virtually certain that Phog will be able to produce a successful drug. The patent is harder to predict. If another company made the same breakthrough earlier, they might get the patent instead. Tulips was working on a similar project, though it was Chris's project and probably was slowed by Chris's departure. The patent, therefore, seems likely. In the process, Chris stumbled upon a new approach to cancer that Chris would like to pursue. Phog, instead of rewarding Chris, fired Chris on May 1, 2005. Chris believes this is an effort to avoid paying the stock bonus (and the remaining three years of salary). Phog claims that his discharge was an effort to limit its potential liability for misconduct that Chris may have committed. Phog was not specific, but Chris believes this is a veiled accusation that Chris used Tulip trade secrets in the research.

Chris could seek out other employment, but similar positions probably pay much less—closer to the $200,000 Chris earned at Tulips than the $300,000 Phog had promised, plus reduced research budget, benefits, and perks. Chris would prefer to continue work at Phog; with the research support Phog promised, Chris is confident that the cancer project will be even bigger than the arthritis project. If Phog pursues this idea without Chris, Chris probably will earn nothing for the new cancer treatment. Chris cannot make progress fast enough without the kind of support Phog provided.

Phog's conduct is a breach of contract. Ms. Stree asks you to prepare a memorandum (informal, but thorough and insightful) evaluating the remedies Chris might seek and the prospects for success. Be sure to consider any arguments that Phog might raise in opposition to those remedies and how you would persuade a court to take your position—or, if their arguments are unassailable, what effect they have on your remedial recommendations. In addition, consider any risks your client may run in raising these issues. Ms. Stree mentions one risk: a lawsuit might come to Tulips' attention, spurring them to make a claim against Chris. Consider this and any other danger you foresee in evaluating Chris's remedies. Ms. Stree will meet Chris for cocktails. In preparation for that meeting, she needs your memorandum by 3:00 p.m. If you need additional information, identify the questions Ms. Stree should ask Chris. She will not be able to consult you after getting the answers, so be sure to explain how the answers will affect your conclusions or advice.

California law applies. Unless you have read (for this class) California cases or statutes to the contrary, assume that California follows the general rules of remedies that we have discussed, including (when applicable) those portions of the Uniform Commercial Code, the Restatement (Second) of Contracts, and the Restatement (Second) of Torts that we addressed in class. Do not discuss remedies unique to the federal patent laws, which we did not discuss this term. You may make an argument for any remedy independent of that statute, but not an argument that relies entirely on that statute.

SAMPLE ANSWER

Our client (Chris or C) wants to return to work for Phog (P). A court could order for specific performance, compelling P to reinstate C. An injunction would be available if the remedy at law is inadequate. Damages are inadequate if they are not as complete, practical, and efficient as an injunction. Damages seem likely to compensate C for most of the losses, such as salary and shares of stock. To the extent that C might be entitled to additional compensation for the cancer discovery, damages are unlikely to suffice. The discovery is very preliminary, making it impossible to assess whether, let alone how much, profits might result from the discovery. Thus, damages might be uncertain, making an injunction a better option. Because Chris may not be entitled to any profits from the cancer discovery (beyond salary and stock), this deficiency may not justify an injunction.

Even if the remedy at law is inadequate, courts may not order reinstatement. Courts never award specific performance of personal service contracts against employees. But sometimes order reinstatement of employees who request it. P can object that reinstatement creates an awkward employee relationship, forcing them to deal with an employee they do not trust and whom they suspect will be unhappy with the company (because they tried to fire C). As a result, C may not perform as loyal employee's should, forcing P to discipline C, probably resulting in claims of retaliation and additional hearings for contempt. These problems make an injunction a very poor choice, especially since damages come very close to being adequate.

P may also raise unclean hands, alleging that C violated his noncompetition clause with Eli Tulip (ET) to work for P and may have used ET's trade secrets while working for P. The latter allegation is troubling and should be investigated. If C in fact gave ET's trade secrets to P, awarding C the benefit of the wrong (including stock and salary) may be troublesome. C might argue that this misconduct is a wrong against ET, not a wrong against P, and thus should not preclude a remedy against P. C may also allege that the large salary and stock bonus were intended to induce C to reveal trade secrets and that P is disingenuously in claiming to object to the revelation—though this would require C to admit misappropriating the secrets, which will produce more problems for C down the road.

Re the noncompetition clause, C may argue that P should be estopped to complain about this breach. Estoppel requires that P's words or actions suggest they do not intend to assert a claim, and that C relied on those words or actions in a manner that will prove detrimental if P now may change its mind. P told C that the noncompetition clause was not valid. In reliance on this assertion, C began work before the one-year expired, violating the clause. Having induced C to violate the clause, it would be inequitable to allow P to rely on that violation in order to argue unclean hands. P should be estopped from raising this issue.

C may want to seek immediate reinstate via a TRO or Preliminary Injunction. If reinstatement is essential to give C a chance to continue the cancer research, then every day out of the lab gives P another day of head start in reaching patentability first. A TRO would require notice to P: they are easy to find and, having already fired C, cannot accelerate the wrong if given notice. To show entitlement to preliminary relief, C must establish irreparable injury, likelihood of success on the merits, the balance of hardships, and the public interest. Irreparable injury focuses on injuries that will become unavoidable before trial on the merits. Here, the delay in C's research cannot be avoided later, making it essentially to award some remedy immediately. C seems likely to succeed on the merits: P clearly discharged C before the expiration of the 5 year term, though they may have been justified if C's conduct (using another's trade secrets) amounts to good cause. (If so, C loses on liability, and the entire remedy issue is moot. Thus, I will assume liability.) The public has very little interest in whether C works for P or not. The hardship to P is financial, having to pay C in the interim. Retaining C seems unlikely to increase their liability to ET, since secrets already have (or haven't) been revealed. But P might face some hardship protecting its secrets from possible misappropriation by an disgruntled reinstated-ex-employee. These hardships may balance, making it hard to predict whether C can obtain preliminary relief. Note that under the Posner formula, the better-than-50% chance of success might outweigh a slight balance of hardships favoring P. It is not clear that courts would award preliminary relief where the balance of hardships tilts in defendant's favor even if the likelihood of success strongly favored the plaintiff.

One other remedy might be sought: an injunction ordering P to stop pursuing C's cancer discovery—or perhaps to stop pursuing the arthritis research. Arthritis is a harder case, since it is complete and damages seem adequate to compensate C for that loss. Indeed, C may want P to patent it quickly, thus satisfying the condition on C's claim to stock. The cancer research poses a closer issue. Here, however, the public interest probably weighs in favor of P. The public wants the cure studied faster rather than slower. While reinstating C might facilitate this, preventing P from working on the cure would only slow matters down.

Damages are available, though the amount is unclear. Salary for the remaining 3 years would total $900,000. The value of fringe benefits and perks (health insurance, retirement contributions, company car, etc.), if quantifiable, also should be added to this sum. C, however, is capable of working elsewhere. Thus, P will seek to offset the amount that C could earn with other companies against the recovery. C need only make reasonable efforts to find substitute work; C need not seek or accept employment if that would cause undue risk, burden, or humiliation. Thus, C need not seek work in a different location or in a different field. But work as a researcher appears to be available for $200,000 a year—about what C earned from ET, so it would be hard to argue this salary is humiliating. And even if it was, the damages will make up the difference. Thus, recovery is likely to be limited to $100,000 a year, plus the difference between the new fringe benefits and the old.

The shares of stock pose a different problem. The patent has not yet issued and, thus, C is not entitled to them. If the patent has not issued by the time of judgment, uncertainty may preclude recovery. Lack of a patent makes the existence of loss, not merely the amount, uncertain, since C is entitled to no shares unless the patent issues. But it seems likely that the patent will issue (or not) before trial, removing this uncertainty. The value of the shares on that day would compensate C for the loss of the shares. Ideally, C would purchase substitute shares on that day, to minimize the loss of investment opportunity. (Interest on a loan needed to cover might be recoverable, though the court may employ the statutory interest rate on the purchase price instead of the actual rate at which Chris borrowed.) Owning the shares allows C to choose when to sell them and invest in other companies instead of P. If C cannot find money with which to cover, Chris may want an injunction ordering P to deliver 20,000 shares. Unfortunately, the shares probably will be awarded after trial, preventing C from selling them between the date the patent issues and the date of judgment. Thus, C will face any loss in stock value after the patent. Of course, the stock should go up in light of the good news, so perhaps this concern is minor.

C may also attempt to recover profits lost on the cancer research. These are unlikely to be established with any certainty. The discovery is very new and may not produce any results before trial, let alone any patent and profits. Thus, even the existence of lost profits may be speculative here. In addition, at the time the contract was made, lost profits on a cancer breakthrough was not in the contemplation of the parties as a probable result of breach. C was to do arthritis research. The cancer discovery was fortuitous. C's best bet is to avoid this loss by finding another company will to sponsor the cancer research. (Perhaps C needs to start a new biotech firm to pursue it.)

All legal remedies may run up against P's defense of in pari delicto. As with unclean hands, C might avoid this by arguing that C's wrongs were against ET, not against P. In addition, C was not equally in the wrong because P's wrongs exceed C's. If they were each equally guilty re the wrongs against ET, P is the only party guilty for breach of the contract, making it the greater wrongdoer.

C may want to pursue an action for Unjust Enrichment. This action requires C to establish that P received a benefit at C's expense and that it would be unjust for P to retain the benefit without compensating C for it. Here, the benefit would be C's breakthrough in arthritis—and perhaps the cancer discovery, too. P definitely has this benefit. Although the patent and profits remain somewhat uncertain, they should be resolved by trial. C was not a donor or volunteer, working under what C thought was a valid contract. P may argue they have a contract right to keep the benefit. They would if they had performed the contract instead of committing a material breach. But firing C 3 years early is a total breach, allowing C an opportunity to cancel the contract and resort to unjust enrichment instead. (The Restatement (Third) of Restitution may produce a different result, if it receives widespread acceptance.)

The amount C may receive in restitution may be measured by either (a) the increase in P's wealth as a result of the benefit or (b) the amount it would have cost P to obtain the benefit from others. The latter may not favor C. The going rate of researchers appears to be less than P promised to pay C. P might argue they could have received the same benefit for $100,000 less per year at the market rate. Yet their willingness to pay more than the market suggests that they could not have obtained the benefit from these less expensive employees. It may be hard to estimate how much it would have cost to obtain the benefit from others. On the other hand, the estimated value of the benefit is $40 million, the amount of profit P expects to make on the drug if patented. P might claim that amount—especially since P is the wrongdoer and, thus, not entitled to the benefit of the lower measure. P may argue that the $40 million represents the efforts of others, not just C: P's labs, P's employees assisting C, P's legal department pursuing the patent, P's production facilities, P's advertising, etc. Apportioning the benefit among these contributions may be more equitable. Whether C's share of the apportionment would exceed the value of 20,000 shares is hard to foretell. Efforts to include the benefit of the cancer research seem unlikely to produce much increase given the uncertainty of any profit from this discovery.

C is concerned that litigation against P might produce a claim by ET. This might be preempted by a declaratory judgment action in California asking the California court to apply California law or public policy to declare the noncompetition clause invalid. If this fails, however, ET certainly will assert a counterclaim for damages. (An injunction is too late, since the one year has already expired.) ET might even assert a claim to the arthritis discovery, if it can maintain that if C had sat idle for one year, ET would have beaten P to the patent. Opening this can of worms is problematic. Negotiating a waiver from ET might be more successful, though not if ET smells blood. If ET has known of C's employment all along, their inaction may create a waiver or an estoppel. By letting C and P continue to invest in the drug, planning to claim the profits of that investment if it succeeded, but to avoid any risk if it failed, ET prejudiced C and P by its delay.

If C opts to keep a low profile, a suit is dangerous. But P, also, must fear claims by ET. P was enriched by the benefit of C's research. If P claims C used ET's trade secrets, the benefit was at ET's expense. Justice might require P to compensate ET for the benefit, perhaps the entire $40 million expected profit. That risk—even the risk of protracted litigation on such a claim—may scare P as much as C is scared by a potential claim by ET. Threatening to sue P may cause them to relent on the contract. Defense against ET remains difficult if they come forward.

Table of Cases